DATE DUE

MR 27 02			

DEMCO 38-296

The Weightless World

The Weightless World
Strategies for Managing the Digital Economy

Diane Coyle

The MIT Press
Cambridge, Massachusetts

First MIT Press edition, 1998

First published 1997, Capstone Publishing Limited, Oxford

Library of Congress Cataloging-in-Publication Data

Coyle, Diane.
  The weightless world : strategies for managing the digital economy/Diane Coyle.
    p.   cm.
  Includes bibliographical references and index.
  ISBN 0-262-03259-7 (hc : alk. paper)
  1. Economic history—20th century. 2. Electronic commerce. 3. Information technology—Economic aspects. 4. Cyberspace—Economic aspects. 5. Unemployment. I. Title.
  HC54.C74   1998
  330.9'04—dc21   98-24518
                                                                        CIP

This book was printed and bound in the United States of America.

Contents

Introduction

A millennium from now historians trying to summarise the twentieth century might characterise it in many ways: the age of total war, an era of environmental degradation, or of permanent technological revolution. But if they have an inclination towards either economics or optimism, it will have been for them a century of unprecedented improvement in human prosperity. Unfairly shared, to be sure, with almost all of the increase in wealth enjoyed by fewer than 30 nations, but still a hundred years of astonishing economic progress.

The industrialised countries are about 20 times better off at the end of this century than they were a hundred years earlier. Most of their inhabitants lead lives that would have been considered luxurious beyond imagination by their grandparents. The curious thing, though, about this huge increase in well-being is that the output of the developed economies weighs about the same as the 20 times less valuable output of the same economies at the end of the nineteenth century.

Laurie Anderson, the American performance artist, introduced a new show called *Speed of Darkness*, which she described as a 'dark look' at technology. Explaining it, she said: 'Where people once wanted bigger cars and bigger offices, now they want smaller, tinier things. The aesthetic of the small is very interesting: the tiniest chip, the smallest watch or car phone.'[1] Miniaturised desires are characteristic of the weightless world.

The credit for first characterising the economy as increasingly weightless goes to Alan Greenspan, the chairman of the United States Federal Reserve

Board. Mr Greenspan is perhaps most famous for having remarked: 'If I've made myself clear you must have misunderstood me'. A banker's irony. In a characteristically lucid speech in October 1996, he pointed out that economic output used to consist of big, physical things – steel, huge cars, heavy wooden furniture and so on. During the past half century or so, technological and economic changes have meant that we produce things of much less bulk: transistors rather than vacuum tubes, fibre-optic cables or satellite broadcasting rather than copper wire, plastics rather than metals. Materials have changed and miniaturisation has been pervasive. 'While the weight of current economic output is probably only modestly higher than it was half a century ago, valued added adjusted for price change has risen well over three-fold', Mr Greenspan said.[2] Indeed, it probably weighs little more than at the beginning of the twentieth century. The average weight of a real dollar of US exports halved between 1990 and 1996 alone, according to estimates from the Organisation for Economic Co-operation and Development (OECD), which reckoned half of member countries' national output to be 'knowledge based' by the mid-1990s.

Although here he emphasised miniaturisation and the use of new materials in making the same value of physical output lighter, the Fed chairman could have added the expansion of services as opposed to manufacturing, or in other words the switch away from physical output in all the developed economies. This switch includes not only the 'knowledge' economy, the growth of services ranging from management consultancy to the music industry that make extensive use of computer technologies, but also low-technology services like fast food restaurants.

Although some of the technological leaps driving weightlessness are not all that recent, their embodiment in our economies is new – it takes upwards of 40 years for businesses to adopt new technologies. It requires advances in design and organisation before it can take place. For instance, new buildings weigh less than those of equal floor space erected in the 1950s because of improvements in architecture and engineering design and because of organisational change as much as the use of improved materials and the replacement of heavy machinery and furniture by computer workstations, or heavy wires by light cables. Open plan offices require far fewer internal walls, hot-desking means less furniture.

For me, the proof that new technologies are finally being implemented throughout the economy lies in the now well-known factoid that the microchip in a musical greetings card contains more computer power than we had on the entire planet in 1945.

After electrification, computerisation. Profound technological change always involves economic upheaval. It also has always meant very rapid growth in living standards in the past. Unfortunately, the gain follows the pain by some distance. Alan Greenspan said in his speech: 'Radical transformations in what we produce in the way of goods and services and how we produce them occur perhaps once or twice a century, at most'.

He went on to explore the implications of increasingly weightless growth for measuring prices and productivity, both of particular concern to a central banker charged with keeping inflation low and employment high. Defining and measuring both becomes tricky.

Weightlessness, symbol of the economic effects of the cluster of advances in information and communication technology, has much wider implications, however. Like any technical development, it interacts with other fundamental changes, such as demographic and social trends and the grand sweep of political history. These are playing together in ways that make us feel that ours is the age of insecurity. Consider some of the facts about the modern industrialised world.

In one half of it, continental Europe, more than a tenth of the population of working age is unemployed. In most of the other half, there is less joblessness but much greater inequality and dissatisfaction with work. Poverty, stress, social tension and political discord are the result.

At the same time, the population of the industrial countries is ageing very rapidly. The proportion over 60 in the industrialised countries that make up the OECD is predicted to rise from less than a fifth in 1990 to a third in 2030, on average. The combined effect is an unbearable pressure on the kind of welfare state that almost all the Western nations have had in place since after World War II. The shrinking proportion of the population that pays tax −

both of working age and still employed – is unwilling to carry on footing the bill.

Predictably, politicians' first reaction was to borrow money to fill the gap. A huge explosion in government borrowing since the late 1970s has created a Frankenstein's monster, the international financial markets, whose power is such that they can hold national governments hostage.

Weightlessness can be spied at several points here. The industrial restructuring that is inevitably following the step-change in technology underlies the rise in both unemployment and inequality. If employment law and other regulations make it hard for an economy to adjust, there will be an increase in joblessness, concentrated in the dying industries, and little new job creation. If the economy is relatively deregulated, like the US or, painfully so, the UK, the adjustment shows up in the much wider variation in the price paid for different kinds of work and know-how.

Weightlessness also manifests itself in the crisis of the welfare state and the sense that our governments can't really do very much for us any more. The loss of confidence in national government is certainly due in part to the end of the Cold War – if there are no evil empires out there, why do we need the security apparatus of the modern state? But in addition, increasingly weightless economies are ones in which the link between production and place, between the economy and the nation state, is breaking down.

Big companies can easily split their production between different countries thanks to the new technology. Capital is very footloose and has no respect for the national boundary. Weightless output is also non-material and in some puzzling sense does not exist anywhere – when you watch a television film, it was filmed in one place, the transmitter is in another, the TV set is in your home, but the economic value of the movie is not located in any of these. It is the intangible act of communication that is valuable.

Likewise, in the international financial markets, traders sit in particular cities, but the value in what they do is in the bytes of data whizzing over the fibre-optic cables and to and from the satellites. The financial markets are the vanguard of weightless economics. They exist in cyberspace.

The result of all this change is a kind of helplessness – fertile ground for populism. If governments seem not to be able to do much to help their people, and if people think they cannot do much for themselves, any plausible leader who says he's got easy answers will seem attractive. So far, luckily, these characters have not made much headway in Western democracies with their sophisticated electorates. Even so, for the first time since World War II individuals rather than corporate bodies – companies or governments – are being required to bear the economic risks of everyday life.

The result is that we are living in an age of anxiety or insecurity, rather than the culture of contentment some thinkers have diagnosed. It is only a small minority that have not worried at all about how they will guarantee their future security, when no job is for life and when no boundary seems secure. In order to restore a sense of progress people need to be equipped to manage risk and to be responsible for their own prosperity.

This must start with the obvious – better education and more of it, and also more equal access to it. The fundamental natural resource of the weightless world is human creativity and intelligence. For all that most politicians now pay lip service to improving education, few have delivered the goods. Few understand that it is about more than cramming young heads with more and better information. Unequal access to high quality education is the root unfairness in our economies. The eminent, maverick British industrialist Sir John Harvey Jones once gave his analysis of the country's essential economic failure:

> 'Our people spend their whole time being told they can't do things, and believing they can't do things. It's just not true. You've only got to look at the people who are written off in this country and see their ability to teach themselves to play the guitar or use computers, to do a host of things outside the system. Get them inside the bloody system, and it becomes smart not to win, smart not to improve.'[3]

His medicine: cultural change. 'Education' is shorthand for altering attitudes, encouraging creativity and enthusiasm, as well as putting more information inside pupils' heads.

As well as developing the human resources of the economy, governments will have to introduce flexibility in the law and the tax system to match the increased flexibility that is demanded of people. To take one example, if none of us can now expect a job for life, and know that we will have to hop from job to job, be unemployed, be self-employed or even emigrate, the tax authorities must not penalise us for this. Our pensions and social security entitlements must be as mobile as we are. No industrial country is anywhere near providing a sufficiently flexible framework. None has modernised its welfare state to cope with changed demands and altered risks.

Economic policies in many countries still discourage the creation of work in the likely areas of employment growth. This means that the 'shadow' or illegal economy is often the most vigorous. Research suggests that the smallest shadow economies, in France and Germany, are about a sixth of the size of the official economy. The proportion rises to as much as a half in countries such as Italy. Sometimes this is because extra taxes make it too expensive to create an 'official' job. Often there is just too much red tape. This might have made some sense when governments had an idea where jobs might be created. One of the phenomena resulting from increasing weightlessness is increasing uncertainty. Top-down control of the economy has to go. This is where the free market comes into its own.

This applies equally to other facets of national economic policy-making. Governments will need to devolve power, probably to the level of cities, which are the natural dynamos of an industrial or post-industrial economy. One of the problems in managing a weightless economy, for the foreseeable future, will be lack of information. Local politicians will know more about what is happening in the economy than national leaders can gain from the official statistics and surveys.

The economics profession is only just starting to investigate the properties of weightlessness, which makes much conventional economic analysis outdated. The key is *dematerialisation*. The value in our economy – whatever it is we are willing to pay money for – has less and less physical mass. Whether it is software code, genetic codes, the creative content of a film or piece of music, the design of a new pair of sunglasses or the vigilance of a security guard or helpfulness of a shop assistant, value no longer lies in three-dimensional objects in space. We will pay for amusement, for style, for convenience, for speed, for creativity, for beauty – but when it comes to things, commodities, we have turned into skinflints, and want the cheapest possible. We will buy either a cheap T-shirt made in Macau or Morocco, or we will buy a designer shirt for 20 or 50 times the price.

One of the characteristics of dematerialised output is that its use by one person does not preclude its use by another. Danny Quah, a London School of Economics professor who has pioneered weightless economics, calls this property 'infinite expansibility'. It is the 'superdistribution' referred to by Brad Cox, writing in *Wired* magazine in 1994, and the basis of the magazine's optimistic philosophy of abundance.

Just because I am using a Claris programme to write this, it does not mean nobody else can use the software at the same time. Nobody else can wear my Agnes B cardigan at the same time as me, but countless others can wear the same design simultaneously. This stands the conventional economics of scarcity on its head. Value used to be determined by rarity. Now, nobody is sure how to price weightless products. It helps explain the value of global brands and designer labels. It explains why there are such tussles over pricing power in the media and intellectual property industries: if it costs virtually nothing to transmit a TV programme to an extra million people, or copy a computer programme over the Internet, or repeat a fashion design, how on earth is anybody going to charge for it? In the face of the abundance of ideas, the dismal science is still at a bit of a loss.

The first chapter of this book explores weightlessness in more detail, what it is and what it means. Later chapters turn to the implications, starting with what many would consider to be the most pressing economic issue: unemployment. Chapter 2 describes the pattern of joblessness in different industrial countries, and debunks some of the most misleading myths. Chapter 3 explores the potential causes of unemployment, rejecting the idea that either restricting trade with developing countries or increasing government spending on jobs will provide an easy cure. The fashionable isolationism shared by the old-fashioned left wing and the populist right wing is completely off-target. Technology is the reason for much unemployment but also the best hope for the growth of new jobs, and governments should gear their policies towards embracing and exploiting change.

The next chapter looks at where modern economies will create new jobs, as the industrial structure shifts irreversibly away from manufacturing and also away from some conventional services like banking as computer technology leads to swathes of redundancies here too. It explores the prospects for the social economy, or 'third sector', where demand is likely to grow enormously, and discusses what policies will be necessary to encourage this. The social economy remains over-regulated and hedged about with unhelpful restrictions in most Western countries. It is often forced to embrace the illegal or underground economy.

This is followed by a broader assessment of the costs of weightlessness, the resulting inequality and insecurity. For the burden of transformation is falling not just on those who do not have work but also on those who do. Work and income are unfairly shared, as are the dangers of losing them and the costs of upheaval. All individuals face much greater economic and financial risks than was normal only 20 years ago. A minority is gaining much greater rewards. While greater inequality is probably inevitable, it is not necessary for those at the bottom of the heap to be getting worse off. Indeed, it is obscene and immoral in a world of greater abundance.

The book then turns to how governments can help us handle those increased risks, with an assessment of how much trouble the conventional welfare state is really facing. Chapter 6 concludes that we have an expensive system that now spends our money on the wrong things. It protects citizens against risks that have long vanished, those of the post-war years which were, in economic terms, remarkably stable, but not the new risks of the weightless world. As a result the crisis in the welfare state is one of legitimacy as much as funding.

Chapter 7 makes a short detour to look at the ageing of the population. Pension payments will continue to be one of the biggest burdens on government budgets, leading some economists to warn of a demographic time bomb. It is a time bomb the UK has defused by cutting pensions, and one the US has and will defuse by allowing increased immigration. There will be other solutions, too. One is weightless – virtual immigration in the form of investment in faster-growing countries with a more youthful work force. The other will be a demographic counter-reaction that also relies on new technologies – later retirement as people stay healthier longer, and a recovery in the birth rate as it becomes feasible for older women to give birth. The expectation of spending the last third of your life on the golf course will turn out to have been an aberration in history.

The next section looks at two important and sweeping developments in the weightless world. The first is the growth of the global capital markets and their power. Exploring the financial markets through the prism of weightlessness rather than globalisation sheds fresh light on what governments should and can do to keep market power in check. The markets present a case study on the need for some economic policies to operate transnationally.

Although I argue that the financial markets are not the bogeyman many believe and have basically been the agent of necessary discipline on irresponsible national governments, they need to be regulated and monitored. This cannot be done at the national level. Increasingly, government action will become a question of co-operation between national jurisdictions. Policing the use of fancy financial derivatives is one example; setting Internet domain names, agreeing product requirements, setting ethical standards in biotechnology are others. The task of governments is to set international regulatory standards. Just as business transactions have always needed a framework of contracts and trust covering the area in which they take place, weightless activities need to be tethered by an appropriate, and necessarily international, legal and social network.

The second development is the changing location of economic activity. Weightless activity takes place in no place, but rather than leading to a dispersion of work thanks to telecommunications, I argue that cities are poised for a big revival in the weightless world. The idyll of the telecommuter in a country cottage is phoney. Being close to as many other people as possible will be central to economic success, whether because of the need for cultural interaction and excitement to generate the valuable content of weightless products such as computer programmes or movies, or because of the fact that the social economy, composed of people-to-people services, is where more and more of us will find work.

Both the importance of global financial markets and the importance of urban regions emphasise the point that the nation state is no longer the natural location of government. This is far from being a novel observation, although there are signs the nation state is fighting back. But the final chapter of this book discusses how the economic decline of the nation state transforms the nature of the economic policies governments ought to be applying. The old set of levers – interest rates, exchange rates, levels of taxes and spending – is still available, in a limited way, but the best a national government can hope for here is that it does not make any big mistakes. These decisions are much less important than the choices made from the new menu. They include international co-operation, the provision of infrastructure including education, and the decisions about what to regulate – and what to leave for either individuals or smaller units of government.

One night in the spring of 1997, when I was part way through writing this book, the BBC's main evening news bulletin started with the following four items. The lead story was about riots in Albania following the collapse of pyramid investment schemes in which many people had lost their life savings. 'You can not contain a civil conflict of this kind,' said an expert interviewed by the reporter. The financial and social collapse indeed triggered a mass exodus of desperate Albanians over the sea to Italy, where the government's emergency refugee camps in Brindisi were soon overflowing.

This was followed by a report on plans for the single European currency. The then British foreign secretary, Malcolm Rifkind, warned that the plans presaged the end of the nation state. One of the German Chancellor's political advisers said he wanted to see monetary union postponed. But the presidents of Germany's Bundesbank and the European Monetary Institute said there must be no delay to the start of the project.

Third came a special report from Korea where there had been unprecedented industrial action by workers in the big conglomerates. One of the best performing 'Tiger' economies was not so tigerish any more, with high labour costs making it vulnerable to competition from overseas. Jobs and benefits were being cut for the first time. David Roche, a commentator who appeared in the report, said: 'The girls want to have nice handbags and the boys want to have fast cars'. Rampant Western consumerism had replaced the traditional ethic of hard work and sacrifice, he implied.

Finally, green protesters in northern Germany had cemented themselves to the railway tracks to try and delay shipments of nuclear waste for reprocessing. It was the first of several days of civil disobedience which ended in failure. Slowly but inevitably, the waste got through.

It was only in the second half of the news bulletin that we got on to the reassuringly familiar territory of domestic political trivia, accidents, sport and human interest. It was a bit of a surprise to find the weather report had no news of hurricanes, earthquakes and floods in the natural world to mirror the upheaval in our human world.

This one news bulletin appeared to me to illustrate why many people feel that we are living through an economic nightmare. There is no safe haven: horrors in one country spill over into others. The number of refugees from local conflicts who seek to cross over the borders between them and us has reached epic proportions. Environmental degradation in one nation imposes costs beyond its boundaries, and the environmental costs of economic growth have – rightly – given birth to one of the most vigorous political strands in the industrialised world.

The pressure of global competition means no workers, even in the most successful young economies, are safe from the risk of losing their livelihood and social protection. What hope, then, for the unemployed in Europe, where wage costs are higher and productivity growing less quickly? How are the big industrial countries supposed to react to the forces of globalisation?

Indeed, what can their governments do at all in a world where the foreign exchange markets trade a trillion dollars worth of national currency every day, and no central bank can hope to control the resulting fluctuations? One of the motivations for creating Europe's single currency is the possibility of creating a counterweight to global market forces. While national politicians and many voters fear the loss of power this implies, the bankers see supranational structures as the only possibility of reclaiming power from the markets.

No wonder that many have come to dislike what we describe as 'globalisation'. There is a political backlash against these phenomena, and one that has produced strange allies. Opposition to global forces links the extreme right-wing American militias, environmental groups, prominent businessmen of extraordinary wealth, some aid organisations and very many people on the left. They all speak the language of apocalypse. If we do not cut off the tentacles of globalisation, these varied groups argue, the results will be social dislocation, riots, urban breakdown, class warfare. The impulse to withdraw from engagement with the world is very strong, and particularly worrying coming from the left-wing of politics where internationalism has been a central strand of belief since at least the 1930s.

The point of this book is to show that talk of impending apocalypse is nonsense, and dangerous nonsense. The idea that disengagement is possible is equally wrong. This varied catalogue of doom-mongers is getting away with it, though, because the metaphor they are using for economic change, globalisation, is misleading. It is, equally, both nonsense and politically unsophisticated – just so much globaloney – to embrace the opposite point of view, that there are unlimited benefits to be reaped from globalisation if only everybody would stop grumbling.

The idea that what is happening to the world is globalisation has become a cliché. It dates back to Marshall McLuhan's 'global village', and has adhered to our mental processes through all the subsequent technological changes, resurfacing again most recently as the 'death of distance'. But it does not capture the essential nature of the transformation we are living through. Consider the fashionable argument that the degree of trade and investment and migration between nations is no greater now than it was a century ago, and therefore there is nothing special (and nothing that governments cannot handle using conventional economic policies) about what is happening now.

This is faulty logic. If the degree of international linkage has barely returned to where it was at the start of the twentieth century, then globalisation is not what is special about today's world economy. For things are different now.

We live in a weightless world, not a global village.

Viewing the world through the lens of a different metaphor, weightlessness, suggests a radically different approach to the policies needed to react to the genuine economic dislocations that are taking place. It is a more realistic vision, neither inevitably apocalyptic nor necessarily utopian. You do not have to become an extremist about weightlessness. It restores the possibility of normal political debate.

However, the weightless world is in danger of being seen as the playground of a privileged, international technocracy. You could call them yuppies. Robert Reich called them 'symbolic analysts'. They are the glossy, healthy, glamorous executives of countless advertisements and television series, presented as the models for our aspirations. You will not find them in Albania, or at environmental protests, or shouting through a cloud of tear gas on the streets of Seoul.

This fortunate minority of mobile professionals, which has so far reaped the fruits of technological change, cannot be allowed to get away with presenting the economic transformation of our world as a merely technical question, a matter of hard facts not difficult choices. A new politics of weightlessness is needed so that the economic benefits can be captured and shared, the technocrats made accountable for economic success or failure.

There is now a strand in political philosophy that detests economic progress, linking it to the fundamental modern liberal agenda. For example, John Gray has criticised the 'elite of opinion formers' who have paternalistically imposed conformity on the world. It is a political tendency 'for which progress is more important than liberty'. He quotes George Santayana approvingly: 'We all feel at this time the moral ambiguity of mechanical progress. It seems to multiply opportunity, but it destroys the possibility of simple, rural or independent life.'[4]

Everybody feels the appeal of the simple life.

I have desired to go where springs not fail,
To fields where flies no sharp and sided hail
And a few lilies blow.
And I have desired to be where no storms come
And the green swell is in the havens dumb
And out of the swing of the sea.

The anti-progressives have been given their ammunition by the economic elites. To caricature it only slightly, the technocratic menu presents only two options: extreme free market liberalism, embracing change; or foolish old-fashioned corporatism, resisting it. It is a dichotomy that cuts across the traditional left–right division, which is why we find deep green environmentalists allied to paranoid militias on the one hand, and centre-left parties embracing raw capitalism on the other.

The experts' unpalatable 'either-or' menu is bogus. This book is my contribution towards the creation of the radical centre. Economic progress is possible in the weightless world. The fresh wave of technological advance can bring decent standards of living within reach of very many more people than in the past. Sharing the benefits fairly is a matter of political will, and can be achieved with the right set of policy tools.

Notes

1. Interview in *The Independent*, London, 31 May 1997.
2. This and other speeches can be found at www.bog.frb.fed.us/BOARDDOCS/SPEECHES.
3. Interview in *Marxism Today*, November 1991.
4. In *Post-Liberalism*, 1994.

Acknowledgements

I owe thanks to many people without whom this book would not have taken shape. The biggest debt of all is to Rory and Adam for their love and patience during the year I spent huddled over the computer when I should have been spending more time with my family.

My editor, Mark Allin of Capstone, and agent, Sara Menguc at David Higham Associates, come next, especially for their confidence in me when mine flagged. Mark deserves special praise for both spotting all the weaknesses in my arguments and suggesting how to overcome them – no author could wish for a better editor.

There were many people who were incredibly generous with their time and ideas. Danny Quah of the London School of Economics deserves special mention for planting the seeds of the ideas in this book. I must also thank Bill Allen, Jane Ashley, Ed Balls, Ruth Ben-Ghiat, Simon Briscoe, Lindsay Fraser, Paul Gregg, Gerry Holtham, Will Hutton, Vinita Juneja, Mervyn King, Denis McShane, Bethan Marshall, Richard Marshall, Bill Martin, Ed Mayo, David Miles, Henry Neuberger, Gus O'Donnell, Trevor Phillips, Penelope Rowlatt, Peter Sinclair, Jamie Stiehm, Raj Thamotheram, Nick Timmins, David Walton, and Martin Weale for helpful suggestions and friendly criticism. Thanks also to Edward Glaeser at Harvard University and Paul Krugman at MIT for providing references and papers.

I owe a great debt to *The Independent*, especially my editor Andrew Marr and his deputy Colin Hughes. The newspaper has not only allowed me to try out ideas, but has also proved a constant source of stimulus thanks to the wonderful people who work there. Anthony Bevins, Yvette Cooper, Matt Hoffman, Andrew Marshall, Hamish McRae, Suzanne Moore, John Price, Polly Toynbee, Roger Trapp and David Walker all – whether they knew it or not – made an important contribution to *The Weightless World*.

Finally, I'd like to express heartfelt gratitude to those people at the Organisation for Economic Co-operation and Development who went out of their way to look up all sorts of figures and publications for me, in a true spirit of wanting to further our understanding of the world.

Responsibility for the finished product, with all its infelicities, warts and omissions, is mine.

Diane Coyle
June 1997

Chapter One

The Weightless World

A single imported greetings card with a microchip that plays *Happy Birthday* when the card is opened contains more computer power than existed on the planet 50 years ago. It weighs a gram or so.

This might seem an odd choice of example to illustrate economic progress, but weightlessness is the key to understanding the new industrial revolution we are living through. People have the deeply ingrained habit of thinking about economic value as something with physical presence, with weight and mass. This is less and less true. Economic value is dematerialising.

In 1885 the United Kingdom imported nearly 16 million hundredweights of wheat meal and flour, and 1.1 billion pounds of raw cotton, amongst other things. Its main exports in the same year were 3.1 million tons of iron and steel and 4.4 billion yards of cotton fabrics.[1] The concept of the balance of trade started out as a literal description of how the quantity of imports and exports was assessed: the weight of imports on one side of the scales and the weight of exports on the other.

It was a conceptualisation still alive in 1985. In that year the volume of computers imported into the UK was assessed by weighing them. Within less than another decade, this had become an absurdity. Computers had become simultaneously so much smaller and so much more powerful that their weight was meaningless.

The things where economic value was once concentrated used to be big, heavy objects: from steel girders and machine tools to cars and mahogany furniture. From the 1950s onwards miniaturisation, new materials and fashions allowed the same value to be embedded in less weight. For example, cars have become steadily smaller and have used more aluminium and plastic in their construction compared to steel and wood. At the same time, they have become much more sophisticated, with electronic windows, power steering, catalytic converters, stereos – and, increasingly, gizmos such as car telephones and on-board navigational computers.

There are many other examples of physical goods that have become lighter over the years. But this is the less important part of the trend towards weight-lessness: for more and more of the economy does not consist of goods at all. This is one way of saying that the share of manufacturing in the developed countries has been on a declining trend for the past quarter century. Services have been taking an increasing share of the economy.

It only takes a few moments' thought to confirm this observation. We all still shop for food and clothes, and want to own cars, TV sets and home computers. But the share of income these absorb is shrinking compared to the money we spend on child care, eating out, video rental, health care and school-ing, insurance policies, lottery tickets, and the TV licence or fees. However, it is essential to distinguish (at least) two types of activity that get lumped to-gether in the services category.

On the one hand, there are the traditional occupations that statisticians call 'community, social and personal services': haircuts, cleaning, babysitting, teach-ing, nursing, government administration and so on. On the other there are 'high value added' services such as currency trading, creating financial deriva-tives, software development, gene research or making programmes for satel-lite television. Most of these are high-technology, depending for their exist-ence on modern computer power and telecommunications. They are also dematerialised, or weightless.

Weightlessness has in a sense become a commonplace. It is not too surpris-ing to learn that a third of the increase in global output during the past half-century has gone into health and education and a third into 'leisure', broadly defined to include the media; nor that since 1990 American companies have spent more on computers and communications than all other types of equip-ment combined; nor that more people work as data processors than, say, for oil companies.

Yet it is a fact of life whose implications are not widely understood. For one thing, it is economic weightlessness rather than the growth of trade or deregulation that is driving the globalisation of which we hear so much these days. According to the cyber-guru William Gibson, 'The Internet could one day be seen as being something terrifically significant, something akin to the building of cities … It's postnational and postgeographical'.[2] Danny Quah, a professor at the London School of Economics, and one of the pioneers of weightless economics, writes: 'Dematerialised commodities show no respect for space and geography'.[3] This is due to a property that he calls 'infinite expansibility'. Put simply, this means that the use of a dematerialised object by one person does not prevent another from using it. Other people can simultaneously use the word processing code I use as I type this. It is an economic good whose ownership cannot be transferred or traded, but simply replicated – and at almost no transmission cost, in almost no time. Trade in such goods is not an exchange, but nearly costless reproduction.

The spread of weightless economic activity is down to the phenomenal cluster of technological advances in computer and telecommunications technology. The computing power of a microchip doubles roughly every 18 months – an observation known as Moore's Law, first made by Intel chairman Gordon Moore. The cost of this computer power, astonishingly, has fallen at about the same pace, halving every two years. For example, a mid-range $2000 personal computer contains about a hundred million transistors (the same computer power as a big mainframe a decade ago). So the information processing power that cost me a precious $1 on a Digital Equipment Corporation VAX mainframe as a hard-up economics student in 1980 would today cost less than 0.01 cent.

Likewise, telephone costs have fallen literally exponentially since 1945. A three-minute transatlantic call that costs $0.84 today would have cost nearly $800 in today's money 50 years ago. Between 1995 and 1996, Internet access charges fell from an average of more than $60 a month to less than $20 a month.[4]

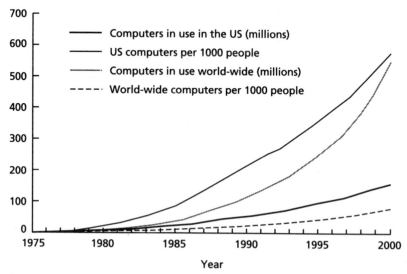

Fig. 1 Computers in use, 1975–2000. (Source: *Computer Industry Almanack*.)

These price falls, a measure of the speed of technical progress, have given a huge boost to economic activity that relies on computer and communications technology, and will continue to do so. This kind of activity has no specific location, and no clear points of entry and exit across national boundaries. Danny Quah says: 'With dematerialisation, the natural marketplace is unbounded'. It is global.

Consider the survey of foreign exchange trading conducted every few years by the Bank for International Settlements. The latest survey showed that in 1995 more than $1 trillion-worth of currencies was traded around the planet every day.[5] Most of this trading takes place in London, with New York and Tokyo a distant second and third. The first thing to note is that the only way the BIS, the foremost international banking authority, can get this information is to send a questionnaire to banks asking them to estimate what foreign exchange business they carry out and where. Neither it not its member central banks can actually measure what is happening in this key financial market. Secondly, the commercial banks' replies to the questionnaire assign the trading to one centre or another depending on where their traders have their desks and book their profits or losses; but all the action takes place between computers distributed around the world, and the assignation of the business to one country rather than another is notional. The world's biggest centre for foreign exchange dealing, one of Britain's biggest industries, is actually cyberspace.

Invisibility

Those of us who claim that computers are transforming the world economy have one big obstacle to overcome: there seems not to be much evidence of it. The spread of computers has been astonishing. According to the annual industry bible, the *Computer Industry Almanac*, there was one computer for every 100,000 Americans in 1965. By the end of 1996 there were two computers for every five people in the US, and this is expected to climb to three for every five by the end of the century. The US is ahead of other countries, but there has also been a wildfire spread world-wide. The number has gone up from seven computers for every 100,000 people in 1975, or about one for every 14,000 people, to one for every 500 people in the world by the end of 1996 and a predicted one for every 400 by the year 2000.[6]

Yet the hard economic benefits of information technology are so far invisible. The period of fast growth in computing power and swift decline in costs have coincided with a sharp slowdown in average growth in the industrial countries. Productivity has been increasing more slowly than in the pre-computer era. There have been three severe recessions in less than 20 years, leaving high levels of unemployment as a legacy. It takes some suspension of disbelief to argue that the industrial countries are blossoming in the white heat of a new technological revolution.

Obviously, computers have made some difference. They have made it easier to book an air ticket or to draw money from the bank. They have usurped typists from their jobs. It is easier to look up information. On the other hand, anybody who has seen computers introduced into their workplace can vouch for the incredible inefficiencies they bring with them. Office workers waste time playing games or looking for that fabled pornography on the Internet. Internal networks are used for gossiping and broadcasting the latest football score. Unnecessary documents with beautiful graphics are generated, delivering little additional information for a lot of extra effort. Impatient shoppers spend minutes waiting for an under-trained sales clerk to figure out how to enter a purchase on the terminal, which will control the inventory, and for their credit card to be validated.

Economists have dubbed this the productivity puzzle. Nobel Laureate Robert Solow famously joked: 'You can see the computer age everywhere but in the productivity statistics'.[7] So why have computers not generated extra growth in output? There are at least three answers: under-measurement of the output of industries using information technology; over-estimation of the importance of computers relative to all other types of capital equipment; and over-optimism about how quickly new technologies spread.

The first point is simple. The output of many industries that have been computerised cannot be measured directly and statistics for output are derived from measurement of the inputs used. By definition, productivity growth, or extra output per unit of input, is zero.

The second point is that we have an inflated perception of how far computerisation has spread. Recent research[8] indicates that even though investment in information technology has been growing very rapidly, computers still form such a small part of the nation's capital stock that they could not possibly have made a big difference to output yet.

The third, and perhaps most interesting, answer is that it takes a long time for new technologies to be diffused. The sewing machine is one example. Elias Howe, a Boston inventor, built the first lockstitch sewing machine in 1846. It could out-sew five seamstresses. Local tailors shunned the new machines, however. They were expensive, less versatile than human stitchers, and would have destroyed many women's livelihoods. Sewing machines were an immediate hit on the domestic market, but it took 40 years for the design to be refined to make them simple and cheap enough for most households. It was not until the 1890s that industrial machines good enough for garment manufacturers went on sale. It took half a century to get from the invention of the sewing machine to the birth of the rag trade sweatshop.[9] Another well-known case study establishes that it took 40 years for commercial gains to result from the introduction of the electric dynamo in the 1880s.[10]

In fact, there is an entire sub-branch of economic research into the generally slow speed with which new technology is diffused through the economy. As far back as 1935 the French historian Marc Bloch noted that it took a millennium for the water mill to be widely adopted because people moved about so little in the Dark Ages and mediaeval times. Linking technical progress with actual productivity growth is fraught with difficulty. It depends on how profitable the new technology is, how expensive it is – and how fast its price is falling, and on how much organisational change is needed to use it. Two American researchers have concluded that the costs of business reorganisation have been one of the biggest impediments to the delivery of higher output by computerisation.[11] Companies have had to develop software, train workers and reorganise – generally by 'delayering' and giving more responsibility to individual employees. All slow, expensive and painful. But it does not mean there will be no pay-off at all from new technology in terms of greater productivity and prosperity. It will simply turn out to have taken two or three decades.

Insecurity

Getting from here to there is always the problem. Just as there are type A and type B personalities, the world seems to divide between the geeks who love computers and think in terms of the boundless new opportunities they provide and the technophobes who do not trust the technology and see computers putting people out of work.

The futurist manifesto published by the magazine *Wired* is resolutely optimistic:

> *'Today's leaders scorn the possibility of a golden age in which economies are based on limitless ideas, not limited materials. They refuse to see that abundance, not scarcity, drives the future, and that widespread connection can replace widespread alienation … The digital society is a place of abundance, not limitations; of choice, not* diktat.*'[12]*

Contrast a gloomier prediction made almost simultaneously by one of the world's foremost economists in a special futurology issue of a magazine. According to Paul Krugman of the Massachusetts Institute of Technology, and by no means an extreme pessimist about jobs, writing as if at the end of the next century:

> 'When something becomes abundant it also becomes cheap. A world awash with information is one in which information has very little market value. In general when the economy becomes extremely good at doing something, that activity becomes less, rather than more, important. Late twentieth century America was supremely efficient at growing food; that was why it had hardly any farmers. Late twenty-first century America is supremely efficient at processing routine information; that is why traditional white-collar workers have virtually disappeared.'[13]

These contrasting predictions were taken to extremes by two men who sought the Republican nomination for the 1996 US presidential election campaign. Neither succeeded. Both on the right wing of their party, their concerns were not seen as mainstream. But both were looking further into the future than the men, Republican Bob Dole and Democrat Bill Clinton, who finally competed for the presidency.

Pat Buchanan, on the one hand, is a fierce and demagogic opponent of the global, technological economy. Trade, computerisation, big corporations are destroying ordinary people's livelihoods, he argued in an ultra-populist primary campaign. He addressed one audience: 'This New World Order is being constructed not for the benefit of you and other American families, but for the benefit of a corporate and financial elite that has no loyalty except to the bottom line of a balance sheet'.

The multimillionaire businessman Steve Forbes, on the other hand, praised the possibilities opened up by this new world order. He said:

> 'The economic transformation that we are on the threshold of will unleash an expansive future for America, a future far greater than anything we've seen before. The industrial machine was about hierarchies, big companies,

big unions, big cities, big government. The thrust of this new economy is more Jeffersonian. It gives power to individuals. It gives power to people.'[14]

Populism versus techno-populism, perhaps. For a while the Buchanan version made all the running. The *New York Times* ran a special series of long articles on corporate 'downsizing', and *Time* magazine made it a cover story in the early stages of the election campaign. According to the *New York Times*, more than 43 million jobs had been erased in the US since 1979, and nearly three-quarters of households had encountered a layoff. In a special poll that the paper carried out at the end of 1995, half of all respondents thought it somewhat or very unlikely that the next generation would be better off than the current one. In other words, the American dream was over for half the population. Fully three-quarters said companies were less loyal to their employees now than 10 years ago.

The paper's report said: 'Everything, seemingly, is in upheaval: not just the jobs and lives of tens of thousands of people, but also the big corporations, the banks, the schools, the religious and cultural institutions, the old relationships of politics and power, and, especially, people's expectations of security, stability and a shared civic life'.[15]

As it happened, the US economy turned out to be so strong that year that the unemployment rate fell to 5 per cent, and the preoccupation with economic insecurity receded. However, other industrialised countries took up the baton. In the surprise British bestseller *The State We're In*, journalist Will Hutton struck a chord with his description of the '30–30–40 society': 30 per cent of people in stable, core jobs, 30 per cent with insecure work, temporary or part time, and 40 per cent either officially unemployed or marginalised from the labour market.

On the Continent, where unemployment remained far above US and UK levels, the sense of insecurity was even stronger. In France, for instance, this took the classic Gallic form of unrest on the streets at the end of 1995 and in later half-hearted outbursts. Jean-Marie Colombani, the distinguished editor of *Le Monde*, diagnosed the last gasp of the system of *dirigisme*, state planning, first introduced by the seventeenth-century finance minister Colbert and consolidated this century by the Gaullist constitution of the Fifth Republic. Last gasps tend to be violent: nearly one in five of French voters has supported the right-wing and xenophobic *Front National*.

Insecurity is an infectious emotion at the *fin de siècle*. The late 1990s are years of AIDS, flesh-eating bacteria, deranged massacres, moral decay and uncertainty on every horizon. Science fiction movies like *Strange Days* and *Crash* set the dystopian future only a year or two away from now. The economic disruptions due to weightlessness, the dematerialisation of the economy – well, most people could do without it, whatever long-term promise it holds out.

The next chapter explains in detail that the trends set in train by new technology have indeed destroyed jobs. Profound industrial restructuring always does. It is creating more jobs too, but that does not make the turmoil necessarily welcome.

Insecurity has become a key theme of the 1990s. Most human beings dislike disruption. As the poet Edmund Spenser noted in *The Faerie Queen* four hundred years ago,

> *'What man that sees the ever-whirling wheel*
> *Of Change, the which all mortal things doth sway,*
> *But that thereby doth find and plainly feel*
> *How Mutability in them doth play*
> *Her cruel sports, to many men's decay?'*

Inequality

In the novel *Microserfs*, hero Daniel has a job testing Microsoft programmes for bugs. Several times every day he checks the company's share price. 'The stock closed up $1.75 on Friday. Bill has 78,000,000 shares so that means he's now $136.5 million richer. I have almost no stock, and this means I'm a loser.'

An economy which is creating winners and losers is one where inequality is growing. The billionaire Microsoft founder Bill Gates is so much richer than almost everybody else on the planet that it defies imagination. Like insecurity, inequality is one of the overriding characteristics of the weightless world. It is something that has generated no end of journalistic indignation, especially in Britain, where inequality has risen faster since 1980 than in any other developed country.

Executive pay is one area where unequal earnings have become very obvious and politically contentious. Top executives in the biggest UK companies making more than £250,000 a year are not unusual, and a handful earn more than £1 million. Million-dollar plus pay is more widespread in the US. Average earnings increased less than twofold to £18,000 over the same period, and the vast majority of Britons in work in 1995 earned between £8000 and the average. The four million or so either unemployed or unable to work have even less income. The ratio of incomes in the top tenth of the pay scale (above £30,000 a year in 1996) and the bottom (below £9000 a year) increased by nearly a full point in the 17 years after 1979.

Inequality has increased even more sharply in the US, where it is also a divisive political issue although less so than on the other side of the Atlantic. Columnist Gary Wills noted that a fifth of the delegates to the Republican Party convention in San Diego in 1996 made more than $1 million a year, and another fifth more than $200,000.[16] Although incomes became fractionally less unequal in 1996 than the previous year, according to Census Bureau figures, the authoritative *State of Working America* report the same year concluded: 'Since 1979, the most important development regarding American incomes has been slow growth and increasing inequality'. The average income of the top 1 per cent rose by 87.5 per cent between 1979 and 1989, while income for the bottom 40 per cent of families declined. The typical American family was worse off in the mid-1990s than 20 years earlier, but the wealthy were very much better off.[17]

In fact, the Institute of Policy Research in Washington DC has calculated that the 447 mainly American dollar billionaires listed by *Forbes* magazine in 1996 had a stock of wealth in excess of the annual income of the poorest half of the world's 3 billion people. Although it does not compare like with like, it is nevertheless a graphic illustration of the extremes of wealth and poverty on the planet.

With exceptions like New Zealand, most of the other advanced countries have not suffered the same increase in inequality. However, the differences between them and the UK are not large, and many Europeans in particular fear that they will be forced down the same path. They interpret their painfully high unemployment rates as the price of resisting the trend towards greater inequality.

It is a trend that seems as remorseless as lava flow. The American economists Robert Frank and Philip Cook have characterised it as the *Winner Takes All Society*. They blame deregulation and a changed political culture as well as a phenomenon identified as 'the economics of superstars' a decade and a half ago.[18]

There are two reasons a field with stars, such as sport or the movies, gener-

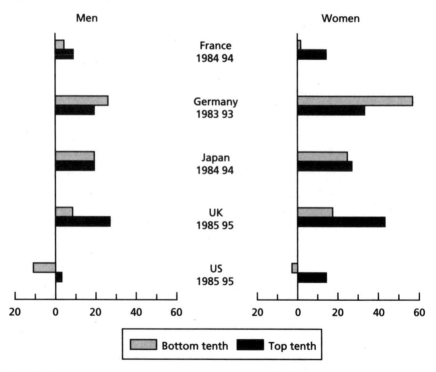

Fig. 2 Real wage growth over the last 10 years for low- and high-paid workers: percentage changes, not annualised. (Source: *OECD Employment Outlook 1996.*)

ates a more unequal distribution of income than teaching or accountancy, say. First, the economic output of a movie star has no marginal cost. Keanu Reeves makes the film once. It can be shown to one or one million people with no extra effort by the actor. Secondly, audiences will prefer to watch a film starring him than one with an unknown actor – even one who is objectively almost as handsome or talented. These supply and demand factors combine to deliver the biggest market share, and biggest incomes, to those who become stars. Trivial differences in talent are magnified into huge disparities in earnings.

Weightlessness is extending superstar economics into more and more fields. The number of fields where both conditions – effectively zero marginal cost to generating extra output and a concentration of demand on the stars, the first in each niche – is growing rapidly. For example, it is increasingly true of all the multimedia industries, from software to music and TV. It is also true for any profession where the expertise of the stars can be reproduced using the new technologies – for instance, surgeons who can operate, advise or teach through video links and software; or successful currency traders, like George Soros, who can leverage the amount of business they do in the financial markets and the degree to which those markets move in their favour when their trades become known.

The fact that there are widespread 'network externalities', or benefits from using something that grows with the number of users, in the dematerialised industries will reinforce the superstar trend. For example, the Apple Macintosh operating system has always been acknowledged as better than Microsoft's by industry experts. But Apple has never broken out of its market niche whereas almost everybody uses Microsoft's Windows. If almost everybody does, almost everybody always will because it makes life much simpler. The externality put the billionaire into Bill.

The mitigating factor in the winner-takes-all trend, Danny Quah notes, is that dematerialisation is also helping to reduce the costs and difficulty of becoming a superstar. You do not need to be born with a great bone structure or have the huge amount of capital needed to start up a pharmaceuticals company. You need an idea, a cheap computer and a telephone. He writes: 'At the same time that income inequalities become more extreme, *mobility* between rich and poor also rises'. It is a bit like Britain's National Lottery fever, he argues. People are willing to see a few win millions of pounds because they can also have a chance at untold riches for just £1 a ticket.

Weightless politics

Politics will be transformed by the weightless world. The economic problems will be different and unexpected. And conventional solutions will no longer work.

Take inequality. Since World War II, the Western industrialised countries have all had a compact whereby governments guaranteed a minimum standard of living to all their citizens. This implied an effort to keep unemployment low and the maintenance of a welfare state. The successful relief of poverty meant incomes became more equal. But providing the welfare guarantee meant sealing the boundaries of the nation to limit payments to citizens. It is no longer clear that the welfare state can continue in its existing form. The bill for current entitlements has risen painfully high, yet governments are not achieving the basics their citizens expect: there are more paupers on the streets of our cities; there are, in Europe at any rate, more people without work than at any time since the Great Depression.

Even trickier for the existing social contract, as the average productivity and income in Western society rises, a small group of citizens is getting left behind. Their productivity is not rising but their expectations keep pace with the rest of us. They will not accept the exploitative jobs in which they might be employable, preferring the informal economy or even the illegal, drugs-based economy. Meanwhile, the grotty jobs that still need carrying out – we still need the cleaners, the auxiliary nurses and the all-night sales assistants at the convenience store – become harder to fill because of the political classes' mania about keeping out immigrants.

A first attempt to provide some answers to these dilemmas follows later, after an exploration of the current tensions in our welfare state in Chapters 5 and 6. Policies for the weightless economy need to accept that governments have simply lost some of their powers. The domain over which the public sector has any power has shifted and shrunk but our political institutions have not caught up with it.

If there are two certainties in life, death and taxes, looking at these demonstrates pretty comprehensively that the arm of government can no longer reach as far as it used to. No government could now significantly increase the amount of tax it raises from business. The barriers to companies moving around the world have almost entirely crumbled. The German government wants to increase corporation tax? A large number of big companies would simply move some of their operations across a nearby border to the Czech Republic or Romania. Or perhaps to an even cheaper, low-tax newly industrialising country in Asia such as Thailand or Indonesia. Or to Ireland or the UK, where the government would be more likely to subsidise an inward investor than tax them. Or they could simply rearrange their internal transactions in order to minimise their tax bill.

German politicians have complained about competition from 'tax havens' within the EU – naming the UK, the Netherlands, Ireland and Belgium.[19] But simply to list the countries they have complained about is to realise how unlikely politicians are to be able to reverse the trend. Indeed, as one German minister complained, another gave a speech about the need to reduce the tax burden on German businesses.

Similarly, it is almost impossible for governments to raise much more income tax from their wealthiest citizens. Try increasing the top tax rate above 50 per cent. Those affected would move money to offshore centres and would set their accountants to minimising the amount of income liable to tax. They might perhaps move to another country. The executive classes have become much more mobile. There would be no point – it would raise very little revenue and generate a lot of wasteful tax avoidance. It is a problem at the margin because most people will not uproot because of taxes. Nevertheless, it marks the limit of government's ability to tax.

These arguments have led Mervyn King, chief economist at the Bank of England, to argue that the tax system in industrialised countries is directed towards taxing spending rather than income.[20] But even then, he observes, a lot of governments' ability to raise revenue is being chipped away by computer technology. Before long, we will be able to buy almost anything over the Internet. Since information on the Net is shipped around on varying routes and broken up into small packets of information which do not mean anything until reassembled, it will be impossible for tax authorities to monitor all transactions.

What's more, it would be impossible to say where those transactions had taken place even if they could be monitored, and therefore knotty to decide which government is entitled to any tax on them. If on-line shopping grows as much as expected, even taxing spending could prove much harder. Governments might be left relying on very high taxes on things whose physical presence means the taxation possibilities cannot dematerialise – such as duties on petrol, for which you have to take your car to the petrol station, or road tolls, or landfill fees. Or perhaps taxes on the distribution companies that ship the goods we buy over the Internet, or the individuals to whom they are delivered.

Weightlessness has already set limits on governments' ability to tax citizens in a deeper sense. The financial markets provide investors – which means almost all of us through our savings and pension plans – with the means to veto government budget policies of which they disapprove. They can easily and cheaply move their money to another country. Peter Huber, a senior fellow at the Manhattan Institute, says: 'By far the most effective way to vote against new government spending is to buy some other government's bonds'. The 'modernisation' of finance, he says, accounts for the mass conversion of Western governments to the notion of a balanced budget, at least in principle. 'Whether they talk left or right, governments world-wide have little choice but to abandon fiscally suicidal policies, most notably the practice of issuing long-term debt to finance current entitlements.'[21]

This argument, explored in Chapter 9, makes sense of a famous remark by James Carville, adviser to Bill Clinton in his 1992 presidential election campaign. He wrote in the *Wall Street Journal*, as the President was inaugurated:'I used to think if there was reincarnation, I wanted to come back as the President or the pope or a .400 baseball hitter. But now I want to come back as the bond market. You can intimidate everybody.' It is its weightlessness that gives the market its reach and power.

The new geography of government

It has become a commonplace to argue that the nation state has had its day. Nicholas Negroponte, the MIT technology guru, puts it pithily: 'Nations today are the wrong size. They are not small enough to be local and they are not large enough to be global.'[22] Although usually couched in terms of economic globalisation rather than weightlessness, many authors have realised that national governments no longer have their traditional reach over economic policy. For example, Andrew Marr notes that if power has really shifted to markets, 'It could be there is simply less need for politics'.[23] He interprets the rise of the global market and information technology as 'respectively, the extreme logical developments of the liberalism and science of the eighteenth century Enlightenment'. They have undermined the power of existing national political institutions and left us for the most part with rule by technocrat.

He notes, later in the same book, that globalisation is generating a political reaction in favour of localism. Some people see new technology providing a vehicle for a revival of local and individual influence on politics as well as creating the need for it. Lawrence Grossman, for example, writes of 'The electronic republic'.[24] He writes: 'The world of finance has already adapted to an environment of instantaneous voting by interactive telecommunications technologies ... The world of politics is next.' We can already use new media to influence politics through talk radio, phone-ins and opinion polling. Lobby groups in the US and UK have certainly leveraged their influence through use of the Internet to circulate material and instructions to members. Similarly, political parties have used e-mail to co-ordinate activists, for instance to call into particular chat shows. Grossman predicts that the time might soon come when it is possible to hold instant electronic referenda on a wide range of issues by voting at a computer terminal or on the telephone, although he is agnostic about whether or not this is desirable.

This type of analysis of the politics of globalisation does not translate to economic policies, however. Weightlessness means that a growing share of economic activity does not have any national physical location at all. It is not a question of finding the right area over which politicians can set policies, nor even necessarily about international co-ordination of policies although this will have an important role in the weightless world.

One possibility is that multinational companies will start to act as quasi-governmental organisations. After all, they have a lot of power through their decisions about where to base the activity that does need a physical location, and their border-hopping can virtually hold governments to ransom. Science fiction writer and journalist Bruce Sterling opts for this conclusion. In his novel *Islands in the Net* he has the representative of a Japanese company over-ride the objections of a politically squeamish colleague: 'A treaty is only a contract. You're talking like my grandmother. It's our world now … Why work through governments any more? Let's cut out the middleman.' This view is widely shared. Many people do believe that 'the free market' – which means, in effect, big international companies and banks – has defeated politics.

Yet even if economic power has eroded political power, it is dangerous to proclaim the end of politics. It is the location of politics that is changing. One dimension of this will be the revival of great cities – already evident in London and New York, in Hong Kong and LA.

To understand this, it is necessary to think about the way new technology has increased economies of scale and reduced transportation costs, for it is these that determine economic location.

The economist Paul Krugman has revived the discipline of economic geography by drawing attention to these factors. The basic insight is that the existence of any economies of scale will favour the concentration of an activity in one place unless transport costs are high enough to mean this makes no sense.[25] Companies will want to be where their market is biggest and it will be biggest where they are. This self-reinforcing effect helps to explain the fact that industries are for the most part astonishingly concentrated in their location.[26]

In economic geography, the key to the location of economic activity is concentration. The obvious manifestation of this is the fact that most people live in urban areas. US economist Robert Hall puts this in extreme form when he says a city and a boom are essentially the same thing, one in space and one in time. In addition, most urban areas are very specialised because of the economies of scale. Hollywood does movies, Seattle does aircraft, Paris does couture. Just as in sixteenth-century Italy or nineteenth-century Britain, cities will become the focal points of the twenty-first century economy.

In the weightless economy, information technologies imply both greater returns to scale and lower transportation costs. The latter point is straightforward: it is extremely cheap and getting cheaper to move information, the basic material of weightless industries, around. The economies of scale are only slightly harder to explain. There are many 'network externalities', which mean that the biggest company can capture a disproportionate share of the market because of the need for compatibility of software or equipment. Thus VHS drove out Betamax, and Microsoft's Windows dominates the Apple operating system, except in publishing where there exists a subsidiary network because the superiority of the Apple Mac software is so pronounced.

London's triumph

One example that illustrates the new geography is the growing dominance of London as a centre for financial market transactions.

The financial services industry is on the frontier of the information technology revolution in economics. The 'Big Bang' reforms in the City of London in 1986 and similar changes in other financial centres were defined as much by huge investment in information technology and telecommunications as by regulatory change. This investment, the need to stay in the technological wild west, remains the hallmark of the financial markets – the first and biggest cyber-industry. William Mitchell, Dean of the School of Architecture at the Massachusetts Institute of Technology, calls complex financial derivatives 'pure creations of cyberspace'.[27]

The economic engine of the financial services industry is the production, transformation, distribution and consumption of digital information. It is in the front line of the shift towards weightless world. But digital industry can take place anywhere – why do financial services continue to be focused on London, New York and Tokyo?

Take the first of these three financial centres. It is a paradox that as its activity has dematerialised, London as a place has become ever more important. Obviously, some things that were done in London have moved thanks to high technology. This includes back offices, registrars – any functions where the information can be put on a production line. And there has been geographical dispersion within London itself, out of the Square Mile of the City of London to Docklands and the West End. But the high value added functions remain and are becoming increasingly concentrated in London rather than any other centre in the same time zone as more foreign banks move in.

There are certainly cost pressures to move out. Rents and taxes are high in the City, the burden of commuting is heavy, deliveries and logistics are difficult, there is even the threat of terrorism. With cost of telecoms falling and quality rising steadily, acting as a powerful decentralising force, there must be some pretty strong glue.

So what explains the paradox? A lot of the standard explanations for London's appeal seem pretty weak. There is a pool of skilled labour, the English language, the time zone – but this is just as true of small-town Luton 50 miles away as it is of London. And a lot of City workers probably live a lot closer to Luton than to London.

Another common explanation is that processing and exchange of information is essentially social – that you're not in the know if you're not in the bar – that rumours, gossip, sensitive conversations, spin doctoring don't work on the phone. There may be something in this. But frankly, anyone who says you cannot gossip down the line has not listened to a teenager recently.

It is the weightless economics that explain London's magic pull. One key is the existing infrastructure, representing enormous fixed investment – in expensive equipment, in the initial concentration of information, as well as the ease of connecting with other people. History matters in economics, like path-dependence in science – just think of enormous cost of laying cable and installing screens in other locations. It puts its imprint on the map of the weightless world.

A related element is the 'oasis' effect of access to high bandwidth cable connections, the fibres whose capacity to transmit digital bits is effectively infinite. The cost of using these channels increases enough with distance that users cluster together.

However, most important is the fact that computers and telecoms allow for concentration as well as decentralisation, to exploit economies of scale. It means that trading operations for international banks are increasingly centred on London. Deutsche Bank's decision to base its European trading in the City is emblematic. London increasingly embodies the circularity of economic geography that companies want to be where the market is biggest and the market is biggest where the companies are.

City politics

Professor Krugman focuses on an entirely different set of reasons for expecting urban revival. In his futurological essay he writes:

> *'The jobs that could not be shipped abroad or handled by machines were those that required a human touch – face to face interaction between people working directly with physical materials. In short, they were jobs done best in dense urban areas.'*

Whether for reasons of weightlessness or the reverse, some cities at least will become important centres of economic power. Perhaps, as in mediaeval and renaissance times, the city state will become the key political unit. This development was foreseen by Jane Jacobs in her wonderful book *Cities and the Wealth of Nations*. The assumption underlying conventional economic analysis, she argues, is that the national economy is the salient unit, an assumption dating from the mercantilists of the sixteenth and seventeenth centuries. Only Marxist economic theory has diverged successfully from this assumption.

She analyses the economy instead in terms of city units, hubs of trade and the centre of webs of economic relationships. Cities form the base of wealth and taxes milked for the benefit of the national economy. They are wells of spontaneous creativity and enterprise, organic and volatile, prone to boom and bust, impossible to develop successfully from scratch. It is a messy, unpredictable interpretation of the economy far removed from the austere and tidy models of conventional economics.

However, this is what economic policies for the weightless world will have to address. If the politics of the nation state have become irrelevant, the city state is where politics will re-emerge. The new pattern of government, explored in Chapter 10, will be a compact between citizens of cities and their mayors or between citizens of the world and the authors of international rules.

Time is money

The other key to forming economic policy in the weightless world is understanding where value lies. Here is a clue. The weekly *TV Guide* in the US in some years makes bigger profits than the four major television networks combined. Guiding people around information is more valuable than producing information; knowledge is more or less free but time is money.

The Nobel Laureate Herbert Simon put this another way:

> *'What information consumes is rather obvious: it consumes the attention of its recipients. Hence a wealth of information creates a poverty of atten-*

*tion and a need to allocate that attention efficiently among the over-abun-
dance of information sources that might consume it.'*

This is the kind of consideration that makes Paul Krugman rather pessimistic about the weightless economy. 'A world awash in information is one in which information has very little market value', he writes.

It is time or attention, the ability to process the endless flows of information, that will be valuable in the weightless world. Digital resources are not scarce at all. The limits are set by our capacity to use them.

This will make the boundary between home and work a social battleground. Modern technology and communications mean the link binding work to workplace is crumbling. Not too long ago a building would correspond one-to-one with a company or employer. It rendered the institution visible and concrete. This is no longer true. It is people not places who define the institution these days – and a shifting group of people at that.

Equally, work is making greater claims over people. Work follows most of us everywhere thanks to phone, fax, pager, mobile and laptop. We could be seeing the start of a reversal of the trend towards the divorce of home and workplace that dates from the Industrial Revolution. In most professions, work now attaches itself to the person not the place. For the people whose problem is not that they do not have a job, it will be that they cannot escape their job and the demands it puts on their time. The distribution of work in the weightless world, like the distribution of income, is extraordinarily uneven. New technology creates new policy problems.

This is a point emphasised, perhaps surprisingly, by Karl Marx in *Capital*, where he insisted that technology is a social process, not merely a mechanical one.

'Technology discloses man's mode of dealing with Nature, the process of production by which he sustains his life, and thereby also lays bare the mode of formation of his social relations and of the mental conceptions that flow from them.'

Political tension results from the fact that although technical change is caused by social change and in turn reshapes society, the social transformation lags far behind the technological.

Economic policies have always had to address the scarcity of resources and the question of distribution, although few theorists have addressed them since the heyday of classical economics. The scarcities were different in the nineteenth century, when capital or land set the limits to production. Just as the great inequalities generated by the Industrial Revolution created the political dynamic that led to the extension of the vote, the creation of social insurance and the redistribution of income through the national economy, the scarcities and inequalities of the late twentieth century will prompt a political reaction.

It is one that will bring to an end the identification of citizenship with the nation state. Cities will rise in power and the movement of people will become more fluid, ending the social contract that guarantees the welfare of a citizen within fixed borders. The idea of full employment, of a full-time job paying enough to support a family for all who want it, is also in its dying days. Both the nature of work and the influence governments have over employment have already changed irreversibly, although tax and regulatory policies have not yet adapted to the more fluid, riskier and more unequal world.

Weightlessness is inexorable, but there is nothing inevitable about the way technology is going to shape the industrial societies. The next few chapters explore the most obvious manifestation of the weightless world and its risks and challenges: unemployment, new patterns of work and inequality. They are all features of the transition to weightlessness.

Notes

1. *Statistical Abstract for the United Kingdom 1871-1885*, facsimile edition HMSO 1986.
2. Interview in *The Independent*, London, 24 October 1996.
3. In *The Invisible Hand and the Weightless Economy*, LSE, March 1996.
4. OECD Communications Outlook, 1996.
5. Published by the BIS, July 1996.

6. *Computer Industry Almanac*, Glenbrook, Nevada, December 1996.

7. 'We'd better watch out', *New York Times Book Review*, 12 July 1978.

8. For example, *Computers and Output Growth Revisited: How Big is the Puzzle?* Stephen Oliner and Daniel Sichel, Brookings Papers, Vol. 2, 1994.

9. See *Moths to the Flame,* Gregory Rawlins, p116.

10. 'The Dynamo and the Computer', Paul David, *American Economic Review*, May 1990.

11. 'The Competitive Crash in Large Scale Computing', Timothy Bresnahan and Shane Greenstein, NBER Working Paper No. 4901, 1995.

12. October 1996 issue.

13. *New York Times Magazine*, Sunday 29 September 1996.

14. Both reported in 'It's The New Economy, Stupid' by John Heilemann, *Wired* magazine, San Francisco, CA, March 1996.

15. 'The Downsizing of America', *New York Times* special report, Times books, 1996.

16. *The New York Review* , 3 October 1996.

17. *The State of Working America 1996-97*, Employment Policy Institute, Washington DC. (http://epn.org/epi/epswa-ex.html).

18. 'The Economics of Superstars', Sherwin Rosen, *American Economic Review*, December 1981.

19. See report by Peter Norman in the *Financial Times*, London, 23 December 1996.

20. 'The Tax System in the 21st Century', Mervyn King, Bank of England paper, September 1996. See also 'Globalisation, Tax Competition and the Future of Tax Systems', Vito Tanzi, IMF Working Paper No. 141, 1996.

21. 'Cyber Power', Peter Huber, *Forbes*, 2 December 1996.

22. In *Being Digital*.

23. In *Ruling Britannia*.

24. In *The Electronic Republic*, Viking Penguin 1995.

25. See *Geography and Trade*, MIT Press, Cambridge, MA, 1991.

26. There are many examples in *The Competitive Advantage of Nations*, Michael Porter, Macmillan, London, 1990.

27. *City of Bits*, MIT Press, Cambridge, MA, 1996.

Chapter Two

Where Have All The Jobs Gone?

By 1990 there were more people without work in the world's richest countries than ever before. The level of unemployment has scarcely fallen from its all-time high of 35 million since then. In Europe, where the situation is the most serious, more than one in ten people who would like work cannot find it. That means that Europeans all know somebody who is or has been recently unemployed – a son, a cousin, or the husband of a friend. Some of these are people who deserve better – talented, hardworking, decent. Or perhaps they are just unlucky or desperate.

However safe we are in our own jobs, the blight of unemployment has spread much closer to us during the past decade. Some, living in unemployment black-spots such as France's bleak urban estates or mid-western rust-belt towns in the US, know very few people who are *employed*. As the century draws to its close, and our societies reach levels of wealth unprecedented in history, mass unemployment is not acceptable. It is the top priority for politicians in the worst afflicted countries. How can the one in every eight or ten without work be found a satisfactory means of living? How can those cut off from normal society by the loss of income and status that accompany unemployment be reincluded?

The picture gets bleaker than it first seems. Millions more have opted out of the workforce to stay at home and subsist on whatever welfare or illegal work they can find, or are working part-time shifts, or making do for a while with dreary low-paid jobs. How many? There is no precise figure, but at a guess more than a hundred million and perhaps three hundred million are underemployed in the OECD. It could add up to more people than the entire population of the US.

The 1990s have brought with them the greatest economic trauma and loss of human dignity since the Great Depression – and the Industrial Revolution before it. This misery has its patterns, patterns which offer clues about its causes and possible cures.

Before about 1970 unemployment was an American problem. The US jobless rate was well above the European and Japanese rates. Since the early 1970s Europe has fared worse and now has significantly higher unemployment than North America or Japan. European unemployment has hovered around 10 per cent of the workforce, about twice the US rate and three times the Japanese rate – although in Japan's jobs market many people simply opt out of the struggle. Add back in the discouraged, and its unemployment level is actually close to America's.

Although unemployment is now very much a European phenomenon, it has not hindered continuing economic growth in Europe. Quite the reverse. The average growth rate in the EU has exceeded American growth by a wide margin. This has led at least one Continental academic to suggest somewhat controversially that unemployment is not an 'economic' problem so much as a social one. Daniel Cohen writes: 'A society in which the unemployed are so numerous, as in Europe, suffer less from the foregone growth than from the loss of social cohesion that the high unemployment brings'.[1]

The high social cost is therefore one reason for worrying about why some Western countries are stuck with high unemployment levels. Another reason is that joblessness is a side-effect of the industrial restructuring that characterises increasing weightlessness; there is a danger that it will be seen as a reason for resisting economic change. There is no shortage of policy prescriptions that hark back to a pre-weightless world, calling for higher government spending or trade barriers as a panacea. These misdiagnose the causes of unemployment. This chapter sets out briefly the patterns of joblessness. The next analyses the potential culprits.

The unfairness of unemployment

The social cost of unemployment, the reason it matters to those of us who have work as well as the minority who do not, is that it falls unevenly on different groups of people. It falls unfairly, building up resentments and tensions between have-nots and haves.

Unemployment in the 1990s is still a working class problem, to use very old-fashioned terminology. The risk of losing a job has increased a little for white collar workers, but it is mainly manual workers who suffer unemployment.

To put it another way, unemployment for skilled workers has risen since 1990, but unskilled workers still have a significantly higher unemployment rate and lower wages than those with educational or vocational qualifications. Headlines like *Business Week*'s 'I'm worried about my job! The only security for today's migrant managers and professionals is in the portfolio of skills they can sell', which launched a thousand newspaper features about the 'white collar' recession in 1991, were simply misleading. The myth persists. A recent *Wall Street Journal* front page headline trumpeted: 'Grim Reaper: Europe's jobless crisis is cutting a broad swath through middle class'.[2] Nibbling at the edges of middle class privilege would be more accurate. It is only in perception that unemployment has hit professional and white collar workers harder this time. The unskilled are faring much worse.

In addition, other groups suffer disproportionately. Young people have the very highest unemployment rates – about twice as high as the corresponding rates for adults in most industrial countries and more than four times higher in Italy, Spain and Greece. For more than a decade one in four or five people under the age of 24 has been without work. Unemployment rates for the under-25s range from 8 per cent in Germany, where most young people either stay in education full time or find an apprenticeship, to 34 per cent in Italy and 42 per cent in Spain. The experience has shaded the social attitudes of an entire generation, and it should come as no surprise that their values are different from those of the in-work, older majority. The radicalism of youth is

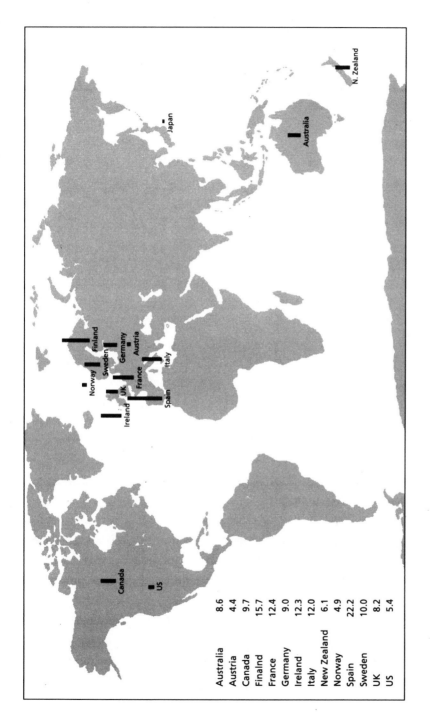

Australia	8.6
Austria	4.4
Canada	9.7
Finalnd	15.7
France	12.4
Germany	9.0
Ireland	12.3
Italy	12.0
New Zealand	6.1
Norway	4.9
Spain	22.2
Sweden	10.0
UK	8.2
US	5.4

Fig. 3 Standardised unemployment rates in 15 OECD countries. (Source: *OECD Labour Force Statistics* No. 1, 1997.)

Fig. 4 Unemployment rates by age and gender (1996).

Country	Sex	Age		
		15–24	25–54	55–64
Canada	Both sexes	16.1	8.6	7.7
	Male	17.5	8.7	7.8
	Female	14.6	8.5	7.6
France	Both sexes	26.3	11.0	8.6
	Male	22.1	9.3	8.6
	Female	31.9	13.0	8.6
Germany	Both sexes	8.0	8.0	17.9
	Male	8.4	7.0	15.2
	Female	7.5	9.3	23.0
Italy	Both sexes	34.1	9.3	4.3
	Male	30.0	7.1	4.3
	Female	39.2	12.9	4.3
Japan	Both sexes	6.6	2.7	4.2
	Male	6.8	2.5	5.1
	Female	6.7	3.2	2.3
UK*	Both sexes	14.7	7.0	7.1
	Male	17.8	8.0	9.5
	Female	11.1	5.6	3.4
US*	Both sexes	12.0	4.3	3.4
	Male	12.6	4.2	3.3
	Female	11.3	4.4	3.4

*Age group 15–24 refers to 16–24.

something that always alarms their elders, but more so now that an understandable nihilism, escape into drugs, violence and political apathy marks so many twenty-somethings – something fully reflecting in popular culture from *Trainspotting* to *La Haine*.

Outside the US and UK, women also have higher unemployment rates, particularly in Catholic countries and particularly if they are single parents. In addition more than a quarter of women work part-time, some proportion of which is low-paid and exploitative work. And members of ethnic minorities have higher unemployment rates everywhere throughout the rich industrialised world. Lastly, there is tentative evidence that unemployment is becoming more concentrated geographically. The highest rates of joblessness have always been seen in certain regions within countries, and especially certain towns and inner city areas. Some unemployed people live in enclaves of poverty and dispossession so isolated that they, too, lose contact with the values of the wider society. This is getting worse. European nations have begun to fear the development of American-style urban ghettos, the geographical expression of all of a country's worst social problems, joblessness, poverty, crime, drug abuse, domestic violence and decaying social and physical infrastructure.

Some of these categories of joblessness obviously overlap. After ten years mass unemployment, mainly in Europe, or poverty-level income, mainly in the US, has become the heritage of millions of citizens. Children are born to it, they grow up into it as young people, and have little chance of escape from it as adults. To have no work is their grim inheritance.

Behind the figures

People's experiences of unemployment depend on where they live. In America flows into and out of joblessness are very high but the typical spell is short, keeping the unemployment rate low. A move from one job to another will normally involve a short period of unemployment. This is because there are more moves into and out of education, more temporary layoffs, and because short holiday entitlements in the US make the gap between jobs the only time to take a break.

Fewer Europeans become unemployed, but once there they tend to get stuck. This means that the ratio of people who have been without a job for more than a year is much higher than in North America – typically between a third and a half of the total in the former, compared to only a tenth in the latter. The oldest and youngest workers are the most likely to suffer long-term unemployment.

Everywhere in the Western world rates of job turnover, as opposed to un-employment turnover, are astonishingly high. Europeans move directly from job to job, North Americans more often move from job to unemployment to job. In all cases, though, the number of people changing their job in any year is truly phenomenal.

Flows of jobs created and destroyed in any given period are far greater than the net increase or decrease in employment. Up to a fifth of jobs have turned over every year on average in almost all OECD countries since the mid-1980s. There is no marked transatlantic difference in turnover. The one ex-ception was the UK, where job turnover is an unusually low 9 per cent. And even that corresponds to about one in eleven jobs (that is, around two mil-lion) being destroyed or created every year. The high turnover rates contrast with net job losses or gains of about one in fifty. It adds up to a lot of churn-ing.

Downsizing blues

Most weeks during the past few years an announcement of big layoffs by a major company will have hit the headlines in most industrial countries. In the 1996 US Presidential election campaign, the 'downsizing' phenomenon became a political football thanks to the efforts of populist Republican hope-ful Pat Buchanan. His attacks on corporate America's trashing of thousands of members of its workforce put candidates Dole and Clinton on the defensive about jobs. Even though President Clinton could point to the creation of 10 million new jobs, net, during his first term of office, no politician could get away without criticising companies for mass redundancies.

One Wall Street economist made news around the world when he re-canted his earlier view that downsizing was the way to make companies more productive. Stephen Roach, head of economics at investment bank Morgan Stanley, concluded that there would be a worker backlash if big companies carried on shedding labour without ever expanding again. 'The so-called productivity resurgence of recent years has been built on the back of slash and burn restructuring strategies that have put extraordinary pressures on the work force. This approach is not a permanent solution. Tactics of open-ended downsizing and real wage compression are ultimately recipes for industrial extinction', he wrote in a newsletter for clients.[3] He called the downsizing phenomenon the 'hollowing of smokestack America'. And it is worth stressing that he wrote this as the unemployment rate in the US was heading down towards its lowest for nearly 20 years.

In fact, it was nothing new in 1996. The only obvious difference in the 1990s is the fractional increase in white collar redundancies compared with previous decades. For factory workers, large-scale downsizing has been going on ever since about 1970, long before management consultants came up with their inelegant phrase for it. In *Rivethead*, his tale of life and layoffs from the General Motors truck and bus plant in Flint, Michigan during the late 1970s, Ben Hamper describes the experience of being thrown out of work by the car giant which had once provided its employees with a meal ticket for life:

> *'Drinking all night was fine, but I needed something to fill up the afternoons. That was one of the problems with unemployment. So often it wove itself into unenjoyment, sentencing you to a vague sprawl where the days all lumped together in one faceless herd. Working was almost preferable. Almost.*
>
> *'It was truly difficult to understand. I had hired in during such a boom era that the overtime alone would have provided enough income to survive on. Yet here I was four years later with nothing but a crop of serious sloth and one mighty pickled liver.'*

Within another four years, under the leadership of the infamous Roger Smith, the plant was shut. From boom to bust in less than a decade – a decline and fall shared by all of the West's industrial regions.

The early 1980s recession brought more redundancies as old industries shrank, with bitterness and pain. The American commentator James Fallows described, in a long article in *The Atlantic Monthly* in March 1985, the ruined lives left behind by South Chicago's retreating steel industry.

> *'To the steelworkers of South Chicago everything about the 'new' economy is bad. They see the movement of jobs to the American south-west or to Taiwan as just another way to undercut the workingman's wage. Few of them see a way to adapt to the new order. Why should they even think of moving? Everyone has a story about the friend or nephew who drove to Houston or Denver, found himself stacking bottles at the Seven-Eleven or competing with illegal Mexican immigrants for construction jobs, and drove back home.'*

The panic about downsizing needs to be kept in this perspective. As the MIT economist Paul Krugman sees it, anecdotes and headlines cannot do justice to the full picture – much as reports of plane crashes make us over-estimate the risks of air travel. He writes: 'The destruction of good jobs by American corporations is just not an important part of what is happening to the American worker ... The people who are doing really badly are those who do not have good jobs and never did'.[4]

Creative destruction?

Turning to fact rather than anecdote, large-scale hiring and firing is simply what happens in Western capitalism (at least outside Japan, although increasingly there too). But we are clearly a lot more worried about it now.

One detailed study of job turnover patterns in American manufacturing[5] finds that recessions are marked by a sharp increase in average job destruction rates and little change in job creation rates, meaning that job turnover rises during recessions too. The variation in job destruction over the business cycle is more pronounced among bigger and older firms, which helps explain why the news of thousands of job cuts by a big company tends to make the headlines. Smaller and younger firms display a much weaker pattern of boom and bust.

These facts suggest that a recession is a period of faster industrial restructuring, rather than simply an economy-wide reaction to a common shock such as higher oil prices or a surprise increase in interest rates. An event like that plays a role as a trigger, but individual industries and companies react differently. The pace of restructuring subsides during a long recovery. The long-term trend decline in employment in manufacturing is due to slower job creation rather than faster job destruction.

As changes in the underlying job opportunities account for about half of the moves workers make between jobs or into and out of unemployment, unemployment also rises during recessions. During a recovery, moves into unemployment are dominated by new entrants and re-entrants to the labour market. During a recession, the rise in job destruction is the main reason.

The US differs from Europe in this respect. Europeans are far less likely to move from job to job via a short spell of unemployment, so even during good times inflows into unemployment on this side of the Atlantic are mainly due to job destruction. However, in America about one in twelve of the workforce moves into unemployment in an average quarter, and about the same proportion moves out of unemployment. Both flows into and flows out of unemployment rise during a recession – 'consistent with the view that recessions are periods of intense restructuring activity in the economy', the authors comment.

The rates of job creation and destruction are remarkably high. Huge numbers of US manufacturing jobs disappear every year and almost as many new ones are created. The minimum turnover in any year between 1973 and 1988 was one in twelve jobs.

The changes were concentrated on factories that were either closing or expanding hugely. Plants that close account for fully a quarter of job destruction. Large-scale job flows characterise all sectors of industry. Even shrinking industries display massive job creation and destruction, although the rate of turnover varies widely from less than 15 per cent in chemicals and petroleum to more than 25 per cent in the clothing industry.

Small firms create proportionately more jobs than big ones, but destroy more too. They do not make a big contribution to net growth in jobs. High wage jobs – which are typically in big firms – are more durable, and there is much faster net growth in jobs in high wage and high productivity industries. The US figures confirm that job opportunities for the low-paid shrank during the 1970s and 1980s.

For everybody, this is clearly not the stable golden age of the 1960s. The increasing weightlessness of the economy might not have resulted in a lot more turnover in total, but it is obvious that the world of work feels a lot more unpredictable. Some traditional manufacturing industries are without doubt dying. The visible rapid growth in jobs is occurring in areas such as high technology, entertainment and the professions, where many people feel that there are no opportunities for them; they feel redundant even if there are jobs somewhere in the economy. Even if industrial restructuring is the norm, it has moved onto a higher level during the past decade or so. This will continue. It is something we are all going to have to get used to.

Insecurity: in the mind?

One of the commonplaces about the jobs market in the 1990s is therefore that it is a much more insecure place. Certainly, it is clear from opinion polls and all kinds of anecdotal evidence that a sense of insecurity has entered our culture. Take a late 1980s novel that recorded the faltering pulse of yuppie America: Jay McInerney's *Brightness Falls*. The main character, young New York publisher Russell Calloway, starts with everything: great career, beautiful wife, artistic friends and the chance to buy his employer's family firm in a leveraged buy-out. The novel ends soon after the October 1987 stock market crash. By the end his marriage has crumbled, his best friend has died of AIDS and the market has put paid to the buy-out bid: 'The upshot of Russell's takeover attempt was that Corbin, Dern had been cut up into pieces, thirty or forty people had lost their jobs, and a man who was already too rich had turned a ridiculous profit'.

The novel ends with lines from a poem by Thomas Nashe, *A Litany in Time of Plague*:

> '*Rich men, trust not in wealth,*
> *Gold cannot buy you health …*
> *Beauty is but a flower*
> *Which wrinkles will devour;*
> *Brightness falls from the air;*
> *Queens have died young and fair;*
> *Dust hath closed Helen's eye …*
> *Lord, have mercy on us!*'

Welcome to the weightless world. Yet in mundane economic terms, in terms of job insecurity, the heightened sense of apprehension is a bit puzzling as it does not show up clearly in various official statistics. This is a fact that the Conservative Government in Britain highlighted in its defence, during the run up to its 1997 landslide electoral defeat, of policies which had been introduced to deregulate the UK labour market since 1980. For instance, the number of redundancies in all industrial countries has been lower this decade than last – most noticeably in the UK, where the insecurity blues are perhaps the deepest. In addition, job tenure – the length of time the typical employee has spent in his or her current job – has declined only slightly during the past 15–20 years. For women it has actually increased. The decline is entirely explained by shorter job tenure for prime age men, and mainly in blue collar and unskilled jobs rather than the professions or white collar work. In addition, typical job tenure varies widely between countries – lowest in the US, highest in Japan.

However, these figures capture only part of the story. They describe the experience of a shrinking part of the population and a smaller and smaller part of the jobs market. Job tenure measures only the jobs that survive, not the short-term ones. Nor does it reveal anything about the options available outside these core long-lasting jobs, such as the pay and prospects offered by new jobs or the lack of generosity of unemployment benefits.

The changes that probably explain the sense of insecurity involve the switch to part-time, temporary and contract work, much of which has taken place since the start of the eighties but was disguised by the boom at the end of that decade.The changing experience of working life is discussed further in Chapter 5. First, the causes of unemployment and insecurity. Finding solutions depends on identifying the right causes.

Notes

1. In *The Misfortunes of Prosperity*.
2. European edition, 19 June 1996.
3. Morgan Stanley, 6 May 1996.
4. *Down-sizing Downsizing* in Slate, http://www.slate.com/Dismal/96-06-24/Dismal.exp
5. *Job Creation and Destruction*, Davis, Haltiwanger and Schuh.

Chapter Three

Weightless Work

The blame for mass unemployment tends to be pinned on one of three culprits: technology, trade and deflationary government policies. This chapter examines each of them, and concludes that the real cause is that many governments have failed to adjust to the profound changes in economic structure resulting from increasing weightlessness. Deregulation – another way of saying the government has to get out of the way of the economic transformation – is a necessary precondition for reducing unemployment, although it is not a complete answer.

False diagnoses carry real dangers. Those who blame trade with the third world want to put up protectionist barriers, whereas trade is the ultimate engine of prosperity. The experience of the 1930s stands as a constant reminder of the dangers of a retreat into protectionism. The old-fashioned Keynesians who reckon a dose of extra government spending to reflate the economy is the right medicine have forgotten, already, about the costs of inflation and the impossibility of running big budget deficits for very long. This solution has been tried and failed. First, though, we will consider those who blame technology, the move towards weightlessness itself.

Technology and luddism

One man who blames machines for putting us out of jobs is American polemicist Jeremy Rifkin. The few who work in the computer and communications industries will do very nicely in the future, he argues. But he claims – incorrectly, as it happens – that these high-technology industries create very few jobs compared to the number destroyed in other industries. In his provocatively titled book, *The End of Work*, he writes:

> 'While the entrepreneurial, managerial, professional and technical elites will be necessary to run the formal economy of the future, fewer and fewer workers will be required to assist in the production of goods and services. The market value of labour is diminishing and will continue to do so.'

It is an argument that hints of a terrible future of social chasms between the elite, living safely and comfortably in their privileged compounds, and the workless and impoverished majority. 'Rising levels of world-wide unemployment and the increasing polarisation between rich and poor are creating the conditions for social upheaval and open class warfare on a scale never before experienced in the modern age', Rifkin writes. 'A new form of barbarism waits just outside the walls of the modern world.'[1]

This is, of course, an argument with a rich history. Technology has frequently been blamed for taking work from people and giving it to machines. The Luddite revolts in 1812 gave their name to the machine-bashing phenomenon – literally in their case. But outbreaks of smashing the machinery of the first industrial revolution took place in England in 1800, 1812, 1816, 1826–7 and 1830.

Luddism was a phenomenon of the textile industry. The worst riot in the cotton town I grew up in, Bury in East Lancashire, resulted in several deaths in April 1826. A crowd of 4000 marched down the picturesque Rossendale Valley from mill to grim mill, smashing the power looms which were destroying the livelihood of weavers scraping a living from handlooms in their cottages. Forty soldiers, defending the Chatterton mill in the hamlet of Stubbins, opened fire. One bullet hit Mary Simpson, a bystander. Another killed James Whatacre, a mill worker who had tried to save the warps from one of the new looms that had enraged the mob but was mistaken for a rioter.

One of the officers reported later: 'The determination of the rioters was quite extraordinary and such as I could not have credited if I had not witnessed it'. According to eyewitness reports one of the crowd ran towards the armed soldiers, shouting: 'I would rather be killed here than go home to starve'. His wish was granted.

The troops prevented that march from reaching the bigger industrial centres of Rochdale and Manchester, where it might have inflamed a serious insurrection. According to some estimates investment in the Manchester cotton mills had reached £20 million as early as 1816. The owners of capital had a lot at stake. The Lancashire inventors of the mule, Samuel Crompton, the spinning jenny, Richard Hargreaves, and the flying shuttle, John Kay, found themselves under personal attack. Kay had to flee the mob, Crompton was burnt out of his home.

Jeremy Rifkin has launched no physical assaults on today's equivalents of the cotton barons, men such as Microsoft's Bill Gates, but he makes it clear that he thinks computers are to blame for depriving people of work. In his book, one of the most dangerous and misleading economic tracts published in the past quarter century, he predicts that 90 million jobs out of a US labour force of 124 million are vulnerable to replacement by robots and computers. Is he any more correct in this gloomy forecast than the Luddites turned out to be in the long run? For the average wage in England doubled in real terms between 1820 and 1870, while there was no upward trend in unemployment during those 50 years. A separate question is, even if the techno-pessimists are wrong again in the long-run, how much short-term disruption and misery is there likely to be?

So far I have singled out, unsympathetically, one extreme book. However, there are many respected scholars, including Robert Reich, the Clinton administration's former Labor Secretary, who share the view that technological developments will make the kind of work that many people in the West currently perform increasingly redundant. Reich sees human intelligence as the most valuable resource at a time when anything else that people can do can be mimicked by machines. He calls the elite of workers benefiting from computer technology 'symbolic analysts'. Rifkin's solution is to tax the computer and communications industries, Reich's is to educate the workforce in order to improve their brain-power and increase the number of symbolic analysts.

Edward Luttwak, the respected director of geo-economics at the Center for Strategic and International Studies in Washington DC, joins in, perpetuating the myth that there are few jobs in high-tech industries. Microsoft and Intel, Apple and Novell, Cisco, Oracle, Sun Microsystems, Sybase, Adobe Systems, Amgen, Cirrus, Informix, Intuit, America Online, MBC Soft, Picturetel – all the 'New Titans' of the US information industries added together – employ only 128,000 people world-wide, he claims, compared with the 325,300 working for Ford.[2]

The technological watershed

In a delicious irony, the analysis by these authors, eminences such as Luttwak, Reich and Lester Thurow, bears a strong resemblance to Marx's theory of underconsumption or overproduction. Philosopher Albert Knox in Jostein Gaarder's novel *Sophie's World* spells it out. The ingenue Sophie asks for an example of the self-destructive nature of capitalism. Albert explains that the capitalist uses his surplus money to buy new machinery. 'Fewer and fewer workers are required, which means there are more and more unemployed. There are therefore increasing social problems and crises such as these are a signal that capitalism is marching towards its own destruction.'

The crisis in turn means the factory owner starts to cut wages. Albert explains: 'The workers would be so poor that they couldn't afford to buy goods any more. We would say that purchasing power is falling. And now we really are in a vicious circle.'

Many scholars believe that technical change this time around is even more damaging in its effect on jobs. Information technology can be used in any industry or service. It is not specific to one, such as textiles. It also coincides with a period of rapid growth in trade and investment between the industrial countries and the developing world – and more on 'globalisation' later.

Is weightless technology going to trigger a crisis of capitalism at the turn of this century? Leave aside also for now the fact that previous technical developments – microelectronics, say, or mass production techniques – were also very widespread in their applications. Economic theory does not imply that labour-saving technology will necessarily destroy jobs in aggregate. But the evidence suggests that the current wave of technical change is favouring some categories of worker over others.

Theory first. Labour-saving technology improves the productivity of workers: the same number can produce more output or fewer can produce the same output. Their firm has lower unit costs and higher profits. An individual firm's demand for workers will obviously tend to fall. However, in a reasonably competitive industry its cost-savings will be passed on in lower prices and stimulate higher demand. Or alternatively the technical change might have resulted in the creation of new products whose prices fall dramatically and for which there is rapidly growing demand. The computer manufacturing industry is itself a classic example of this effect. Five years ago few people had personal computers at home. Yet a fair number of middle-class households in the West now own more computers than cars.

Furthermore, even without this effect, higher profits tend to be followed by higher wages for the employed. Along with increased investment by firms

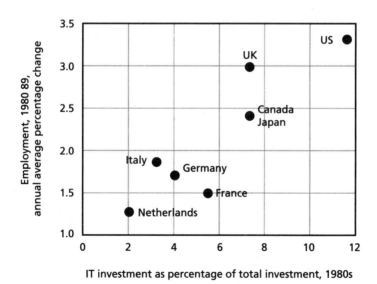

IT investment as percentage of total investment, 1980s

Fig. 5 IT investment versus employment growth. (Source: OECD.)

in the new technology, this tends to stimulate the economy as a whole. Finally, where workers are laid off as a result of new technology, the unemployment puts downward pressure on wages and stimulates the demand for labour as a result.

The net impact of labour-saving technical change on jobs depends on the size of these effects, on the speed with which the new technology spreads and is absorbed by different companies, on how easy it is for new firms to start up and for workers to switch jobs, and on the general economic policy framework. A good education system, competitive industries, flexible labour markets and expansionary macroeconomic policies will tend to favour net job creation rather than destruction.

The structure of the economy is also crucial. Countries that have a history of exporting electronic products for which demand is growing faster than incomes in its markets will do a lot better out of new technologies than those countries that tend to import those items or traditionally export old-fashioned goods to stagnant markets. It is far worse to experience technical change embodied in cheaper new imports than to innovate yourself, as the European countries have discovered with electronics. The moral is that even if it looks as if new technology will cost jobs, the cost will be higher if other countries adopt the new technology first. Keeping pace with the front-runners minimises job losses, however paradoxical that seems to some pessimists.

Industries in the US and Japan were swift to adopt information technology. Companies in countries like Britain and France were slower. For example, in 1991 the US accounted for 30 per cent of industrial spending on computer-aided manufacturing. Japan accounted for 20 per cent. The big European economies trailed with 4–6 per cent of the total each.[3] OECD studies and surveys suggest that European companies have found it harder to adopt the new patterns of organisation and management techniques needed to make full use of information technology. This is not itself conclusive evidence, but the faster automation of manufacturing in America and Japan has certainly not noticeably damaged their jobs records.

In fact, the concentration of the unemployment problem in the European Union countries makes it unlikely that any world-wide phenomenon like the information technology revolution can take sole blame for job losses. America has raced ahead in the use of information technology without suffering permanent mass unemployment – although whether it has paid the price for generating jobs in lower incomes for many workers and greater income inequality instead is something that is discussed in more detail later.

Neither theory nor evidence supports the conclusion that computers have destroyed jobs in the aggregate. What the available evidence from a series of studies does indicate is that lagging behind in information technology has probably hindered long-run job creation in Europe. Especially on the Continent, there has been scant growth in employment in the private sector at all and especially not in the high-technology sectors that have grown very rapidly in the US and Japan. In those countries computers have probably helped create jobs. They are just not the kind of jobs that everybody can do. There has been a change in the structure of employment, one that is just as disruptive and costly in human terms as the mythical large-scale destruction of jobs.

The next wave

Most jobs created during the past 20 years have been in the service industries, a wide category that covers everything from nursing and policing to working as an accountant or designing video games. The reason has been the shift in demand in the industrial countries. Manufactures now make up only a small portion of what we buy, and in most cases manufacturing industry accounts for less than a quarter of the economy.

There is therefore a clear pattern over time of employment shifting from the high to the low productivity parts of the economy: from farming to factories, from factories to services. The thing that is troubling about this pattern is that it is hard to see where the inefficient and labour intensive areas are going to be in future. For now even service industries are using new technology to improve productivity. This is the phenomenon that created so much *angst* during the recession of the early 1990s. The risk of redundancy for white collar workers remains much lower than for blue collar workers, but it was the first time professional and office jobs had been at risk.

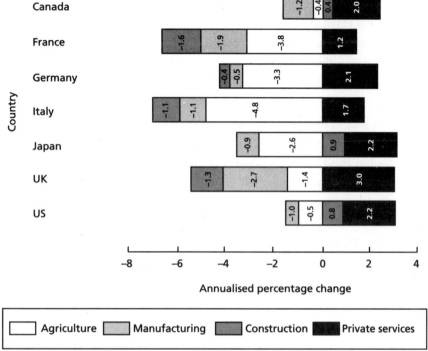

Fig. 6   Employment growth 1979–93 in G7 countries, by sector. (Source: *OECD Labour Force Statistics*.)

My own industry, print journalism, was at the forefront of this trend, which without doubt explains why it was brought to public attention so swiftly. Technological advances meant that the craft of printing could be eliminated. That happened in the 1980s, with new printing equipment to replace the old hot metal type and, eventually, the computerisation of newsrooms which could transmit the material for publication directly to the printing plant. Information technology has also allowed papers and magazines to economise on the number of reporters they need. Direct computer input and on-line news wires allow a smaller number of writers to process a larger amount of information.

Other service industries such as retailing and banking have followed the pattern of downsizing as a result of computerisation. There are very many white-collar jobs in which bytes are a cheap and efficient substitute for brains.

Companies can reduce their costs by millions of pounds once they have made an initial capital investment in the right information technology – the right stock tracking system or network of automatic cash machines. Even teaching, where it would once have been impossible to imagine replacing the human being standing at the front of the classroom, is becoming increasingly mechanised. One teacher can reach many more students through video links and on-line methods.

This fits in with the broad historical shift from agriculture to manufacturing to services. As the share of manufacturing in the economy has shrunk – a trend that started in the early 1960s, long before computer technology had any impact at all – so the number of jobs in industry has declined too. However, across the OECD area the number of jobs in 'high-technology' manufacturing has either increased since 1970 or decreased far less than the number in traditional 'low-technology' sectors.[4]

For example in France there was a tiny increase in high-tech jobs between 1970 and 1991, but a fall of nearly 2 per cent in low-tech jobs. In Japan high-tech employment expanded by nearly 2 per cent while low-tech jobs contracted slightly. In only a few countries – Australia, the Netherlands and the UK – were there losses in all kinds of manufacturing jobs, and then they were proportionately far smaller in the high-tech sectors.

Thus the main force driving the pattern of employment within industry is productivity growth. This goes wider than the suggestion that greater use of microchips has replaced human labour, for the type of humans who are most likely to have been fired during the past two decades have been the unskilled. They typically do jobs that a computer cannot, such as cleaning or labouring. Computers tend to replace people with middling skills, such as machinists.

It is the industries where productivity has increased at the fastest pace which have been the ones creating work. These enjoyed a virtuous circle of rapid growth, improvements in productivity and efficiency, and high wages. The sectors of decline were the traditional industries such as textiles, steel and shipbuilding. However, as these made up the vast bulk of manufacturing industry in the early 1970s, their job losses overwhelmed the number of new jobs created in sunrise industries like microelectronics.

The twin migration of job opportunities, out of older industries into newer ones and into services, looks paradoxical: for the expansion of employment in services is explained by the fact that the level of productivity is much lower than in manufacturing, so a lot of workers are still needed. On the other hand, the move within manufacturing has been into the higher-productivity areas, which in theory need fewer workers. Both moves occurred simultaneously because demand was growing for both services and high-tech manufactures.

In the longer term – over a period of 30 or 50 years, say – an economy creates jobs where the level of productivity is low. During the late nineteenth and early twentieth centuries the countries that now make up the industrial West saw a massive switch in employment from agriculture into industry. Agriculture became steadily more efficient and simply did not need the masses of labourers living in the countryside. They flocked to the towns instead, becoming the factory fodder who then saw the arrival of more efficient machines in the mills.

The trend away from agriculture has continued since 1945 due to its ever-improving productivity performance. In her evocative portrait of French village life during the past century and a half, Gillian Tindall explains the diminishing need for people to work the countryside.

> 'While, between the wars, farms had still continued to occupy large numbers of people, and the loss of men in the Great War helped to disguise the declining need for labour, the far greater mechanisation that came in gradually after the Second World War changed the whole nature of farming. A squad of men out in the fields was, simply, no longer needed.'

By contrast, a mechanical threshing machine in use before World War II still required a team of at least fifteen men, 'sweating from sun-up to sun-down in the noise and the flying chaff'.

Only the UK, which industrialised more and earlier than other nations, has seen little further shrinkage in its farming sector since World War II. The growth of farm productivity, the amount of food produced per worker, has continued to outpace industry and services. For example, between 1960 and 1990, average productivity growth in agriculture ranged from 3.1 per cent a year (the US) to 6.3 per cent a year (Germany). This compared with growth rates in industrial productivity of between 1.6 per cent (US) to 5.9 per cent (Japan) and in services of 0.9 per cent (US) to 3.8 per cent (Japan).

The third sector

If even bedrock services are undergoing their own productivity revolution, what will be left for people to do? The American economist Paul Krugman has one answer. He argues that as the computer revolution matures, the highly skilled elite of professionals and programmers which has done well during the past two decades will itself become obsolete. 'The time may come when most tax lawyers are replaced by expert systems software, but human beings are still needed – and well-paid – for such truly difficult occupations as gardening, house cleaning, and the thousands of other services that will receive an ever-growing share of our expenditure as mere consumer goods become steadily cheaper', he writes.[5] The computer-adept professionals of today will be like the cottage weavers of the nineteenth century who cashed in on the earlier technical revolution in spinning until the development of the power loom made them redundant in their turn.

There are certainly signs that the use of technology in financial services, for example, is eliminating a lot of routine jobs in the banking sector – it started with automatic teller machines and has now got as far as the current introduction of electronic imaging of cheques to avoid the need for human staff to key in values. So perhaps he is right, and as our prosperity continues to increase more people will hire the services of gardeners, cleaners and, who knows, personal trainers and aromatherapists. But there is a far more significant sector of the industrial economies, one that is growing by leaps and bounds. It incorporates some of the subsector of services economists describe as 'community, social and personal' and much of the voluntary or non-profit sector. Some writers have taken to calling it the 'third sector'.

This sector, intrinsically weightless, is the focus of the next chapter. It includes some of the fastest-growing services such as long-term and health care, housing, education and training, charities – all areas for which demand in the ageing, high-income countries will continue to expand well into the next century, and which can therefore be expected to provide jobs. And the fact that many of the jobs in these fields are now low pay and low status does not mean that they will remain so. To predict the importance of the third sector is not to condemn a growing chunk of the workforce to a ghetto of undesirable work.

The trade red herring

Before turning to this, there are two fashionable and dangerous explanations for unemployment that need knocking down. Public enemy number one, in the eyes of many commentators, is not computerisation but rather trade with developing nations. This is a theory with more resonance in some countries than others. American scholars often link it with the spread of information technology – if a computer doesn't get your job, a third-world coolie will. Many French economists and businessmen, true to their mercantilist heritage, also blame trade and investment overseas.

Take the late Sir James Goldsmith – a French resident who of course had direct experience of a cheap labour country thanks to his luxury Mexican holiday home. In his polemic *The Trap* he argued – or perhaps ranted would be a better word – that free trade will only benefit capitalists. It will impoverish and destabilise the industrial world, sacrifice social stability, and destroy livelihoods and society in the third world too. It even threatens the stability of the family.

These claims resonated in his adopted country. There has been more public uproar about *délocalisation* in France than any other industrial nation – even Japan, which has exported many jobs directly to low-cost countries in south-east Asia. Protectionism has many supporters in America too. Ross Perot, the mega-wealthy businessman who ran for President in 1992, criticised the North American Free Trade Agreement. There was, he said, a 'giant sucking sound' of American jobs rushing south of the Rio Grande.

It is a view that has started to cross to the other end of the political spectrum. Edward Luttwak, a respected researcher, argues that it would be worth having a lower GNP if tariffs on imports would save jobs. Americans would suffer from their inability to buy cheap imports, but: 'They would gain greatly overall because the production of those more expensive and/or inferior US goods behind tariff walls would do wonders for their wages by increasing the demand for their labour'. The US trade deficit has translated into a net loss of 1.4 million jobs, he has claimed.

Britain has had such a strong history of free trade, since the repeal of the Corn Laws in 1848, that protectionist sentiments are extremely rare. Left-wingers opposed the extension of the free market during the Thatcher years but did not query trade liberalisation – until recently. The opening shots in the campaign to make protectionism acceptable were fired by David Marquand, often described as one of the 'gurus' of Labour leader Tony Blair. The spread of trade will cause society to fragment, he predicts, fuelling protectionism and isolationism of the Ross Perot or Pat Buchanan type. In a recent article[6] he concluded: 'Economic and political liberalism no longer live together. Globally and nationally, we shall sooner or later have to choose between the free market and the free society.'

The difficulty with the argument that trade destroys jobs is that there is scant evidence for it. If we think there is, it is the anecdotal bias again. Most job destruction is no more the fault of cheap imports than most accidental deaths are due to plane crashes. It happens, but the evidence is that it is not – not yet, at least – very common. To suggest otherwise is dangerously misleading. Trade has always been the engine of growth. It is the fundamental economic activity. To argue for restrictions on trade is to head back down the path that proved so disastrous in the 1930s.

Trade in perspective

The people who see trade destroying jobs are often the same ones who point out that the world is not nearly as global as it was a century ago. The amount imported and exported, and the value of capital flows overseas, is significantly lower now as a share of GDP than at the end of the nineteenth century.

For example, at the pre-World War I peak in 1913, the share of imports and exports in GDP in Great Britain was 60 per cent, in the Netherlands nearly 250 per cent, and even in heavily protected France and Germany above 30 per cent. These compare with a maximum of about 90 per cent in the UK and Netherlands now. Britain, the world's prime exporter of capital, invested the equivalent of 7 per cent of its GDP abroad each year in the late nineteenth century. This compares with 12 per cent of GDP for the UK, once again one of the biggest international investors, in the first half of the 1990s, and a typical ratio of 2–7 per cent for other OECD countries.

Most of the more limited modern openness involves the industrial countries trading with and investing in each other. Trade between the industrial countries and the developing world has grown very rapidly since about 1980, but from a very small base. Trade between OECD countries and non-members amounts to just under 4 per cent of total GDP in the OECD, compared with 11 per cent for trade with other industrialised economies. That is, trade within the first world is nearly three times as big as trade between the first and third worlds. All trade has grown very fast since the early 1960s. Exports and imports of manufactures have grown fastest, up from the equivalent of 3.5 per cent to 9 per cent of GDP.

The OECD countries have a trade surplus with the developing world, and were also in surplus with those bogeymen, the newly industrialised Asian economies, up to 1980. Most industrial countries exchange goods overwhelmingly with each other. Both imports and exports have grown rapidly for all the industrial countries. Mainly they have been exchanging manufactures with each other.

It is sheer common sense to accept that there are some industries that have suffered severely as a result of trade. The textile industry is one of these. The only industrial economies that still have any significant clothing and footwear manufacturing are the poorest – Portugal and Malta, for example. Footwear, clothing and textiles account for a quarter of OECD imports of manufactured goods from non-OECD countries. The effect of the power loom on employment in Lancashire last century was trivial compared to the impact of cheap imports in the 1980s. The industry's capital stock was shipped direct from mill to scrap yard or textile museum in the space of less than a decade.

This is just what economic theory would predict. Countries should export the goods in which they have a comparative advantage (that is, goods which make intensive use of inputs that are relatively cheaper in those countries – unskilled workers, in the developing world). An increase in trade will tend to raise the return to the relatively abundant input world-wide, which should mean higher wages in the third world, but a decline in demand and lower wages for these workers in the developed world. The return to other inputs – capital and skilled labour – ought to rise in the industrial world. The point of international trade, the reason it brings benefits, is that countries specialise in what they do best. The West has its sweatshops, but we do not do sweatshops as well as poor nations.

The fact that it seems plain common sense that trade with cheaper countries is putting people in low-skilled industries out of work means that free trade is beginning to acquire the status of villain. But there are flaws in the argument. One is theoretical. Economics also predicts that as the wages of the unskilled fall and wages of the skilled workforce and capital rise in the industrial countries, if the trade effect is operating, companies should economise on the use of skilled labour. The ratio of skilled to unskilled employed should fall across the economy. It has done precisely the reverse. In addition, the mix of industry should shift towards sectors that use skilled labour intensively, reflecting the increasing specialisation. There is no overwhelming evidence of this either.

The second type of objection to blaming trade is that the developed economies do not do very much of it with the developing world. Even though the surge in trade with the Pacific Rim economies has been one of the most spectacular economic developments of recent years, their exports to members of the OECD amount to at most 1 per cent of the latter's GDP. According to the calculations of Paul Krugman for the US economy, even America's massive trade deficit during the 1980s was not big enough to have more than a small impact on the total output and employment of the nation. If trade had been in balance between 1970 and 1990, the manufacturing sector would have shrunk from 25 per cent of GDP to 19.2 per cent rather than the 18.4 per cent actually observed. The impact of international competition on wages could only have been, at most, 0.07 per cent of national income, he calculates.

This relaxed view is disputed, of course. The most convincing counter-argument is that these figures exclude two adverse influences on jobs and wages. One is that the industrial nations have dropped out of some types of labour-intensive manufacturing so completely as a result of trade that the lost jobs are not measured. The other is that technological changes to boost productivity have been a defensive reaction to foreign competition. Add these in, and the impact of trade on unemployment is ten times greater than conventionally measured, the argument goes.[7]

This is fair enough, but leads into definitional problems about what exactly we mean to measure. Trade has certainly had some impact on the structure of the industrial economies. It might in future have a far greater effect. Yet it is clear that some of the more excitable commentators have got the issue completely out of proportion. And even if their worse fears proved true, it does not mean that trade with poor countries has become an evil to be expurgated. Hard as it is to remember now, Japan was seen as the same kind of threat during the 1960s, mass-producing cheap plastic goods and later electronics that 'flooded' into Western markets. Funnily enough, Germany was never seen in the same light, even though it adopted the same export-oriented industrial strategy to rebuild its economy after World War II. Could the economic analysis of the Japanese 'threat' have been tainted by racism? Or the fear of trade with Asian countries now?

Most discussion of trade suffers from an attitude forged by the mercantilism of the seventeenth century, the notion that exports are Good and imports Bad. Imports are Good too. They bring consumers cheaper, better and more varied products than they could otherwise buy, increasing our purchasing power and releasing our income to buy other products. Would we be worse off without our Taiwanese stereos, Japanese microwaves or cheap Chinese cotton clothes? Without doubt. What's more, the Western nations export more to the developing world as a whole than they import. Few countries have had a big trade deficit over a long period of time. The US is one of the exceptions, and its trade deficit has been the result of huge government deficits rather than underlying trends in trade.

Even without trade with the third world, the industrial structure of our economies would be changing. The personal traumas and tragedies that arise from seeing an industry die, a town wither, would still exist. This does not mean that it is acceptable to cast entire workforces onto the scrap heap of the capitalist economy. It does mean that blaming other countries for changes that would occur anyway is dangerous nonsense. Those who consider themselves left-wing but are prepared to agree with populist demagogues about the 'dangers' of allowing other countries to raise their own living standards by exporting to the West should be ashamed of themselves.

Exporting jobs

There is a second strand to the view that the rest of the world is to blame for the economic ills of the West. As well as importing goods that destroy jobs, big multinational companies are exporting jobs directly by investing in cheaper countries. It is an easy headline: 2000 jobs here go to the Philippines, 3000 there to India. This is a fear that now has half a decade of history behind it. Some of the first to cause uproar occurred during the recession of the early 1990s.

Direct investment by multinationals in developing countries has increased by leaps and bounds during the 1990s but from a tiny base. It is still not as sustained as in the late nineteenth century, when Britain regularly exported capital amounting to 7 per cent of its GDP.[8] In the 1980s the fast-growing Asian economies were actually net exporters of capital to the rest of the world. However, within the past two years total foreign direct investment has reached about $250bn at an annual rate. But this differs from the larger flows at the turn of the last century in a key political aspect. It is the first large-scale non-imperial investment in the third world. The money last century flowed to countries run by white men.

Most of the investment by the developed world in the developing countries – around four-fifths – is concentrated on about ten mainly middle in-come countries in the Pacific Rim and Latin America. In other words, it is not going to the poorest and therefore cheapest countries. Wages in places like Brazil and Thailand are not incredibly far behind wages in Portugal and Greece. The exceptions are China and India, both very low wage.

Investment in India by multinationals has been the source of one of the big scare stories of the 1990s. Seeing jobs in textiles and electronics assembly go to India was one thing. The Bangalore software industry is another. Here was one of the sectors we in the West had been counting on to provide our jobs in the next century. It looked as if information technology had made it possible to export almost any work to cheap-labour countries, and was inevitably bound to lead to our impoverishment. It seems, however, that the demand by international computer firms for Indian programmers has led to the enrichment of the Indians instead, in a pleasing illustration of the law of demand and supply. Wages for programmers have climbed. More examples like this will remind us of the lesson of economic history, which is that growth tends, on average, to level up rather than level down.

Fears about investment by Western companies overseas should also be calmed by the fact that, although capital has become very mobile, people are substantially less able to move between countries than they were at the end of the last century. Research suggests that the aspect of nineteenth century globalisation that was most responsible for falling wages and growing inequality in some countries was mass immigration. It was the doubling of the size of the population in Chicago and New York within the space of a decade, the quintupling of Detroit's population between 1900 and 1930, that undermined wages for the uneducated masses. This is a phenomenon that is not going to be repeated as this century draws to a close, if politicians succeed in their desire to stem the flows in the tide of humanity from war and famine zones. One of the ways that tide will be shrunk, however, is by investment in the world's poorer economies. If home offered the hope of some work and income, there would be far fewer economic migrants.

A later chapter suggests that there are other reasons that the industrial nations should not raise the wall against immigration from the third world, mainly to compensate for the shortage of productive workers that many of them will start to experience about three decades from now. If today's middle-aged

Germans and Japanese want a pension, they should be thinking about how their economy will be generating the wealth to pay it. Equally, investment by the OECD countries in newly industrialising and youthful economies is a way of generating future returns to pay first world pensions in the year 2030.

Is the government to blame?

The most obvious culprit for high unemployment is the least fashionable, at least in official policy-making circles. This is hardly surprising, for it is the suggestion that economic policy is to blame at least for triggering mass joblessness, even if structural problems then help to keep it high. This is a view with a lot of currency on the left of centre.

There have been two episodes when governments made macroeconomic policy mistakes. The first was in the mid-1970s, after OPEC quadrupled the price of oil in 1973, when most Western governments reacted by relaxing their interest rate and budget policies to try to offset the impact of the shock on jobs. It was the wrong reaction to what economists would describe as a 'supply' shock, a sudden change in the conditions under which businesses made the investment and employment decisions. Trying to manipulate the level of demand in the economy in reaction cannot alter the underlying change in circumstances. It can only raise inflation. That is precisely what happened. Stagflation – the combination of stagnant growth and high inflation – entered everyday language.

One of the few countries not to fall into the trap was West Germany. The ultra-orthodox central bank, the Bundesbank, fended off political demands to loosen up. There was a short, sharp recession. The economy emerged from this with more energy-efficient industry, somewhat higher unemployment and low inflation. Other Western economies had made less adjustment to the higher cost of energy, had much higher unemployment and much higher inflation too.

Germany took a different path after its decision, following the fall of the

Berlin Wall in November 1989, to reunite the western with the eastern provinces at an exchange rate between the Ostmark and the Deutschmark of one for one. East German industry was so profoundly less productive than West German industry that economists had recommended a rate closer to five Ostmarks to the Deutschmark.

However, Germany's leaders concluded that parity was a political necessity for the unification to succeed. An economic necessity too – the alternative would have been massive immigration from eastern to western *länder*. Along with large-scale borrowing by the Government to finance investments and social transfers to the east, it unleashed an economic boom in the east. The Bundesbank decided to offset the inflationary consequences by keeping German interest rates high.

Other members of the European Exchange Rate Mechanism had to follow suit if the currency links were to survive. They chose to do this rather than accept an official devaluation which would have cost less in terms of jobs but more loss of face and credibility. For two years from 1990 to 1992 they struggled with the consequences of high interest rates during a downturn in the business cycle. Britain and Italy dropped out, and other countries later adopted wider bands of fluctuation against the Deutschmark in one of the most dramatic currency crises for well over a decade. European countries paid a high price in mistaken response to the German policy – massive unemployment was the alternative to a profound loss of the credibility of their interest and exchange rate policy.

It is easy enough to identify these mistakes with hindsight. The role of macro-economic policy in creating high unemployment in Europe does not mean, unfortunately, that tax and interest rates could be used to stimulate activity and reduce unemployment now. One reason is that past policy mistakes interacted with structural features of the European economies, such as generous unemployment benefits, to cement the high level of joblessness. Another is that identifying a macro-economic policy that will work is difficult – if it were easy, nobody would have made the mistakes in the first place. Thirdly, the increasingly integrated financial markets make it hard for any single country to go it alone. This is a subject that will be explored further in a later chapter. For now, it is enough to describe France's experience in 1981

– an episode whose memory still burns in the minds of central bankers.

The Socialist Government of President François Mitterrand had been in power for only a year when it decided to try to reflate the economy and cut unemployment. It expanded government spending and cut interest rates enough to avoid the 1981–2 recession that afflicted its neighbours. But the balance of payments deficit soared and the punishment from the financial markets was swift. The French franc came under such dramatic speculative attack that the Government decided it had to switch its policy to ensure that the currency did not breach the limits of the Exchange Rate Mechanism. This has been the cornerstone of French economic management ever since. The episode was the first example of the international capital markets vigilante effect on the policies of national governments following the widespread deregulation that started around 1980. It sent a shiver of fear through the hearts of finance ministers around Europe. It was, after all, less than half a decade since Britain had had to call in the International Monetary Fund to restore confidence in its macroeconomic policies.

The lesson has not been forgotten in policy-making circles, even though it took place 15 years ago. After all, financial markets have demonstrated their powers on subsequent occasions, notably in breaking up the ERM in September 1992, with a repeat crisis a year later. In a sense, European monetary union is an attempt by Continental politicians to evade the constraints placed on policy by the power of footloose capital.

There is not a lot of scope for macroeconomic policy to cut unemployment anyway. All Western governments are running big budget deficits. In both absolute terms and relative to the size of the economy, the shortfalls between their revenues and spending are unprecedented in peacetime. You do not have to be an ultra-orthodox central banker to believe there is no scope to boost demand by expanding the scale of government borrowing, even without taking into account the likely future cost of health and pension spending.

That leaves lower interest rates as the only macroeconomic tool available. It is one that governments have used where possible. Germany and Japan took their official interest rates to historic lows in the mid-1990s. It was not enough by itself to solve the unemployment problem.

Structural policies

That leaves the possibility of actions that affect the underlying structure of the economy, to dissolve the cement that has left unemployment at unacceptably high levels. These are slow-acting, incremental and undramatic. They are often extremely unpopular too. But they are about the only weapon left in the armoury of the industrial governments.

Structural policies can be divided into two categories – those which are controversial and those which run motherhood and apple pie a close second. The former include any deregulation of the labour market, reduction of union powers, withdrawal of employment protection. Adopted by the UK and New Zealand governments during the 1980s, they have coincided with an apparent trend decline in the unemployment rate in these countries since the early 1990s.

Critics argue that the price has been greater inequality and insecurity. They are right, although they overdo the criticism. The two countries have experienced a bigger increase in inequality than any other industrial countries since 1980, even though both remain in the middle of the league in terms of the degree of inequality. Incomes in France, for example, remain more unequal than in either.[9] The proportion of the work force that is part-time or temporary has risen in both cases, but remains lower than in France and Spain. It is a bit of a heresy to admit the possibility that the Conservative Government's flexing of the UK labour market has not had any dire side-effects, for reasons which are explored in more detail later. But taking the effects of the UK experience in context, it certainly does not add up to a compelling case against deregulation in some of the highly inflexible Continental countries. Equally, although it is suggestive that the 'Anglo-Saxon' economies combine lower than average unemployment rates with increasing inequality, that coincidence does not prove the existence of an unpalatable trade-off between jobs and fairness.

The uncontroversial type of policy involves measures to help the unemployed with their job search, retraining, relocation and so on. Such 'active labour market policies' focus on reducing the amount of friction that can slow up the matching of people to jobs, especially when the people have been out of work for long enough to have lost the habits and skills needed to hold down a job. The experience of the past two decades suggests that it is near-impossible to get anyone who has been unemployed for more than a year back to work without this type of government assistance. The only reason governments have not all introduced schemes of this sort already is that there is disagreement over their design and cost. The devil is in the detail. In reality there is no excuse for not implementing schemes – almost any schemes – that help marry someone who has been out of a job for more than a year with some kind of work.

Almost all economists now acknowledge that some countries have to deregulate their labour markets. A high national minimum wage for young people, high payroll taxes and 'social charges' on employing the unskilled, laws making difficult for companies to vary overtime hours and staff numbers, shop-floor agreements that prevent them using their employees flexibly – all tend to increase unemployment among the most vulnerable groups.

Summary

Unemployment is easy to bemoan, harder to diagnose, hardest of all to solve. The combination of the OPEC shocks, the diffusion of new technology and bad policies cemented high levels of unemployment in Europe from the mid-1970s on. With a vastly different structure to its economy and better policies, the US has reversed its unemployment bulge, although at a high cost in terms of poverty and inequality.

By now it is possible to be clear about which solutions to unemployment will not work. Turning a blind eye to new technology in the mistaken belief that it will save jobs will prove damaging. It would prevent progress in industry that would eventually encourage growth and job creation. So would putting up barriers against international trade. Protectionism would protect a minority of employees in the industrial countries at the expense of the majority and at the expense of third world countries for which trade offers the best hope of economic advancement. More expansionary macroeconomic policies would help stimulate employment, but their scope is limited.

That leaves a range of microeconomic policies to reduce frictions in the labour market and to overcome the legacy of high long-term unemployment in Europe. There is no miracle cure, but active labour market policies targeted on the groups most vulnerable to unemployment could, realistically, cut European unemployment by a third or more within a few years. Governments also need to address the sheer unfairness of unemployment: the current rethink of the welfare state will have to cover the distribution of work and income.

For the longer term the best prospects for jobs growth lie in embracing the changing world rather than opposing it. The next chapter looks at the areas in which modern industrial economies will create jobs in the next half century.

Notes

1. *The End of Work*, Chapter 18.
2. Article in *London Review of Books*, 9 May 1996.
3. *OECD Jobs Study*, Vol. 1, page 134.
4. *OECD Jobs Study*, Vol. 1, page 145.
5. In *Technology's Revenge*, reprinted in *Pop Internationalism*.
6. Prospect, July 1996.
7. Adrian Wood, *North–South Trade, Employment and Inequality*.
8. See Williamson.
9. OECD Employment Report, July 1996.

Chapter Four

Nourishing the Grass Roots

In his fine and funny documentary *Roger and Me* the American journalist Michael Moore pursues the then chairman of General Motors, Roger Smith, for an interview about the massive job cuts the company had imposed in Moore's home town of Flint, Michigan. He never managed to confront the elusive executive, but Moore's quest illustrated the human cost of those redundancies in what had been a company town.

One episode, both hilarious and poignant, concerns a former GM worker who had retrained as an image consultant. She visited other women in their homes to advise them on their best 'colours' and make-up. Not only did she get the colours wrong and come back on camera to admit it, but it was also a doomed enterprise in a depressed town where so many people were unemployed. Only the well-off can afford fripperies like a personal image session. The movie invites us to laugh at the foolishness of this woman's alternative career choice as well as sympathising with her desperation to find another way to earn a living.

But her idea was not as daft as it seems. At different times in history, the growth in employment has occurred in different parts of the economy. In the early years of industrialisation, when agricultural productivity leapt ahead and people started to move from the land to the cities, one group of pessimists in France predicted starvation and mass unemployment. The Physiocrats – the most prominent of whom, François Quesnay, was a physician at the court of Louis XV – saw agriculture as the only productive activity, which generated a surplus on which the rest of the economy depended. For one seed of grain could generate a full field, whereas a manufacturer merely reshaped the same materials he started out with. Manufacturing was 'sterile'.

The Physiocrats' gloom turned out to be utterly misplaced. Industry not only provided the jobs, but it has also been the motor of modern economic growth. Despite the example of this error, however, there are many economists now who see disaster looming in the decline of manufacturing as a share of output and employment. This is a prejudice that dates back to Adam Smith, who updated the Physiocratic theory by arguing that both manufacturing and agriculture were productive, but it was services that were sterile. Services yielded neither tangible products not reinvestable surpluses.[1]

The tyranny of the tangible over economic thought in an increasingly weightless world will prove to be as mistaken as the original Physiocrats. The lesson of economic history is that as the most productive and wealth-creating parts of an economy destroy jobs, this allows the least productive areas to create work. Lead sectors compete on a global level but their earnings are channelled into the local economy, which can be less productive because it is not competing in the same context. Some parts of the economy can be sheltered by regulation, like retailing in Japan. Others are sheltered in other ways, whether by government subsidy, by consumers being willing to pay more as they are at corner shops, or by producers who are willing to work for lower rewards than they would get elsewhere, like 'social entrepreneurs' who work in the voluntary sector.

Much of the growth in employment, especially for the least skilled people, in industrialised societies during the next few decades will be in what is formally described as 'community, social and personal services'. Although not high technology, this is intrinsically weightless work. There are two categories of these. Personal services includes Michael Moore's image consultant, and a huge range of other jobs from child-minders and nurses to aromatherapists and aerobics teachers. A lot of these people will be conventionally employed or self-employed, and their numbers have been increasing rapidly. With ageing populations and rising incomes, this is forecast – by the US Bureau of Labour Statistics and the OECD, for example – to be one of the fastest categories of jobs growth.

Another aspect, the focus of this chapter, is the 'community and social' services – the *third sector* in English, or *économie sociale* on the Continent. The third sector is a varied mixture of activities with rather fuzzy boundaries, some of them outside the formal, monetary economy. It includes charities, voluntary organisations from unions to think tanks and lobby groups, non-governmental organisations including the quangos that overlap with the public sector, not-for-profit businesses, churches, schools, housing associations, museums, and mutual and co-operative organisations.[2] The list could go on. It could be extended to cover all the 'unemployed' people who describe themselves as 'carers', for example, of whom there are about 6 million in the UK. These are just as much part of the weightless world as jobs in the knowledge economy.

The link is that they are all very people-intensive services whose purpose is to provide the service rather than maximise the profit that can be made from doing so. The absence of an emphasis on profit and productivity is precisely what will permit the sector to create jobs. It parallels the way some advanced economies have permitted the existence of an inefficient, sheltered sector as an employment policy, like retailing in Japan, safeguarded from competition by strict regulation, or the public sector in many northern European countries.

The sector is likely to help provide a solution to one of the key social problems in the advanced economies; that is, what to do about the people at the bottom of the economic heap – those who have been unemployed for a long time or have not worked since leaving school, who have no skills and no work habits. It includes the feckless adolescents failed by the education system, and the fifty-something men made redundant from declining industries and unlikely to work again.

It is a pure political myth to pretend that most of these long-term unemployables can be retrained for 'good' – well-paid and skilled – jobs. On the other hand, they are very unlikely to want to accept low-paid bad jobs that are fitted to their low level of productivity. For everybody's aspirations are set according to what they see other people around them bringing home. Low-productivity workers want average-productivity wages. It is a mismatch that is likely to get worse as the average standard of living rises.

The development of the social economy will provide part of the solution. Apart from anything else, it reveals the bankruptcy of economists' typically dualistic division of activity into state versus market or public versus private sectors. The social economy is neither. It will be supported by the wealth-creating and productive sectors – agriculture, industry and the other parts of the service sector such as financial and information services – because we all want some of the services provided by the third sector. Lester Salamon, who heads a big research project into the third sector at Johns Hopkins University in the US, claims: 'The rise of the non-profit sector may well prove to be as significant a development of the latter 20th century as the rise of the nation state was of the latter 19th century'.[3]

One example in the East London borough of Tower Hamlets, the poorest in the capital, offers a signpost to the role the social economy will play in the next century. In late 1996 the East London Communities Organisation (Telco) was launched, linking churches and mosques, Sikh gurdwaras, tenant groups and schools, and hoping to persuade union branches to join.[4] Telco is trying to build links with the powers that be in the area, the big employers, local and national politicians, hospitals and so on. So far, Telco has persuaded big local companies to consider pledging that a small proportion of the new jobs they create will go to local people, and got a factory to reduce its emissions of bad smells. Small beer, but there will be more groups like Telco, and they will grow in confidence and achievements as well as numbers. Telco is the sixth such organisation to be formed in the UK since 1990.

The finance for the social economy is likely to come – as it does now – from a mixture of sources: some self-generated, some from government funding and some from charitable contributions. According to the Johns Hopkins project, charity forms the least important source of funds, accounting for less than 20 per cent of the total in the US, where it is most developed, and a far smaller share elsewhere. Self-generated income from fees, sales and invest-ment accounts for a half, on average, followed by government funding, which provides 41 per cent of total income on average – less in the US and Sweden, more in France and Germany. Whatever the make-up, affording a social economy is not a fundamental problem for the wealthy, developed countries. The industrialised countries have always transferred resources from the most to the least productive areas, although the mechanisms change.

One way forward is illustrated by a range of schemes in France, a country where concern about the social exclusion of the long-term unemployed has been at the top of the political agenda. Unemployed people agree a contract with a social worker on a project, often a cultural or craft activity. They receive a small government-funded benefit, the *Revenu Minimum d'Insertion* or RMI. Although the amount of money is small, many French social workers think the scheme helps restore optimism and a sense of purpose to people who have been without work for a long time. The kinds of projects involved, such as community theatre or voluntary environmental work, are typical third sector activities. They differ from the compulsory 'workfare' projects US and British politicians are so keen on by being devised and motivated by the unemployed themselves rather than thought up by a bureaucrat – surely a more productive and sensible approach.

What the process needs as much as funding is a kick-start from government, but few politicians even acknowledge that the third sector exists. They even tend to grumble when key players in the social economy such as church leaders or community leaders 'interfere' in politics. It is an issue that has not appeared on the conventional political radar. This shows incredible myopia. But before long the social economy will be so big that even the most narrow-minded and introverted politicians will have to acknowledge it.

The growing third

In a recent book[5] on third sector organisations, Mike Hudson sets out the following principles for deciding what they are. They must exist primarily for a social purpose rather than having a profit-making objective. They must be independent from the state in its government even if it gets some state funding. They must reinvest any financial surplus in the services they offer. These sound fairly limiting criteria, but even so the sector is surprisingly big.

Until recently, the third sector was the poor cousin in the advanced economies. Until at least the end of the 1970s there was an assumption that the kinds of services it includes ought to be provided by the state. Mike Hudson writes: 'Provision of housing, schools and health care was increasingly seen as a government responsibility. Many services that had historically been provided or supported by charitable institutions were slowly being incorporated into the public sector.' But the efficacy of the state in these areas has come into question – governments have not been notably successful in housing and educating all their citizens, and in providing an acceptable social environment. Even the middle classes, broadly well-served by big government, are unhappy with it. This has set the scene for a revival of the *économie sociale*.

There are no comparable official figures for all the advanced economies. In the US the third sector accounts for 6 per cent of GDP and more than one in ten of the work force, according to Jeremy Rifkin, who grudgingly admits in the dire *The End of Work* that there is actually work here. He adds that 90 million Americans do some voluntary work. In the UK charities alone have turnover equivalent to 3 per cent of GDP and employ 450,000 people, or one in 50 of the work force. The Volunteer Centre estimated the value of volunteering in 1994 – with 23 million people involved – at £41 billion or 8.5 per cent of GDP.

Third sector organisations have played an important role in Eastern Europe since the collapse of the Communist regimes in 1989. With robber capitalism rushing to fill the vacuum in some cases and the IMF administering 'shock therapy' to the economy in others, the social economy has become enormously important. It had its precursor in an array of organisations that were illegal before 1989, often churches, environmentalists and similar dissidents. These groups both helped overthrow the previous authoritarian regimes and have played a unique political end economic role since.

The most comprehensive figures comparing the third sector across different countries have been collected by the Johns Hopkins University Comparative Nonprofit Sector Project.[6] In the first eight countries for which the researchers Lester Salamon and Helmut Anheier collected data – France, Ger-

Fig. 7 Non-profit employment as a percentage of total employment.

Country	Non-profit sector employment	
	Number of people	Percentage of total
France	802,619	4.2%
Germany	1,017,945	3.7%
Hungary	32,738	0.8%
Italy	418,128	1.8%
Japan	1,440,228	2.5%
Sweden	82,558	2.5%
UK	945,883	4.0%
US	7,130,823	6.9%
Average		*3.3%*

Source: The Johns Hopkins Comparative Nonprofit Sector Project.

many, Hungary, Italy, Japan, Sweden, the UK and the US – the third sector employed 11.8 million people, excluding volunteers. The share in total national employment ranged from 0.8 per cent in Hungary, where the sector is nascent, and 1.8 per cent in Japan, where it struggles against legal obstacles, to 4.0 per cent in the UK, 4.2 per cent in France and 6.9 per cent in the US. More significantly for the future, the sector's employment growth has been extremely rapid since 1980, increasing by 15.8 per cent in Germany, 11 per cent in France and 12.7 per cent in the US in a decade. Third sector expenditures as a share of GDP in 1990 ranged from 1.2 per cent in Hungary to 6.3 per cent in the US, with an average of 3.5 per cent.

The focus of the sector differs between countries. In France and Italy, it is heavily geared towards social services, followed by education. In the US and Germany, health is the dominant component. In the UK, education accounts for most third sector activity, followed by culture and recreation – the more so now the latter has National Lottery funding.

The sector is international, too. The UN's Yearbook of International Organizations lists about 5000 non-governmental organisations operating across national boundaries. For instance, Greenpeace has $100 million revenues and nearly 7 million members, up from $24 million revenues and 1.5 million members in the early 1980s. The Worldwide Fund for Nature had increased

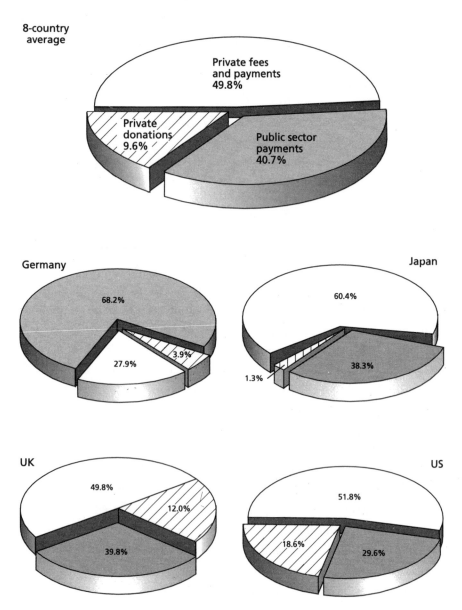

Fig. 8 Share of non-profit revenue centres by source. (Source: Johns Hopkins University.)

its revenues and membership tenfold, to $100 million and more than one million, respectively, by 1991.[7]

These figures indicate that the social economy is bigger than agriculture in turnover – bigger also than the car, coal and steel industries combined. It is not the part of the national economy that will generate rapid growth in output per person or contribute to the balance of payments, but for precisely that reason it is where the richest economies will generate jobs in the twenty-first century.

Politics of the third sector

In an influential article called *Bowling alone: America's declining social capital*, Harvard Professor Robert Putnam described the decline of civic engagement in the US. His headline evidence was the two-fifths fall in the number of people going league bowling between 1980 and 1993, at the same time that the number of people bowling at all rose by a tenth. Americans go bowling by themselves in the 1990s.

Professor Putnam linked this to his magnum opus, a 20-year study of Italian government which showed that a higher degree of civic engagement in the northern regions explained their greater political stability and economic success compared to the southern regions, which had received absolutely huge government handouts over the years. Civic networks partly accounted for the success of economic networks, such as the highly efficient and flexible industrial districts of Emilia Romagna. Putnam called the history and agglomeration of membership of football clubs and choral societies, high voter turnout, volunteering for the Boy Scouts, and so on 'social capital'.

Successful economies have high levels of social as well as physical capital. Social capital refers to the stable framework of law, politics and convention that allows business to be done. It is what Francis Fukuyama would call 'trust'. Where there is a high level of social capital, deals can be struck, bribes are rare, violence does not play a key part in economic life. Money cannot compensate for its absence.

One British social entrepreneur, karate champion and founder of the Youth Charter for Sport in Manchester, Geoff Thompson, is quoted as saying: 'No square mile of the country has had more public money pumped into it to less effect than Moss Side and Hulme'.The most deprived areas of the UK's former centre of industrial might are lacking social capital rather than money. Founders of organisations like Thompson's are trying to build it.[8]

This correlation has been confirmed by other researchers. Stephen Knack at the University of Maryland found that the proportion of those asked in a survey whether they thought 'most people can be trusted' was closely linked, across countries, with rates of investment. In another article[9] Mancur Olsen provides evidence that differences in the amount of their resources and level of capital cannot account for differences in wealth and income between countries. For example, he found that the more land per person in a given country, the *lower* income per head was likely to be. In addition, people who emigrated from poor countries to rich ones became much more productive – as measured by their earning power – simply as a result of moving. Eliminating the other possibilities, Olsen concludes that there is compelling evidence for the view that legal, political and social institutions are vital for economic prosperity.

In *Bowling Alone* Robert Putnam warned that the tradition of engagement is on the decline in the US.'In sum, after expanding steadily throughout most of this century, many major civic organisations have experienced a sudden, substantial and nearly simultaneous decline in membership over the last decade or two.' The argument struck a chord in many other countries.

However, he noted a counter-trend: the third sector. Its alternative name, the social economy, makes its potential contribution to social capital clearer. Putnam concluded that it had not grown enough to offset his gloomy conclusion. But the partial exception he makes for the third sector highlights its political potential. Consider the point raised by Ed Mayo, director of the New Economics Foundation, in an article where he argues against the desirability of conventional full employment. He writes:

> *'The labour market exclusively defines how we organise and validate work within society (where those out of employment are dismissed as "economically inactive"). The results? We have two – twin – evils: mass unemployment on the one hand and a large amount of socially useful*

work remaining undone on the other. It is hard to imagine a worse out-come.'[10]

The social economy offers a way of tackling these twin evils. More than this, its development will provide the serious content to what my colleague Suzanne Moore has memorably described as 'cuddly capitalism'. Many thinkers on the left have urged 'stakeholding' as the principle upon which economic policy and job creation should be based. The central notion is that any economic activity has a number of stakeholders — a business, for example, has its share-holders, managers, employees, customers and neighbours in the local com-munity.

Recognition of the range of stakeholders presents a middle way between the excesses of the free market and the bonds of government intervention, or so its advocates suggest. In a book[11] published in the run-up to the UK gen-eral election, John Plender writes:

> *'The stakeholding solution outlined here is about responsible individual-ism. It accepts that uncertainty is a condition of life for the foreseeable future and that people who have been used to security in a paternalistic environment will have to develop a more robust sense of independence.'*

But these are empty words. Stakeholding is a vague extension of conven-tional politics, recommending a softening at the edges of conventional ways of running the economy. It does not recognise that the social economy lies entirely outside this framework. The stakeholding theory, like communitarianism in the US, does nothing to include the huge numbers of people who are bored by the exclusive nature of conventional politics, alien-ated by the politicians and theorisers, and have an entirely different agenda. Suzanne Moore speaks for them when she writes: 'We are Heretics Anony-mous and maybe one day some pamphleteer or even guru with his eyes off the prize just for a second, may realise that we are the fastest growing political force in Britain today'.[12]

The alienation from politics as usual is not confined to the US and Britain.

The *tangentopoli* corruption scandal combined with the surge in support for the separatist northern parties in Italy, voters' distaste for the cronyism and corruption revealed by investigations in France and Belgium, the strength of the environmental movement in Germany, all point to it being a pretty widespread phenomenon across the developed world. Most of us do not trust our political and technocratic elite. John Gray identifies this as the main failure of modern liberal democracy. Ours is not really a pluralist society, he argues. 'It is instead a society ruled by an elite of opinion formers', he writes.[13] He urges the importance of 'civil association', people getting together for reasons other than the narrow purpose of economic advance. 'Civil society is the matrix of the market economy, which both history and theory show to be a precondition of prosperity and liberty in the modern world.'

In *Primary Colors*, the best-selling novel based on Bill Clinton's 1992 election campaign, there is a compelling scene where presidential candidate Stanton addresses a meeting in a depressed New England town where unemployment is running high. He says:

> *'There are two kinds of politician in this world. Those who tell you what you want to hear – and those who never come around. The second kind, the ones who don't come 'round here, they're the ones who tell the uptown folks what they want to hear ... No politician can bring these shipyard jobs back. Or make your union strong again. No politician can make the world the way it used to be.'*

The candidate goes on to explain the realities of global capital flows, the loss of 'muscle' jobs to cheaper countries, the need for Americans to get smarter and learn new skills. His speech ends by referring to the torrent of newspaper stories criticising his sexual antics. 'Why? Why is Jack Stanton worth the ton of garbage they're dumpin' on his head? ... It may be that there are two kinds of politicians – the ones who tell you what you want to hear and the ones who don't bother tellin' you anything at all. And maybe some folks aren't very *interested* in there being a third kind. You should think about that when you cast that vote next Thursday.'

Addressing the failure of conventional politics to touch on the difficult issues that matter to people proves a vote-winner for Stanton. People want that third way. Reversing the alienation of a majority from their rulers and the depletion of social capital has become an urgent political task for the industrial democracies. It goes hand in hand with the economic task of creating and reshaping work. The *économie sociale* is the economic project of what has been described as a 'world opposition movement', a loose coalition of environmental groups, people seeking alternative life-styles, some unionists, some right-wing nationalists – in sum, all those who are left out of the loop by politics and business as usual. Andrew Marr writes: 'The World Opposition Movement is possessed of a single and priceless truth: there is, in out times, a terrible danger of slipping into an arid economic determinism that becomes contemptuous of anything it can't measure'.[14]

Weightlessness is unmeasured and ignored by conventional policies. One of its positive aspects is that it is creating the flexibility and the economic space for alternative approaches. The next chapter considers new, flexible working patterns, and their contrasting facets – insecurity and inequality on the one hand, and greater freedom and control on the other. The remainder of this chapter looks at two examples of how third sector schemes can work.

Local economies

One of the most promising avenues for the generation of jobs and income in the social economy takes the form of the Local Exchange Trading System, or Lets. Essentially, a Lets scheme allows people in a given area to barter goods and services. They can be seen as an extension of the social bartering that most of us participate in – looking after friends' children, running errands for somebody who is ill, in the knowledge that the neighbourliness will be re-paid if necessary. I used to exchange baby-sitting with a group of close friends in my neighbourhood; we paid with pretend money raided from an old board game.

Many of the formal UK schemes consist of a computer bulletin board, describing the offers or requirements to trade, and an accounting system which records the transactions and keeps credits and debits up to date. The buyer and seller negotiate a price between them. The units of account are an alternative form of money – 'anchors' in Greenwich, 'strouds' in the town of the same name in Gloucestershire. The related US schemes are more likely to have a physical, printed alternative currency instead, such as 'Ithaca Hours' in the town in upstate New York.[15] A swift Internet search reveals a large number of schemes, most seeming to be in the US and UK. The number in the UK has climbed from 5 in 1992 to 350-plus by 1997; in Australia from 34 in 1990 to more than 200 by 1997.[16]

Lets schemes started as a means of overcoming the constraints imposed by lack of money in a poor community or during a recession. The schemes reduce the need for money and potentially offer a social network and sense of self-worth to the people taking part, often those like the long-term unemployed who have been steadily excluded by the conventional economy. As Polly Toynbee, one of Britain's most experienced reporters of social affairs observes: 'Years of doing nothing drives young men mad'. In a report on riots on an estate in Luton, one of London's satellite towns, she writes: 'Unemployment on the estate is officially 10 per cent but among the young it is far higher. They want what everyone wants, a job, a place to live, a car, some money in their pockets, a future.'[17]

There is not much hope that conventional economic approaches will provide the solution for these pockets of urban exclusion, not just in Britain but throughout the industrialised countries. In many low income communities, the little money that enters is often a state payment of benefit, and it will often leave straight away by the payment of rent to landlords from outside the area, or buying food and other essentials from branches of national stores. The Lets currency, by contrast, has to stay in the area, and starts to boost the local economy through an absolutely standard economic 'multiplier' effect, whereby what one person earns is spent in turn on another service.

Many Lets get some support – usually advice and management – from local councils or voluntary agencies. The success record is mixed. A recent series of case studies of UK schemes concluded that there were two main obstacles. One was a combination of a lack of confidence and know-how on the part of the members, and a lack of support from the council or voluntary agencies. The other was the lack of trust – or absence of social capital – in areas such as problem estates with high crime rates.

However, despite these problems, the New Economics Foundation estimates that the UK has at least 300 schemes ten years after they were first introduced. Some Lets have grown to impressive proportions. For example, one of the UK's biggest, in Manchester, has 700 members and has created its own credit union. Paul Glover, organiser of the Ithaca Hours scheme in the US, estimates that transactions in the local currency, accepted in about 300 businesses, have reached a value equivalent to about $1.5 million. A time-dollar system in St Louis, Missouri, has about 3000 participants earning and spending about 50,000 time-dollars. The scheme, started with the help of a grant in 1987, will help Missouri satisfy tough new welfare laws, such as the requirement that a quarter of a state's welfare recipients have to be working at least 20 hours a week.

George Eberle, organiser of the St Louis scheme, asks: 'How do you increase the capacity of a community to respond to its needs? How do you take a neighbourhood and capture the sparks that are there?'[18] It is because Lets schemes seem to offer an answer that charitable foundations such as the Rockefeller Family Fund and the Robert Wood Johnson Foundation – another part of the social economy – in the US are increasingly offering them start-up grants.

Ed Mayo, director of the New Economics Foundation, argues that Lets do not represent a second-class economy. Rather, they are a logical development in a global economy. 'Lets should not create the impression of a dualistic structure of classical work versus local exchange. Instead they point towards multiple ways of organising and rewarding work', he writes. He goes on: 'Localised approaches to work creation should be set within, rather than apart from, broader spheres of economic activity – the aim being greater self-reliance rather than autarchy'.[19]

Lets offer one means of growing the third sector without an infusion of public funds. It is one of many possible forms in which there can be meaningful activity and work in an increasingly weightless economy where many traditional job opportunities are vanishing.

Local financing

Another approach is one born of an astonishingly successful initiative in the developing world known as microcredit. The vision of one man, Muhammad Yunus, who founded Bangladesh's Grameen Bank has grown into a worldwide lending network amounting to hundreds of millions of dollars – all in loans of no more than a few thousand dollars each and often far less than that. Yunus, an economist, founded Grameen in the mid-1970s when he was head of the economics department at Chittagong University. In 1974 Bangladesh suffered a terrible famine. Some estimates put the number who died as high as 1.5 million. Yunus says:

> 'While people were dying of hunger in the streets, I was teaching elegant theories of economics. I started hating myself for the arrogance of pretending I had answers. We university professors were all so intelligent, but we knew absolutely nothing of the poverty surrounding us. Why did people who worked 12 hours a day, seven days a week, not have enough food to eat?'[20]

He recounts that he spent the next two years on field trips to get at the root of the problem, and decided that it was the destitute underclass, the rural poor with no land or assets. These very poor people had no savings or capital. To earn their living they had to borrow, and loans were only available to them from moneylenders charging as much as 10 per cent interest a month. At this cost, they could never do more than survive, never save.

He therefore set up Grameen Bank, which makes small loans to people considered uncreditworthy by conventional banks. In order to keep up repayments borrowers – almost all women – meet in groups and put social pressure on each other not to embarrass everybody else by failing to meet a due payment. Grameen enjoys a high repayment rate and makes a profit.

Yunus argues that its profitability and absence of dependence on government aid is its strength. The relief of poverty lies in self-reliance. He says:

> 'Poverty covers people in a thick crust and makes the poor appear stupid and without initiative. Yet if you give them credit they will slowly come back to life. Even those who seemingly have no conceptual thought, no ability to think of yesterday or tomorrow, are in fact quite intelligent and expert at the art of survival. Credit is the key that unlocks their humanity.'

From these small beginnings, microcredit has been given the seal of approval by the World Bank, which had itself made $200 million available for tiny loans in developing countries by the end of 1995. World Bank figures put the amount of such loans in Bangladesh alone at $520 million by that time, involving 4.8 million borrowers. By the end of 1996 it estimated that there were more than 7000 microcredit programmes serving 16 million people in developing countries with loans worth $2.5 billion. Almost none of the funds came from government sources.

In the light of this success it is not surprising that projects involving microcredit in the developed world should have started to spring up. They are seen as an extension of well-established social investment programmes. One of the best-known of these is Chicago's South Shore Bank. It was founded in 1973 by investors who wanted to put their money to socially useful ends by lending money locally to people seen as bad risks by other banks, and some of the loans have been tiny in scale. Most of the lending has been for redevelopment of the neighbourhood's housing. Community banks in the US are estimated to have financed more than $2.5 billion in loans, and to have a capital and reserve base of $800 million.

A similar bank which includes some microlending, the Aston Reinvestment Trust, has more recently been established in the UK, just outside Birmingham. The UK – where a quarter of adults do not have a bank account – now has around a dozen social or microlending schemes. But the process is less well established than elsewhere, despite the tradition of the mutual friendly societies. The Charities Aid Foundation estimates that unfilled demand for microloans in the UK could amount to £250 million. Social lending has a longer history and takes place on a much bigger scale on the Continent. For example, France has the Caisses de Credit Municipal, serving a million low-income customers, and Germany has a big credit union movement dating back to the mid-nineteenth century.

Sometimes the process is more informal. Jane Jacobs gives the example of the redevelopment of Boston's North End in the 1950s – it has since become an expensive and chi-chi neighbourhood. But after World War II it was a squalid, crowded immigrant area with a very dilapidated housing stock. Banks would not lend for redevelopment in the area. It was a no-hope project, a bad credit risk, in their eyes. The redevelopment did take place, but without outside capital. The North End's inhabitants, a close-knit Italian community, pooled their own savings to pay for the work on the same principles as a friendly society but informally, policed by the fact that everybody knew each other and by social convention rather than the law.[21]

The state and the third sector

The notion that the state has reached its useful limits has filtered across the entire political spectrum. The libertarian right wing obviously believes in rolling back the frontiers of big government. But on the left too there has been growing interest in the notion of the state doing less, and the individual having more responsibility. This idea has had several manifestations, from the US-based communitarianism of Amitai Etzioni and others to stakeholding in the UK and the Continental debate about how to re-involve in society the exclus. The philosopher John Gray argues that the state has usurped the vital role played by civil associations like churches and trade unions – that is, by the third sector. Modern states have grown too big, he argues, so that rather than fulfilling the classic liberal ideal of delivering a peaceful civil society, the state itself has become the battleground of competing interest groups.

For the simple reason that the governments of the rich industrialised countries no longer seem to be able to deliver what they once confidently promised – full employment, an end to poverty, steady economic growth – the most pressing question in public policy is whether governments should carry on as they have, as best they can, or whether instead the state should withdraw from some of the territory it has taken over during the post-war era. The social economy is the borderland. If the boundary of the public sector is being forced by weightlessness to recede, the third sector will take over those areas.

The prospect of governments reducing their ambitions does not alarm the free-market right, with its tradition of emphasising self-help and the family intact. But on the radical left, too, thoughtful politicians are proposing shifting the boundary of government in favour of third sector institutions.

The French ecologist Alain Lipietz speaks of the need to replace the welfare state with a 'welfare community', by which he means the development of local activities. There must be what he calls a social dimension to the guarantee of work to citizens. 'One firm on its own cannot guarantee the same kind of job over a long period.' People will need the option of mobility between market economy and social economy, he argues.

In Britain, the Labour MP Frank Field draws on the Labour movement's tradition of mutual financial institutions – building societies, friendly societies, credit unions – in proposals for reform of the welfare state. He argues that universal provision of pensions or social insurance can be provided outside the public sector. 'Politicians have no idea how to rebuild community', he writes. In addition, the former consensus in favour of redistribution of incomes to the poor has been eroded, people are unwilling to pay higher taxes, and resent the widespread social security fraud. 'Any welfare reconstruction needs to address and channel the differing roles of self-interest, self-improvement and altruism, which are among the great driving forces in human character.'[22]

Field's key proposal, very likely to be implemented in some form in the UK by the turn of the century, is a private sector National Pension Savings Scheme, a compulsory saving scheme that would run in parallel with the state basic pension scheme. He notes that there is nothing particularly novel in this approach. The Commissioners on Friendly and Building Societies (1875) considered a proposal for selling annuities through local post offices.

Traditional left wingers are scathing about the notion that mutual help and organisations outside the public sector can do anything to help the poor and excluded. Their hearts lie with the classic socialism of Robert Tressel. In *The Ragged Trousered Philanthropists* he calls the volunteers in Mugsborough's 'benevolent society' loathsome hypocrites:

> *'"Loathsome hypocrites" may seem a hard saying, but it was a matter of common knowledge that the majority of the children attending the local elementary schools were insufficiently fed. It was admitted that the money that could be raised by a halfpenny rate would be more than sufficient to provide them all with one good meal every day. The charity-mongers who professed such extravagant sympathy with the 'dear little children' resisted the levying of the rate 'because it would press so heavily on the poorer ratepayers ...*
>
> *'To judge them by their professions and performances, it appeared that these good kind persons were willing to do any mortal thing for the "dear little children" except allow them to be fed.'*

Why has the possibility of raising a bit more tax to get the long-term unemployed into conventional jobs dropped off the bottom of the political agenda, even amongst many people with left-wing sympathies? This is a question I return to in more depth in the next two chapters, which look in more detail at the welfare state. The point here is only that after 50 years the state has not been able to eradicate poverty or ensure that large numbers of people are not left on the margins of society. Not only that, state bureaucracies have gone out of their way to make it next to impossible for private sector or quasi-private institutions to step in. Traditional mutual organisations, churches, unions and so on have been marginalised themselves. The public sector has squeezed the social economy.

Yet all the industrial countries have a tradition of social provision predating the corporate state that offers a useful model for the development of the social economy in the next century. It has the potential to become a thriving source of more jobs and greater flexibility. In the weightless world the social economy will take over some of the role that in the past half century has been played by the state in guarding individuals against economic risk.

Measuring the social economy

There is one unexpected hurdle to overcome before economic policy can be properly tailored to the emerging third sector. Which of these two tasks is more like work? Having a chat with a colleague at the office over a cup of coffee, or cleaning the bathroom at home? Although the latter is more arduous, it is the former that is included in Gross Domestic Product, the conventional statistical measure of the size of the economy. Although it is widely accepted that GDP is not a perfect measure of economic well-being, it is the only one we have.

Prior to the Industrial Revolution, which took so many people out of the home and into the factory, censuses classed unpaid housework by women as a productive activity. It was not paid, but it still counted as a job. But by the end of the nineteenth century, housewives were classed as unproductive dependants. It has taken another century for statisticians to realise that tax and social security policies cannot be drawn up properly without knowing a lot more about this unmeasured and invisible part of the economy. It is impossible to assess the impact of policies on people's decision to enter the labour force, on childcare choices or on care for the elderly or disabled without having an estimate of the 'productive potential', paid and unpaid, of households.

The gap in our knowledge will become wider the more people switch to flexible patterns of employment, interspersing paid work in the formal economy with non-monetary third sector activities such as volunteering or Lets. As the social economy grows, an increasing share of total activity will fall outside the spotlight of the conventional statistics.

To see how damaging this could be, think about the way the tax system treats the care of dependants. It makes no allowance for the number of children or elderly relatives cared for within the household, nor does it take account of who does the caring. Children can be cared for by an unpaid parent, or their parents can work and pay for somebody else to look after them. Either the household gives up a big chunk of income or one member pays for a carer out of after-tax income. It is hard to imagine that a tax system would have been deliberately engineered to create such a stark dilemma if there had been figures indicating the scale of the national need for childcare.

Mistakes in tax and social security policies can be expected as the third sector grows. Most tax authorities insist that Lets schemes are just like work paid for with conventional money, but we would never have devised the tax systems we have for an economy in which a significant amount of activity was outside the formal monetary system.

In the UK the Office for National Statistics has begun to construct a set of 'household accounts' to supplement the national accounts and fill the gap. Henry Neuberger, the statistician in charge of the project, explained in an article announcing the move that the best way to do this was to monitor people's use of time.[23] 'How people spend their time is as good a measure of civilisation and social progress as any', he wrote. The biggest switch in time use in the UK between 1960 and the mid-1980s was the shift from blue collar to white collar activities. There were also quality improvements in time spent on housework due to labour-saving equipment. Not only will the quality of time be a sensible measure of people's well-being, it will also be an increasingly important constraint on the economy. For in the weightless economy the amount of time people spend contributing their brain power will be a key resource. Any harassed and overworked professional can testify that this is something their employers are already exploiting.

Although a preliminary version of the statistics will be available in the UK around the turn of the century, we are far from having a consistent set of figures for all the increasingly weightless economies.

Salamon and Anheier argue that better measurement of the third sector will be essential to overcoming its invisibility, both to the general public and policymakers. Without visibility there will be no credibility, they reckon. 'The sector is systematically ignored in national economic statistics, rarely mentioned in public debate, and overlooked almost entirely in public education and scholarly research.' But this problem of measurement is only one obstacle to the expansion of the job-creating third sector.

The new framework

Tax and social security rules are extraordinarily unhelpful to the third sector. This is partly because of the fact that we have few statistics on it so policy makers have no idea of its scale and importance. It is partly because politicians are only just getting round to accepting that there is a role for the third sector outside the public sector – and therefore outside the direct influence of politicians. Meanwhile in some countries such organisations operate in a legal limbo, the tax system discourages charitable donations, and the sector that is going to be absolutely critical for employment and economic stability has little legitimacy.

Economic policy is starting to involve third sector organisations more than before. In the Anglo-Saxon economies, this has been connected to deliberate attempts to roll back the frontiers of the state. Conservative Governments in the UK have achieved this in areas such as housing, by forcing local councils to sell their housing stock. 'Social' home-building is now carried out by housing associations. Although they depend on the government for much of their funding, they are not public sector bodies. The same goes for parts of the National Health Service and the education system.

In the US the radical welfare reform approved by President Clinton is involving third sector agencies in many state programmes to force welfare recipients out of their 'dependency' on government cheques. For example, in

Wisconsin's radical version which makes Aid for Families with Dependent Children depend on attending training and ultimately forces recipients to get a job, it is bodies such as the YMCA which have won the contracts to establish training and job search schemes. Equally, charities and churches have had to provide shelters for the homeless mothers who lose their welfare payments for failing to turn up to their courses.

In France, the other country with a big and thriving third sector, the Mitterrand government created an interministerial agency to co-ordinate its activities, the Délégation a l'Economie Sociale, which has representation on the national economic and social council. The formal recognition, although of limited practical help, has certainly helped legitimise third sector organisations.

Whether the outcome is bad or good, policy is clearly starting to take account of the third sector. But there are many obstacles to the development of the social economy in tax and benefit rules. The legal and regulatory framework is too rigid and bureaucratic. It leaves no room for social provision outside the conventional public sector.

Take the problems Lets face in their interaction with the state. People who participate in Lets sometimes find that their cash benefits are reduced pound for 'pound' (or stroud or anchor) because they have unearned income. Equally, 'earnings' in the scheme are sometimes deducted from benefits. Lets earnings are also formally liable for income tax, although this is, of course, supposed to be paid in formal money. The attitude of the authorities seems to be benign neglect, until a scheme grows to be big enough to trigger the bureaucrats' active hostility. According to the New Economics Foundation, officials do not like the way Lets enable their 'clients' to escape their surveillance. If a scheme grows beyond something the authorities regard as on a par with a baby-sitting circle, their instinct is to harrass it out of existence.

A clearer and more helpful framework of rules is obviously needed. For example, small Lets or a certain number of transactions within any Lets could be exempted from loss of benefits, and the definition of 'small' or the acceptable number of transactions made formal so participants would know where they stood. Australia already does this. Its 1995 Social Security Act disregards Lets income in benefit calculations, and social security offices encourage new claimants to join a scheme. This is an easy and obvious change, on a par with exempting small businesses from paying Value Added Tax in recognition of their importance in creating jobs. Indeed, there is a lot of overlap between formal small businesses and Lets. The social economy merges imperceptibly with the formal economy.

Similarly, volunteering sometimes disqualifies a claimant from receiving unemployment benefit on the grounds that they are not really available for work – yet governments are experimenting with 'workfare' schemes that compel the unemployed to undertake community work. It is a completely illogical combination of rules, and one that arises mainly because politicians do not recognise that volunteering has become a mainstream economic activity and do not get regular statistics showing them how much of it is going on.

Many financial services, including pensions, are devised on the assumption that people have stable and conventional employment. Few are flexible enough to incorporate other patterns of work, and as a result are unavailable to many people who are more active in the social economy than the conventional economy. Credit unions and microloans plug the gap a bit. However, the gap would shrink if the regulatory framework for pensions and investments acknowledged the importance of activity in the social economy. To take one glaring example, married women who do not have conventional paid work – key participants in the social economy – are not permitted a pension in the UK, despite its relatively well-developed personal pensions industry. This is nothing to do with the timidity of the banks and insurance companies. It is a legal restriction.

These examples could be multiplied. The point is that governments will be forced to devolve more responsibility in a world where weightlessness is shifting economic activity, making it harder to monitor, and forcing people to employ their time more flexibly whether they like it or not – as the next chapter explores. The tensions and costs of change will be reduced if the framework of rules and regulations adapt too.

Notes

1. See any economic history, such as *A History of Economic Thought*, William Barber.
2. For further definition see *Managing Without Profit*, Mike Hudson.
3. In 'The Rise of the Non-profit Sector', *Foreign Affairs*, Summer 1994.
4. Reported in *The Independent*, London, by Stephen Godwin, 18 and 22 November 1996.
5. *Managing Without Profit*, Mike Hudson, Penguin 1996.
6. Figures drawn from *The Emerging Non-profit Sector*, Lester Salamon and Helmut Anheier, 1996
7. Cited in Strange, *The Retreat of the State*.
8. In *The Rise of the Social Entrepreneur* by Charles Leadbeater, Demos 1997.
9. *Big Bills Left on The Sidewalk: Why Some Nations are Rich and others Poor*, Journal of Economic Perspectives, Spring 1996.
10. *Dreaming of work* in Meadows (ed.) 1996.
11. *A Stake in the Future*, John Plender, 1997.
12. In *The Guardian*, London, 11 July 1996.
13. *Post-Liberalism*, Chapter 18.
14. In *Ruling Britannia*.
15. This section draws on *Lets on Low Income*, Barnes, North and Walker; 'The Transatlantic Money Revolution' by David Boyle in *New Economics* Winter 1996, and discussions with Ed Mayo.
16. Figures from *LETS Make Money Work for People*, by Gill Seyfang and Colin Williams, Kindred Spirit, August 1997.
17. In *The Independent*, London, 19 July 1995.
18. Quoted in *The New York Times*, 29 September 1996.
19. In Meadows, *Work Out - or Work In?*
20. Interview in *Independent on Sunday*, London, 5 May 1996.
21. *The Death and Life of Great American Cities*, Jane Jacobs, 1961.
22. In *Making Welfare Work*, 1995.
23. In *Economic Trends*, July 1996.

Chapter Five

Fear of Flexibility

'Bill Clinton has created ten million jobs – and two of them are mine.' It was one of the classic jokes of President Clinton's 1996 re-election campaign.The US economy has had an unparalleled record of high job creation and low unemployment since the trough of its recession in 1992. It also has millions of people on low pay, in insecure positions and facing bleak working conditions in a (hotly disputed) proportion of those jobs.

Across the Atlantic, Britain's Conservative Government claimed its policies of introducing 'flexibility' through the removal of employment protection, the reduction of non-wage social charges like pensions and sick-pay and the encouragement of part-time work explained why the unemployment rate in the UK fell substantially while the rest of Europe suffered jobless rates that seemed condemned to stick in double digits. But critics and political opponents saw only the inequality and insecurity of a two-tier labour market, which might help explain the Labour opposition's landslide victory in May 1997. There is clearly something in the charge of unfairness. Earnings inequality increased by far more in Britain and America between 1980 and the mid-1990s than in any other developed economies. In many countries, in fact, there was almost no increase in inequality.

This tension – jobs or equality, unemployment or insecurity – is one of the key political dilemmas facing the weightless world. Although the trade-off is not as fixed or simple as some commentators suppose, modern economies do face some choices that are extremely thorny in the light of their success at reconciling the two for several decades after the war. Many people who place themselves on the left of the political spectrum or who adhere to the European social tradition will not concede defeat on the questions of income equality and social protection. Those of us with the same political roots, for whom that insistence means conceding defeat on the expansion of opportunities for work and growth instead, can only feel ambivalent about flexibility.

Having a flexible labour market is all about transferring the risks of profound industrial and economic change from governments and companies to individuals. This is a planetary phenomenon. In newly industrialised South Korea 1997 dawned with mass protests by workers employed by the *chaebol*, the country's huge industrial conglomerates. The reason was that the government, under pressure from business, had rushed through legislation that started to chip away at the long-term deal between the corporations and their workers. The pressure of competition meant the companies felt they could no longer afford the literally cradle-to-grave welfare – the housing, health care, schooling and secure employment – they had so far provided to their employees. As the economist and Labour peer Meghnad Desai expressed it in a comment on the Korean unrest: 'These circus tigers have to get out into the jungle and face some rivalry'.[1] Like the welfare states of the industrialised West, these mini-welfare organisations wanted to pass the risks onto the men and women they had so far sheltered.

To understand how weightlessness has led to this pass-the-parcel of risk, it is helpful to think about what happened in the last Industrial Revolution, when the building of the railways and introduction of steam-driven travel and telegraphy transformed the geography of production and sales. John Burrows was a merchant in Davenport, Iowa, who had made his fortune in the 1840s by warehousing agricultural commodities that he had transported from across the mid-west and selling them on. His success lay in overcoming the awesome difficulties of transportation on either side and in having the capital to tie up in stocks and warehouses.

The opening of the Chicago and Rock Island railway eliminated many of the transport problems that had created the conditions for John Burrows' success. Others, based in Chicago, with little capital, could enter his business and undercut his prices because they had lower expenses. By 1857, Burrows was bankrupt.[2]

The transformation of business opportunities that is taking place in the weightless world is having similar effects, although of an altogether higher order. It is not just a question of a company based in the UK having to face up to a number of new competitors based in other countries entering their market because of cheaper transport costs and lower barriers to trade, although that is part of it. The dematerialisation of an increasing proportion of economic activity means it is not really taking place anywhere. How can a business get to grips with competition from cyberspace?

As geographer David Harvey argues in a fascinating book, *Justice, Nature and the Geography of Distance*, the changing geographical basis of business has social as well as economic effects. People base their sense of identity on what they do most of the day and where they do it. It is little wonder that anybody living in a traditional manufacturing centre in the industrialised world is profoundly uneasy about the wave of economic change and the flexible manner in which they are urged to react to it. It is not just that middle-aged male steelworkers cannot easily retrain as nurses or computer programmers because they lack the education or the aptitude. They do not want to do it. For them to do so would be a betrayal of their culture and community. The traditional jobs have a dignity and resonant history, a romance, missing from the majority of modern occupations – just as working the land had a romance for the early urban masses, and indeed still does for the French, for many of whom the links to agriculture go back only a generation or two.

This is something that runs very deep. I had always told my young son that I worked on a newspaper. One day, aged four, he asked me: 'Mummy, when you go and work on your newspaper, do you stand on it or sit on it?' For him, work was something that has a physical presence and connotations of strenuous labour. This was a cultural attitude he had imbibed without any conscious teaching.

The degree of risk created by increasing weightlessness varies, and so does the ability of different individuals to cope with it. For people like me, a well-educated and well-paid economist and journalist with a degree of entrepreneurial spirit, the new flexibility of the UK labour market has provided wonderful opportunities. I have been able to work freelance when that fitted my family responsibilities, have been self-employed and have hopped more easily between different jobs and even careers than would have been possible only a decade ago. There are others working in weightless industries like financial services, television or software who have been able to take advantage of the new looseness of the jobs market to turn themselves into 'stars' and make huge amounts of money. They have been able to exploit to their own advantage the economic dynamics spelt out in Chapter 1. But for people without suitable qualifications, adequate family resources or enough savings, increased flexibility boils down to being exploited more thoroughly by employers who are either unscrupulous or under enormous commercial pressure themselves. They are the victims of the ghastly social Darwinism that has become the hallmark of end-of-century capitalism.

I find myself torn between the conviction that flexibility is essential in the weightless world, and a distaste for the inequality and unhappiness that are its results. I would guess that many other people who would regard themselves as left of centre feel torn by the same dilemma. How far has our old-fashioned compassion become redundant? And if flexibility is essential, how can we mitigate its undesirable consequences?

So what's so great about flexibility?

Nevertheless, for now there is a keen irony for most people in describing the kind of jobs market the US and UK enjoy – if that is the right word – as flexible. Flexible for their employer, perhaps. For most employees, there is less choice than at any time in recent memory.

But there is a crack for optimism to slide through in this fashionable gloom about the world of work. There is a hint of it in *Microserfs*. Our hero Dan observes: 'In the 1990s, corporations don't even hire people any more. People become their own corporations. It was inevitable.'

People can become their own bosses. There is a freedom as well as vulnerability in flexibility. Now, it is obviously not given to all of us to build our own equivalent of Microsoft. Mostly we will always be small fish in a shark-infested sea. But there are two points to make. First, computer technology has brought the superstar effect within the reach of many more people. It actually is open to somebody with a bright idea and enough application to become another Bill Gates. The great man himself is aware of it. 'If we stand still we are going to get replaced pretty quickly. Our business is less forgiving than any other I can think of',[3] he said in an interview with John Kennedy. Of course we cannot all achieve this, but in principle any of us can.

The second point is that for those who have the right kind of education and personality, and in the right conditions, it will be possible to exploit peripheral, short-term or part-time work. Flexible types of work can provide freedom from control by line managers, more free time, more variety, possibly less commuting. For highly skilled professionals, this has become known as the 'portfolio career'. The path taken reluctantly by many a redundant middle-aged man, it can come as a liberation.

Management theorist Charles Handy has expressed the range of opportunities by considering the different ways a typical lifetime career of about 50,000 hours (about half its length a generation ago) can be made up.[4] The 'standard' pattern would be 37 hours a week, 37 weeks a year for 37 years. But 45 hours a week for 45 weeks a year for 25 years would be typical of a high-flying professional after a long education and looking forward to early retirement. A high salary, reward for the level of educational attainment, would fund the long retirement. This variant on the traditional norm has a lot going for it.

At the other extreme, 25 hours for 45 weeks a year for 45 years would characterise somebody slogging away in part-time, low-paid work. A job in the periphery is a different matter. A young person on low pay with no career prospects or a mother forced to accept dead-end, part-time work because it is close to home and fits in with school hours does not benefit from the wider variety of working patterns now available in the way a highly paid professional does.

One of the key tasks of economic policy will be to combine the macroeconomic benefits of a deregulated labour market with social and educational measures that equip individuals to cope with the risks this imposes on them, and to have a chance of being in the upper league. Some possible measures are outlined below.

But it is worth emphasising first the fact that flexibility does achieve some of the things its ideologues claim for it. There are few countries in the OECD where the private sector has created jobs on any significant scale since 1980. Those that have achieved this are the US, Canada and Japan. There are 26 million more people working in private sector, wealth-creating jobs in the world's most flexible and insecure economy than there were in 1979, a 26 per cent increase in less than 20 years.

Japan has created jobs without following the American path, but this is simply because until 1990 it grew much faster than the other OECD economies. Since then, its unemployment has set record highs, and Japanese politicians, like those on the Continent, are talking about the urgent need to make the economy less sclerotic. For the countries where there has been almost no deregulation of the markets for jobs and (just as important) goods and services have not created work for their inhabitants outside the public sector, where it has to be paid for out of taxes.

It is as ideologically blinkered of bleeding heart liberals to deny this fact as it is of their free-market, libertarian opponents to deny that flexibility has imposed any costs. Of course there are human and economic costs to the tides of redundancy and the emergence of the second division in the labour market. Even so, it is my view that jobs are better than keeping millions of citizens on the dole. Most people agree: opinion polls consistently show unemployment as the number one worry in countries where the level is high. Research by economists and psychologists shows that having a job is the single most important thing that makes people happy.[5]

The worst consequences of flexibility can be addressed by creative policies. But if private businessmen do not want to hire workers, governments soon run up against the limits to making up for it with public sector employment. Countries like France, Germany and Italy have hit the buffers. These economies have run out of options and, however reluctantly in the face of street protests, their governments are following the flexible path. It is on a par with defending the Maginot line to rant about how terrible the flexible labour market is, how insecure we all feel, and how this should be stopped, rather than accepting the inevitable and concentrating on how policies should react to it.

The personal pluses

Besides, there are advantages to individuals in flexible working patterns. In a famous essay written more than 20 years ago, the radical historian E.P. Thompson described how the advent of the factory system in the Industrial Revolution changed our conception of time. Instead of understanding the passage of time as how long it took to do various tasks, we switched to clock time. People on the left of the political spectrum have always railed against the tyranny of owners over workers' time – the clocking in, the restricted breaks, the petty rules.

It used to be worse. A list of 21 rules from the Waterfoot Mill in Haslingden, Lancashire, dating from 1851 includes the following:

> *'Any person coming too late shall be fined as follows – for 5 minutes 2d, for 10 minutes 4d, and 15 minutes 6d, etc.*
> *'The Masters would recommend that all their workpeople Wash themselves every morning, but they shall wash themselves at least twice a week, Monday morning and Thursday morning; and any found not washed will be fined 3d for each offence.*
> *'Any persons found smoking on the premises will be instantly dismissed.*
> *'Any person wilfully damaging this notice will be dismissed.'*

Times have changed a bit. Even so, people will find that one of the changes in the world of work will be that more of their time is their own. We will become freer to decide what work to do and when. This might raise a hollow laugh from those who work long hours to make ends meet, or professionals whose careers are more demanding and time consuming then ever. But work will inevitably be organised in more flexible ways in weightless economies.

The range of possibilities is wide. Telecommuting is one of them. Technology has made work more mobile. The European Commission's 1995 Bangeman Report on the 'global information society' predicted that 2 per cent of white collar workers could be telecommuters by the end of the century. Most professionals and most people in administrative jobs can do some of their work away from the office, and will do so. It is cheaper for employers because it cuts the requirement for office space, and pleasanter for employees, who can wear their scruffy jeans and pick the children up from school. The fact that the spread of telecommuting has got off to a slow start doesn't mean it is not happening. It is just that organisational change occurs very much more slowly than technological change.

More important, varied patterns and hours of work will become more common. Oddly, there is more acceptance of this idea on the Continent, rather than in the more-flexibly inclined US and UK – partly because European politicians have latched on to the idea of job sharing as a means of reducing unemployment and also have a social preference for shorter working weeks as one of the manifestations of prosperity.

For example, Michel Rocard, the former Prime Minister of France and MEP, argues that reducing working time in a way that gives people an extra free day a week or two hours a day will encourage desirable social developments such as people spending more time with their children, undertaking more voluntary and community work, developing cultural interests and escaping from the habit of spending their leisure time in passive consumption because they are so worn out from working. He concludes: 'We have countless examples in many Member States which show that men and women who work for around 30 hours adapt admirably to this situation and like it despite the lack of official encouragement and publicity for this new potential for a more active life'.[6]

Many Americans desire more control over their own time. Harvard Professor Juliet Schor chronicled the 160 hour increase in the US work year between 1969 and 1989.[7] The Employment Policy Foundation has found that time off has become the most valued benefit a company can now offer its employees, and many American employers are devising ways of increasing the flexibility over time worked, from sabbatical leaves to 'time off banks' which allow 'deposits' of time – holidays, sick leave, maternity leave and so on – to be drawn down as desired.[8]

Flexibility and portfolio careers are potentially far more varied, stimulating and personally rewarding than the tyranny of a life spent in the same or similar factories and offices. People like organising their own time. They will be freer to take career breaks for travel or family reasons, go back to college or retrain, and just be in charge of themselves. According to the programme 'Redefining Work' sponsored by the Royal Society of Arts:

> 'The new big idea is that security does not come from the outside. It comes from the inside – from the work itself, from relationships … above all from marketability, the ability to sell yourself, the versatility to spot, to seize, and to adapt to multiple opportunities in many careers.'[9]

Sceptics and hard-headed realists mock this kind of talk. It sounds utopian – fine in theory for a well-off minority but just irrelevant for most people who have to scrape together a living. In one sense they are right. Although the way in which money is paid for labour is changing fundamentally in a world in which what is intrinsically human – intelligence – is an increasingly important part of economic activity, the social and political structures have not kept up. Tax, pensions and welfare systems are still based on the factory model. Governments urgently need to reform them. If they cannot equip people to cope with the new uncertainties, there will be a dangerous and ultimately counter-productive political backlash.

Why insecurity matters

There could be no more startling sign of the backlash against Anglo-Saxon flexibility than the recantation by financier George Soros of his belief in pure *laissez-faire* market economics. In an article written for the *Atlantic Monthly* magazine,[10] the Hungarian–American who has made billions of dollars from speculation on the international capital markets argued that the unfettered ideology of free markets could lead to a break-down of the global economic system. Markets only work within the context of behaviour and morals established outside the market system, he argued. In particular, Soros attacked the inequalities being generated in the free market economies.

'The cult of success has replaced a belief in principles. Society has lost its anchor', he wrote. 'By taking the conditions of supply and demand as given and declaring government intervention the ultimate evil, *laissez-faire* ideology has effectively banished income or wealth redistribution. I can agree that all attempts at redistribution interfere with the efficiency of the market, but it does not follow that no attempt should be made.'

Now, this was not quite as Damascene a conversion as billed in some quarters. For example, the left-wing *Guardian* newspaper in the UK presented it thus: 'He is a Midas of the money markets. But George Soros explains why his mind and his money are pitted against the system that made him fabulously wealthy.' However, the Soros fortune remains firmly invested in the markets. His argument is with a particular fundamentalist version of free-market economics. The article begins: 'Although I have made a fortune in the financial markets, I now fear that the untrammelled intensification of *laissez-faire* capitalism and the spread of market values into all areas of life is endangering our open and democratic society.' The danger, he believes, is the development of 'robber capitalism', the 'gangster state' – in other words, a world of inequality, exploitation and instability, where a few have the freedom to become rich at the expense of the many, terrorised and lacking in opportunities.

The Soros conversion delighted all those left-wing commentators who had clung to the belief throughout the heyday of Thatcherism and Reaganomics that free markets were undesirable: that they did not work and had unwelcome social consequences. Theirs is an honourable tradition, voiced, for example, by John Kenneth Galbraith. In *The Culture of Contentment*, Galbraith spells out his belief that the affluent majority faced the risk of social disharmony due to the results of extreme free market policies. He writes: 'The possibility of an underclass revolt, deeply disturbing to contentment, exists and grows stronger. There have been outbreaks in the past, notably the major inner-city riots in the latter 1960s, and there are several factors that might lead to a repetition.'[11] The main such factor is endemic unemployment, he believes.

So one of the dangers of an unpredictable and insecure outlook is the danger of urban violence and social chaos, according to critics such as Galbraith and Soros (interestingly, both rich men with more than most to lose from social breakdown).

In another famous book, *The Affluent Society*, Galbraith identifies as the dominant strand in the history of economic thought, 'the haunting fear of poverty, inequality and insecurity.' The world had always been like that. Until mid-way through the twentieth century, life for most people in the industrial countries was scarred by grinding poverty and the risk that even their greatest efforts would not be enough to preserve a family from illness, starvation and early death. The task of economics was to fight against these traditional evils. Hence, Galbraith argues, developed today's emphasis on producing more and more goods. Economic security for the masses demands more and more capacity even though today's existence bears no resemblance to the meagre and starved life most people led a century ago. Fear of insecurity is deeply embedded in the demands we place on economic policy.

He is surely right to argue that economic security, and the absence of grotesque inequalities, are among the main demands occupants of the world's wealthy countries place on their government. Even conservatives who accept inequality and uncertainty as inevitable respect, if they are honest, the ideal of the social democrats. It is an ideal of dignity and humanity. Tracy Chapman's hit song *Mountains O' Things* voiced it:

> 'Sweet lazy life
> Champagne and caviar
> I hope you'll come and find me
> 'Cause you know who we are
> Those who deserve the best in life
> And know what money's worth
> And those whose sole misfortune
> Was having mountains of nothing at birth.'[12]

If an intelligent and sensitive – and successful – capitalist like George Soros has reached the same conclusion and is worried about the direction the advanced industrial economies are taking, there has to be something in the fear of flexibility – to use the word as shorthand for the Anglo-Saxon version of free markets, especially in the market for jobs. This chapter will go on to argue that flexibility *is* inevitable and to make the case for embracing its benefits. It will also argue against the antimarket backlash, whose real target should be the political hijacking of free-market economics rather than competition and deregulation in themselves, while suggesting how governments can compensate for their unacceptable side-effects. But first, some facts and figures on the extent to which the world of work has really changed during the past two decades.

The flexible facts

Measuring the increase in flexibility which we all know in our hearts has occurred in the US and UK, and increasingly elsewhere, is surprisingly difficult. It does not show up in the figures as much as you might expect – to the delight of the free-market ideologues criticised by George Soros. For example, redundancies are much lower than they were at the depths of the 1980s recession. Job tenure – the typical amount of time an employed person has been in their job – has fallen, but only a little.

The flexible labour market has several dimensions. One is the risk of becoming unemployed and staying unemployed. Another is the number and kinds of job available to those hunting for work. Then there is the issue of the quality of work. One sign this might have diminished is the increase in part-time and temporary jobs. In addition, contracting-out of some activities by big business has been a widespread phenomenon, so large numbers of people have found themselves working for different employers under worse terms and conditions.

The risk of unemployment

The danger of redundancy depends very much on the business cycle. The number of redundancies rises during a recession and falls during a recovery. As discussed in Chapter 2, all industrial economies see a lot of turnover in jobs, so the level of layoffs during a given period is always quite high. The ups and downs during the business cycle are less pronounced than the variations in new hires, however. So the unemployment rate will rise during a downturn partly because there are more redundancies but more because there are fewer new jobs created.

Over time, there has been no striking trend in redundancies. The recession of the early 1990s saw an increase in the risk of white-collar workers losing their jobs – especially older men – but nothing on a scale that really justified the tide of press angst about the new uncertainties facing the managerial classes. As the OECD's Jobs Study noted drily: 'While the risk of job loss for white-collar workers might have risen somewhat compared to previous downturns, these workers still experienced less difficulty finding new jobs than did blue-collar workers'.

For instance, in the US, the unemployment rate for men with higher education rose from 1.9 per cent in 1970 to 3.2 per cent in 1979 and 3.9 per cent by 1989. For educated women, the rates climbed from 3.2 to 4.1 per cent and fell back to 3.5 per cent in 1989. Signs of a modest upward trend. For men with only a basic education, however, the unemployment rates in 1970, 1979 and 1989 climbed from 4.0 to 6.6 to 9.7 per cent, and for women from 5.7 to 8.3 to 8.4 per cent. According to the OECD's figures, only in Italy and for Japanese women was unemployment higher for the better-educated at any time. Typically, those likely to be in blue collar work are two or three times more at risk of unemployment than those likely to be white collar workers.

Beyond that, the one striking feature about redundancies is the upsurge during the 1980s recession. It has fallen sharply since. That episode of industrial restructuring has dwarfed any other. One could therefore argue that during the past decade this unwelcome aspect of flexibility has diminished. It is hard to persuade people reading newspaper headlines about 500 jobs going here or 2000 being slashed there of this fact. Nevertheless, the risk of being made unemployed due to large-scale layoffs by an employer is certainly lower than it was ten years ago.

Equally, there is no striking evidence that people on average are staying in their jobs for shorter periods than in the past. The typical length of time an older man has held his job has shrunk – in the UK from eight years and three months in the mid-1970s to six years and one month by the mid-1990s. Median job tenure actually rose for women during the same two decades because more mothers have taken advantage of maternity leave and returned to the same employer. The storms of economic change seem to have inflicted most of their damage on the prime age and older men in the work force, largely because these are the people who held what – once upon a time – were the best-paid jobs in traditional manufacturing industry. The shake-out in industry in the early 1980s destroyed the traditional aristocracy of labour. Other categories of workers did not have as far to fall, and have not seen the same kind of hurricane sweep away their traditional job opportunities. Although younger people do change jobs more often than the older generation, this is out of preference as much as necessity.

The second division for jobs

Neither measure – the probability of redundancy or the average length of time people in jobs have held them – is an ideal measure of insecurity, however. They do not measure whether there are more jobs that last for only short periods. They do not take account of the growth in self employment, part-time and temporary work. They do not assess whether working conditions and pay have deteriorated. These are the areas where flexibility begins to show up.

One of the results has been the division of the work force into a first and second division. The ranks of the second division, or 'peripheral', labour market are swelling. The share of part-time employment in the total, especially for women, has been increasing in almost all the industrial economies for a long time. The chart illustrates this convincingly. Part-time employment ac-

counts for a small proportion of the total in the Mediterranean countries –
6.4 per cent in Italy, 7.5 per cent in Portugal and Spain. In France and Germany the share has climbed during the 1990s to 15–16 per cent. But in North
America nearly one in five jobs were part time in 1995, while in other European countries it accounts for a very high share. A quarter of UK employment is part-time. A phenomenal 37 per cent of jobs in the Netherlands are
part-time, up from 16.1 per cent in 1979, mainly because of the introduction
of a very successful welfare-to-work scheme.

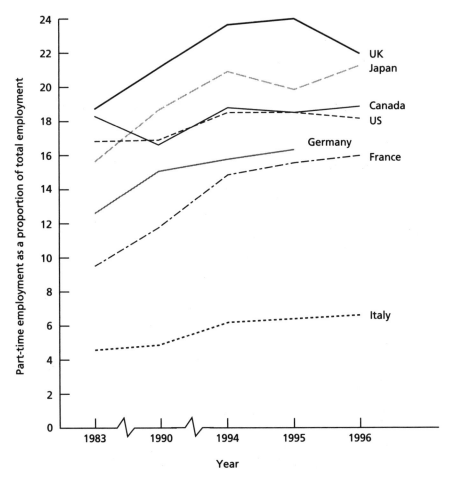

Fig. 9 Part-time unemployment as a proportion of total unemployment over
time. (Source: *OECD Employment Outlook*.)

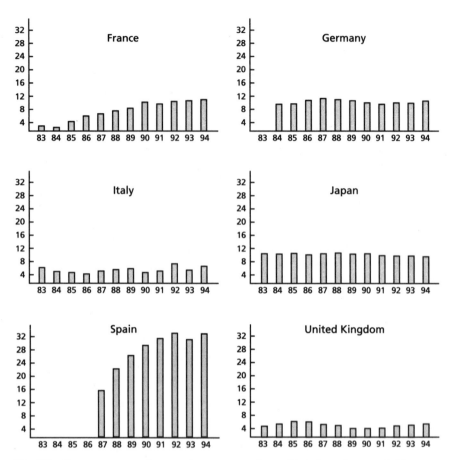

Fig.10 Temporary employment as a proportion of total employment. (Source: *OECD Employment Outlook.*)

Women make up the vast majority of part-time employees – between seven and nine out of every ten depending on the country. It is clear that one of the reasons for the growth of part-time work has been women's increasing participation in the work force when they have children. It is the countries where the most women want to work that have the most part-timers. For this reason the focus on part-time work as one of the terrible aspects of flexibility and exploitation is highly misleading. It is a diagnosis most often made by male politicians and commentators who hold in their mind the full-time male breadwinner as the only desirable pattern of employment.

Surveys suggest that this is the case. At one extreme, in the US, up to 30 per cent of the part-timers asked said they would rather have full-time work. For most countries the proportion of unwilling part-timers falls below one in five. And some of the people who say they would prefer full-time work cannot manage it because of family responsibilities, health, or some other obstacle. Of course, it might be that some of this army of part-time females would prefer to stay home and keep house but are driven out to work by the growing inadequacy of their men's earnings to support a household, and so only say they like to work limited hours because they would rather not work. But, frankly, this is another male myth. Since the 1950s women have discovered that we too like working and earning money. Doing it for only half of the week is ideal, for all sorts of reasons.

Self employment has increased dramatically in scope in some countries. In the UK its share of total employment nearly doubled to 13 per cent between 1979 and 1989, although this subsequently fell back. There were also big increases in Portugal, Ireland and Belgium, and small rises in the US and Germany, but declines in France and Japan. The difficulty with using self-employment as a flexibility indicator is that it varies so enormously across countries anyway for cultural and historical reasons. Nearly a third of the work force in Greece and Turkey is self-employed, but little over 1 in 20 people in Norway and Austria at the other extreme.

Temporary work has grown in scope in some industrial countries, although not all. The OECD's Jobs Study records that there is no general tendency across its member countries for temporary employment to increase. Beyond that, the share of total employment that is temporary varies enormously. In 'flexible' Britain it is about 7 per cent, somewhat below the OECD average. In Spain it is a staggering 33 per cent. Some countries have a tradition offering short-term work to *gästarbeiter*. The ratio of temporary jobs tends to be higher in countries with a big agricultural sector, where the figures represent grape-pickers and cabbage-packers, and this type of short-term employment has declined over the years as the agricultural sector has shrunk in importance and become increasingly mechanised. In the popular analysis this does not count as being really temporary – it is a class of work apart.

Non-traditional types of temporary work excite more concern, and although there are no authoritative figures on this, the UK and US probably do have more temporary work in fields that until recently would have consisted entirely of permanent jobs – that is, clerical and professional jobs, services such as office cleaning, and even once-safe occupations like accountancy, the civil service and teaching.

While the sorts of people who find jobs during the harvest are probably used to their exploitation, accountants are finding it hard to get used to short-term contracts. For most of them, the reason they became accountants in the first place was to play safe, to have a job for life and a secure pension. If they had wanted to make a quick buck they would have become used-car salesmen. A poll in France in early 1997 showed that more than half of young people wanted to become bureaucrats. The only explanation can be the desire for security in an uncertain world – for by then the French Government had removed most of the tax perks formerly enjoyed by civil servants.

If temporary contracts make only a little headway amongst these categories of employees, the psychological toll is therefore high. The industrial economies – and especially Britain with its dramatic transformation from a staid, comfortable and unexciting sort of place to a country where, for the first time since spivs ran the post-war black market, there is an embarrassed admiration for entrepreneurialism and risk-taking – have seen the shattering of the implicit understanding between employers and employees. That understanding was never as all-embracing as it was in Korea's *chaebol* or even Japan's less regimented big corporations. Even so, it was widely understood that loyalty and long service brought low pay but high security. All of a sudden, the deal is low pay and low security. Even though the great majority of civil servants, teachers, accountants and so on still have their jobs, thousands of their fellows have been fired, contracted out or are working on less secure terms or short-term contracts.

Contracting out responsibility

Contracting out is a third dimension of flexibility, and one that has struck manufacturing industry on the one hand and the public sector on the other like a thunderbolt. Again, nobody has collected statistics on how much business is contracted out, not least because of difficulties of definition. But it is clear that the wave of fashion in management for both 'downsizing' and 'delayering' can only have taken place because of the hiving off of activities that used to come under the same company umbrella.

Like other elements of flexibility, there is nothing intrinsically bad about corporations – or hospitals or government departments – deciding that they want to concentrate on what they are good at and hive off the rest. There is clearly some logic to it. The catch is, of course, that working for a smaller, newly spun-off business is not as good a deal as working for a large and safe organisation with a career pyramid and a pension waiting after the required number of years.

For those who do not manage to survive, nervously, in a big organisation, the terms of employment and pay they can find in a peripheral company are likely to be much worse. For one thing, accumulated employment rights can be lost if the clock starts ticking again on job tenure in the peripheral company. Holiday entitlements are likely to be reduced, hours of work to be extended.

This decline in working conditions is starkest where decent public sector jobs have been transformed into the direst of private sector employment – cleaning in hospitals, working as a security guard in a government department or even programming computers to collect local government taxes. Small private companies that have gone through a cut-throat tender to get the business will cut wages, reduce holidays, demand longer hours and harder work, and pay less.

The pattern is mirrored in the private sector, where it is the norm for cleaning and catering at a minimum to have been contracted out. Look around your own office, if you have one, and see the cleaning staff. Chances are they will be wearing the uniform of some other company, and their faces will be grey with fatigue.

Of course, cleaners have some meagre privileges. One tale of the City of London during the recession in the early 1990s records two highly paid financial traders getting into work extra early. They get into the lift with one of the cleaning staff, and ask her to press the fifth floor button. 'Fifth?' she says.

'I've been told not to bother with that floor any more.' This was how they learnt that their entire trading team had been fired overnight thanks to a takeover.

The quality of jobs

In the two countries which have benefited from some growth in employment during the 1990s, there is heated debate about the quality of those jobs. How many are part-time, temporary, or carry impoverished terms and conditions? Defending the Clinton record as the presidential election approached, the Council of Economic Advisers in 1996 published a report which claimed that a majority were good jobs.

The report presented figures showing that two-thirds of the net increase in full-time jobs in the latest two years it covered (early 1994 to early 1996) had been in industries or occupations paying wages above the median level of American earnings. It said: 'Even in the traditionally lower-paying service industries, a majority of the net employment growth has been in managerial and professional specialty positions, which typically pay above-median wages'. The number of Federal Government jobs – a low-pay sector – had fallen. It was the private sector that was creating work, about two-fifths in services. The vast majority of the new jobs were full time, it said. And, taking aim at that joke, the report said the share of workers holding multiple jobs had remained roughly constant.

Joseph Stiglitz, the economist then in charge of the CEA, drew two conclusions. One, that it was a myth that most of the new jobs the economy was creating were so-called 'McJobs' – that is, typical of hamburger-flipping jobs in security, conditions and pay. Two, that the government needs to equip people with 'security of employability' rather than security of employment. In other words, they needed the kind of education, training and attitudes that would allow them to find other work quickly if unemployment befell.

The Stiglitz report fell on a lot of deaf ears. It could not overcome the widespread view that new jobs are not as good as old jobs. Most people who became unemployed, or feared it, believed their subsequent opportunities would not be as rewarding. In the UK, according to research by Paul Gregg at the London School of Economics, the typical 're-entry' wage for somebody leaving unemployment for work is less than half of the typical weekly wage for all jobs in the country. Adjusting for the fact that the unemployed are likely to be the least well-qualified or least experienced workers, the gap between wages before and after unemployment is around a fifth on both sides of the Atlantic. If you lose your job, you are likely to earn a fifth less when you find a new one. (This is not typical in other European countries. For example, a recent Dutch study[13] found that there was no wage gap between the typical job and re-entry jobs.)

Re-entry jobs are also more likely to be part-time or short-term. In the UK nearly a quarter of all jobs are part-time, but around three-fifths of the people leaving unemployment find themselves working part-time.

Insecurity means inequality

This separation of the world of work into upper and lower divisions is forging a link between insecurity and inequality. People in the peripheral jobs are increasingly concentrated near the bottom of the income distribution. However, it is a phenomenon that is, for now, confined to the Anglo-Saxon world. Most other OECD countries have seen little change in the distribution of incomes. The direction of change can be seen by looking at the growth in earnings, adjusted for inflation, of the highest and lowest paid. During the past decade, the richest 10 per cent have enjoyed the biggest increase in earnings in several countries, including the US, UK and New Zealand but also Austria, France, Italy and Sweden. The rise in inequality has been big in the first three cases, small in the others. The poorest tenth of Americans have actually suffered a decline in their real pay.

By contrast, German incomes have become more equal during the past decade. So have incomes in Canada and Finland. Other countries, such as Belgium and Japan, have seen little change in the distribution.

On balance, the picture is one of a gentle increase in the ratio of top to bottom incomes across the industrial world. One or two countries, notably Germany, have bucked the trend. The Anglo-Saxons – Canada and New Zealand as well as the US and UK – have seen a much bigger rise in inequality. The dispersion of earnings is most pronounced, by a long way, in North America.[14]

Economist Richard Freeman describes the change in prospects for unskilled American men, especially young men, as an 'economic disaster'. In one summary of his findings[15] he lists four manifestations of the catastrophic decline in their relative position in society.

(1)   The hourly earnings of young workers who had completed their college education always exceed on average the earnings of their counterparts who left education after high school. This education premium doubled in the 1980s. Similarly, earnings of white collar workers pulled away from those of blue collar workers.

(2)   The ratio of incomes of somebody in the top tenth of the income distribution to somebody in the bottom tenth increased by a fifth for men and a quarter for women between 1979 and 1989. In other words, the distribution of incomes became much more unequal. This growth in inequality also took place within every profession and occupation. This is a characteristic economists describe as 'fractal' – the same pattern repeated at finer and finer levels of distinction.

(3)   There has been little growth in job opportunities for the unskilled, despite the popular perception that a lot of new jobs are low paid and rotten. Unemployment has increased a bit for the skilled, over the long run, but the unskilled are still far more likely to be unemployed.

(4)   Pay adjusted for inflation for the unskilled actually fell by a staggering amount during the 1980s – by a fifth for young males with less than 12 years of schooling between 1979 and 1989.

These facts put flesh on the bones of the observation that some of the industrialised economies are becoming far more unequal.

The two-tier society

There is a neat characterisation of the diverging fortunes of different groups of people in the notion of the '30/30/40 society'.[16] The top 30 per cent (these are UK figures but the idea is internationally comparable) are in secure and relatively well-paid jobs. The bottom 40 per cent are unemployed or trapped in poverty-level, dead-end jobs. The middle 30 per cent earn a decent amout but are just as exposed to unpredictability and insecurity. They might have higher incomes than average, argues Will Hutton, the exponent of this idea, but the unpredictability of that income puts them at a disadvantage.

This notion that security is a key dimension of well-being parallels a division drawn in economic theory between the 'core' and 'periphery' in the labour market, or between insiders and outsiders. The distinction has a venerable history. What makes it fresh now is the way it interacts with another long-standing difference, between the haves and the have-nots. For the US and UK, where deregulation and flexibility have given a new edge to the insider–outsider distinction, have also seen a startling increase in income inequality for the first time in a century.

In fact, inequality might be as pronounced now as it was a hundred years ago. For the earnings of British men are more unequal now than they have been at any time since 1870. The Britain of today resembles the Britain of George Gissing. The novelist painted a grim picture of life not only for the destitute but also for the struggling *petit bourgeoisie* for whom economic disaster was only ever a hair's breadth away. An unfortunate illness or a single mistake could tilt the balance between brave respectability and dreadful poverty.

In his novel *New Grub Street*, Gissing describes the ultimately unsuccessful efforts of struggling writer Edwin Reardon to earn enough to keep his family in genteel poverty. Reardon seldom sleeps, and in his dreams begs for money. An attack of bronchitis confines him to bed.

> *'Had it been a question of gaining a pound a week, as in the old days, he might have hoped to obtain some clerkship, as that at the hospital, where no commercial experience or aptitude was demanded; but in his present position such an income was useless. Could he take Amy and the child to live in a garret? On less than a hundred a year it was scarcely possible to maintain outward decency. Already his own clothing had begun to declare him poverty stricken, and but for gifts from her mother May would have reached the same pass. They lived in dread of the pettiest casual expense.'*

These fears, and the desire for a less uncertain life, will ring a bell with many of that middle 30 per cent a century later. It is the effort of keeping up standards in a world where work and income are insecure that has fuelled the 1990s phenomenon of 'downshifting', the desire of middle-class people to minimise the impact of economic catastrophe on their lives. Although downshifting has been presented as a lifestyle choice by those opposed to relentless consumerism, it is a symptom of insecurity. As Suzanne Moore put it in a review of a guide to downshifting: 'That some of us are choosing time over money marks not so much a move towards "voluntary simplicity" as a pre-emptive strike at an insecure job market'.[17] If you cannot reduce the risk, you can at least reduce the penalties it will impose on your life.

The Anglo-Saxon economies are seeing a growing division between those who have money but no time and those with all the time in the world but little money. Households increasingly have two incomes or no incomes. Academics have charted this using newly available 'panel' data on the same individuals over long periods of time.

The shortage of time in some well-off households is boosting demand for servants. Domestic service was the fastest growing economic activity during the UK's recovery from 1992 to 1997, expanding by more than a third in real terms in five years. This was more than financial services, more than telecommunications. Inequality of incomes threatens to recreate conventional class struggle.

Fat cats of the world unite

The political battle lines for this struggle have been drawn. A typical newspaper article on income inequality is titled *How Fat Cats Rock The Boat* and ends with a prediction of 'the rise of a new politics of envy'. It concludes: 'There are complex economic forces at work, but the basic trend is simple. In future, a few winners will get richer, while the rest of us get poorer.'[18] This is full of hyperbole – after all, most of us are getting richer, a few of us are getting much richer and in the US a minority are getting poorer. The Western industrial economies are expanding, and with them the incomes of most of their inhabitants. But there is no doubt that this type of journalism touches a popular chord. There is a backlash against 'fat cats'.

In the UK the resentment of executive greed was tapped by the Labour Party in the run-up to the 1997 general election. To criticise the ludicrously high salary and share options packages of managers in the privatised utility companies was an easy way for Labour to score points against the Conservative Government which had sold all those companies to the private sector. The highest-paid directors in the biggest UK companies have been enjoying pay rises of about four times the average. The chief executives of the top 300 US corporations earned more than 212 times the average salary paid. Many voters saw the rewards to these executives as pretty much on a par with winning the lottery – undeserved by the men lucky enough to be holding the job when the three bunches of cherries rang up in a row.

This political dynamic means many left-wing commentators and intellectuals have concluded that increasing inequality is not only a bad thing that they must combat but also the result of a deliberate policy choice – or, at least, a deliberate policy decision to accept the trend – by conservative governments and technocrats. The left wants to turn the clock back, stuff the genie into the bottle and put the cork back in. On the one hand this has led to demands for import restrictions because some think free trade is to blame, and to proposals for fresh regulation of industry because inequality is due to the operation of naked capitalism. On the other hand, at the woolly liberal end of the spectrum, the focus is on stakeholding, an unspecific notion that companies can be made more aware of their social responsibilities and that we can all play a greater part in the economic and social communities in which we live.[19] The argument is that in a stakeholder economy there will be no dilemma, no need to choose between unemployment and insecurity, no inevitability about the increase in inequality. Stakeholder theory presents this as a political choice rather than an economic law.

The causes

The stakeholder brigade is over-optimistic. It is the increasing weightlessness of the Western economies that is creating insecurity and inequality. These phenomena are caused by fundamental technological changes, and although there is every need to set a better moral tone in the public policy debate, governments will not be able to choose to reverse the increased uncertainty of working life or make the income distribution more equal unless they accept that this will have other unpleasant consequences like high unemployment and slow economic growth.

For the most likely explanation for the growing inequality in the US and UK on the one hand and rising unemployment on the Continent on the other is a growing divergence in people's ability to create economic value – their productivity, or underlying ability to earn. (The employment expert Andrew Britton calls this the skedasticity theory of unemployment.[20]) If, for some reason, this has occurred, then one of two things can happen. Either the distribution of actual earnings will widen to a corresponding degree and employers will continue to be willing to hire the least productive people because they can pay them relatively less. Or, if the framework of employment legislation and labour relations laws prevents this – if there is a high enough minimum wage, say, or union rules about pay differentials prevent greater inequalities from opening up – then companies will stop wanting to hire the individuals with lowest earnings ability.

Weightlessness is a highly plausible explanation for greater inequality in how productive people are in their work. The case is made clearly by two American economists, Robert Frank of Cornell University and Philip Cook of Duke University in their book *The Winner-Takes-All Society*, although their conclusion is completely the reverse of mine. The argument is that information and communications technology has extended 'superstar' economics – discussed in Chapter 1 – to wide areas of the economy. Thus any opera diva, tennis champion or movie star can easily reach a world-wide audience. Consumers will prefer to see or hear them, even at a slightly higher cost, because they are the known star quantity. There is much less of a market for the tenth best or twentieth best.

Frank and Cook point out that superstar status increasingly applies outside the conventional areas of sport and entertainment. A global brand will make its manufacturer far, far more money than a very similar product that does not achieve the same recognition in the market place. That means that there are superstar product designers, engineers, advertising executives and so on – anybody with a proven record of success will become a celebrity in his or her own field. The authors write: 'The winner-take-all markets ... have become an increasingly important feature of modern economic life. They have permeated law, journalism, consulting, medicine, investment banking, corporate management, publishing, design, fashion, even the hallowed halls of academe.' (The two professors modestly omit to mention that they fall into this last category following the success of their book.)

In my language, it is the increasing weightlessness of the economy that is taking the superstar phenomenon into ever wider areas of activity. Dematerialisation has two effects. It decreases the cost of delivering a service or product and it increases the market for the service. If I am a star opera singer, once I have sung and recorded an aria it can be very cheaply disseminated; and the market for my singing is more likely to be world-wide rather than just the people who can get to the nearest opera house. The same is true if I am a star surgeon. Technology means I can diagnose and treat patients around the world, and that I will be known around the world.

Here I part company sharply with Professors Frank and Cook who go on to argue that this is inefficient in economic terms. They make a series of arguments. First, superstar economies generate income inequality, which is a social bad. True, but not necessarily an economic inefficiency. Secondly, winner-takes-all markets cause effort to be mis-allocated. For everybody wants to be a superstar and therefore too many people pile into professions where the winner-takes-all conditions apply. They write: 'In increasing numbers our best and brightest graduates pursue top positions in law, finance, consulting and other over-crowded arenas, in the process forsaking careers in engineering, manufacturing, civil service, teaching and other occupations in which an infusion of additional talent would yield greater benefit to society'.

Apart from the fact that this contradicts their earlier argument that the superstar phenomenon is spreading, and now encompasses engineers, surgeons and professors, it is also breathtakingly value laden about what careers are 'socially useful'. The despised law, financial services and consulting form a large and growing part of modern post-industrial economies. If they are so much in demand it is hard to see in what sense they are not useful, except to somebody who still thinks that we ought all to make things in factories or perhaps nurse or teach – pure romanticism.

The third argument as to why superstar economies are bad relies on a separate argument about overcrowding into less socially useful areas. Frank and Cook argue that there is an analogy with the 'tragedy of the commons' whereby common land is overgrazed, or seas overfished, because individuals' private benefits carry a social cost. So, they suggest, there is an overcrowding into the field of mergers and acquisitions law because successful candidates do not realise that their job with a prestigious Wall Street or London firm is gained only at the expense of a rival's failure to get the job. And all those failed candidates would contribute more to the economy if they had decided to be teachers in the first place rather than competing to get a job on Wall Street. The analogy is false, of course. Land is in fixed supply; the supply of M&A jobs – or demand for lawyers – is growing. The fact that not all of them become stars does not imply that there is an inefficiently large number of lawyers. If there were, pay for lawyers at the bottom of the heap would decline.

The book's conclusion – that very high incomes should be very heavily taxed – plays well in some political circles. It would be an interesting proposition to put to the voters – should incomes over, say £100,000 a year, be taxed at 75 per cent or some equally punitive rate? Governments that tried it would probably find many of their superstars emigrating, as pop stars have long done. The US Labor Secretary Robert Reich, in his influential book *The Work of Nations*, noted the development of an internationally mobile elite class of highly paid professionals. He called them 'symbolic analysts'; they are the 'stars' in their fields.

Nor would punishment change the underlying economic forces. In a weightless economy individuals' earning power varies more than in a heavy economy. Different people doing the same job will actually be serving different markets – from a small-town solicitor or attorney through a specialist employment lawyer to global star every international corporation wants to hire for its most important legal cases. In fact, the dispersion can only increase.

Take pop music, a traditional 'winner-takes-all' business. There will always be a Madonna or a Bowie, a true international star and big business – Bowie has even issued his own bonds in the financial markets. There are others who come close, pretty well known but not quite as familiar a household name. Then there are national stars who for cultural reasons do not export too well, like Britain's Pulp or France's Négresses Vertes. But increasingly, there are even smaller niche markets – the genres of music that play in different kinds of club. It is cheap and easy for somebody to make an album in their bedroom, transmit it over the Internet, and become a star in their own small field. Thanks to the technology, there are no barriers to entry.

This will limit the tension created by growing income inequality as long as the tide is rising. For all the social horrors and inequality of the Industrial Revolution, it is easy to forget that it had transformed living standards within a generation. The urban squalor turned out to be better than the desperate rural squalor it replaced. Living standards will turn out to be higher in the weightless world too. The inequality and tension is a feature of the transition and the lack of suitable policies for adjusting to a new kind of economy.

The political agenda

The priority for policy makers must be to equip people better to deal with change and uncertainty. A lot of them have understood this. It is why Joseph Stiglitz, former head of the US Council of Economic Advisers, talks about 'security of employability', and why better education has become the motherhood and apple pie issue in election campaigns – everybody is in favour of it.

Unfortunately, few politicians have gone beyond the rhetoric to the nitty gritty proposals. Better education probably means spending more money on more of it. It will require investment in an infrastructure of computers and telecommunications to give a wider range of people access to a flexible education at different stages in their careers. Less than a third of the work force in the advanced economies has had any training at all – on the job or off – in the past 12 months, according to recent survey evidence.

At least the necessity of improving this situation is now widely understood, and a varied range of proposals emerged. The US Government is getting its schools and colleges online, and some states are making sure that there is wider public access to computers for people who do not have them at home. Britain's Labour Government plans to introduce individual learning accounts, which will give people the financial means to dip in and out of education at different stages of their lives.

More difficult and important than the relatively straightforward question of creating a better and more imaginative education system will be the need to put a flexible framework of taxation, financial services and social security in place. Suppose an engineer in his 30s wants to take a refresher course to catch up with recent developments in the field and move on to a better-paying job. If he gives up his current job he will not be entitled to unemployment benefit, and will have to pay his living expenses as well as fees for the training. He will not be making national insurance contributions, which will reduce his future entitlement to benefits, and he will probably have to stop making contributions to his personal pension, if he has planned for a flexible career by starting one. If he halts payments into savings plans he will either get lower interest, lose some tax benefits or both. His mortgage is unlikely to allow for any repayment flexibility. If he tries to do some part-time or freelance work to make ends meet he will find himself entangled in a bureaucratic nightmare with the tax authorities. It is hardly surprising that people just wait for disaster to fall.

The tax and benefit system and the regulation of financial services require a thorough overhaul. If people are being required to take more risks and be more flexible, governments must set in place a legal and regulatory structure that supports them. It should not be a tax nightmare to be self-employed for a year then take up two part-time jobs – but it is. Changing careers should not slash the pension that people can expect, but it does.

With their governments failing them in this regard, people are taking matters into their own hands. Across the advanced economies, the personal savings rate has gone up: individuals are putting more stuffing into their private financial cushion. Credit unions are enjoying a rise in popularity, especially in communities where most individuals do not earn enough to save their own nest-egg for emergencies. People are also educating themselves far more than ever before about personal financial matters. The number of newspaper pages and magazines dealing with personal finance has mushroomed – there is more advertising of products ranging from savings plans to new forms of insurance, as the financial companies spot new types of demand for their services. Even so, most financial services, like the regulations, still assume that people will have a predictable income and steady lifetime employment. Governments can and should make a difference here.

Ultimately, our governments have to offer us a new guarantee. They can no longer provide any certainty about employment and incomes. But they can do two things. The first is to reduce the costs of uncertainty by changing the shape of the regulatory and social security safety net. Middle-class insecurity is one of the factors that has contributed to a debate across the advanced economies on the shape of the welfare state. There is a new interest in making it less of a matter of relieving poverty for those at the bottom of society, and less a question of defining and providing some lifelong entitlements, but rather shaping it into a form of social insurance for people who need it for certain periods of their life. In other words, the typical voter wants the state to offset some of the new kinds of insecurity. This has driven the US debate about health care reform as well as the European focus on value for money in social security.

The second thing governments can do to mitigate the effects of insecurity is to provide a guarantee of a job or training for anybody who is unemployed for more than a short period. This is not the same as workfare – there need be no compulsion, although perhaps there could be a financial incentive to take up the offer. Nor does it amount to either creating public sector 'make-work' schemes or displacing other people from jobs. As the London School of Economics expert Richard Layard has argued,[21] if you increase the supply of labour by providing a jobs guarantee, the real wage level will fall, demand for labour will rise. In a market economy, the jobs will be created, at a lower wage, many of them in the private sector. For there is no fixed number of jobs in the economy – the so-called 'lump of labour fallacy'. If the wage rate is altered by a change in labour supply, the demand for labour will change too. The unemployed can take the new low-paid jobs if they want them, and not if they do not. But the government has offered what it could.

What governments cannot do is change the world back to the way it was before. The next three chapters look at three areas in which weightlessness has completely changed the scope for public action and intervention. The first looks at the limits on the welfare state in general, the next at the provision of pensions and care for the elderly in particular. The third follows on by looking at the power of financial markets over governments – the result of both new technology eliminating national boundaries and economic policy mistakes. The final chapters go on to explore the geography of economic activity and power in the weightless world and the emerging shape of weightless politics.

Notes

1. 'Tigers and Elephants', *Business Standard*, London, 20 January 1997.
2. Cited in *Justice, Nature and the Geography of Distance* by David Harvey, p. 243.
3. In *George*, February 1997.
4. Charles Handy, *The Age of Unreason*, 1989.
5. See, for example, Andrew Oswald, CEP working paper, March 1996, London School of Economics.
6. Writing in *European Labour Forum*, Summer 1996.
7. *The Overworked American*, Basic Books, 1992.
8. A list of examples is given in *Corporate America's Missing Minutes*, Victoria Griffith, Financial Times, London, 6 November 1996.
9. Report of seminar held 30 April 1996, published by the RSA.
10. February 1997.
11. *The Culture of Contentment*, Chapter 14.
12. Tracy Chapman, Elektra/Asylum records 1988.
13. By Maarten Lindeboom and Jan Van Ours, in *Jobs, Wages and Poverty*, Centre for Economic Performance 1997.
14. Figures from the OECD's *Employment Outlook* 1996.
15. In *Working for Full Employment*, ed. John Philpott.
16. *The State We're In*, Will Hutton.
17. Article in *New Statesman*, London, 21 February 1997.
18. *How Fat Cats Rock the Boat* by Charles Leadbetter, *Independent on Sunday*, London, 3 November 1996.
19. See, for example, *The Stakeholder Society*, by John Plender.
20. Essay in *Working for Full Employment*, ed. John Philpott.
21. In *What Labour Can Do*, Warner Books, 1997.

Chapter Six

The End of Welfare

It always seems to be dark, appropriately enough. The city – it could be any American megalopolis, but it happens to be LA – is swarming, noisy, filthy, crumbling, dangerous. Crowds riot as rival gangs fight to the death. The well-off travel in armoured limousines driven by bodyguards. They create their own fortresses of social order. The police leave most of the population to its own lawless devices. Black marketeering, drugs trafficking, prostitution – and the entertainment business, which technology has made ubiquitous and powerful. These are the economic options open to most. Almost nobody has anything resembling a job. The driving ethic is escapism rather than work. It is December 2003. It could be any vaguely futuristic film from *Blade Runner* to *Strange Days* or a William Gibson novel. As the songwriter Leonard Cohen puts it more succinctly: 'Get ready for the Future. It is murder.'

Although the American vein of paranoia about the state has to be treated as a special case, the product of its history, the image of a not-too-distant future in which order has decayed and most of us will lead a dangerous and feral economic existence is resonant throughout the industrial world. It is as if those who try to imagine the future cannot conceive of the survival of anything resembling the existing physical and social security provided by government.

The politics of this bleak vision stem partly from the traditional anti-government passions of the US right wing, and partly from cultural critics who diagnose increasing social fragmentation. On the one hand, academics like Charles Murray have criticised Lyndon Johnson's Great Society for creating a dependency culture.[1] And on the other there are those like historian Christopher Lasch or economist J.K. Galbraith who have blamed the disappearance of a broad sense of civic responsibility on the growth of a selfish, international professional elite.[2] Either way, the vision chimes with the American middle classes who perceive the welfare state as existing entirely to support those dangerous masses in the inner cities, excluded from the ordered citadel of Middle America but threatening to storm its walls. It even strikes a chord with the inner city citizens themselves, such as those who believed wholeheartedly reports (in the *San Jose Mercury News* in the summer of 1996) that the CIA had introduced crack cocaine to the ghettos to undermine and debilitate them.

This is not the European experience. For Europeans, the state is inclusive, and the welfare state in particular is part of the post-war effort to rebuild war-damaged countries as a New Jerusalem for all citizens. In the autumn of 1995 I attended a conference to discuss the future of the social order with young British and American professionals. One speaker asked how many of us regarded ourselves as products of the welfare state. Almost all the Britons raised their hands; none of the Americans did. The British had mainly attended state schools, been cared for by the National Health Service, had the government pay their university fees. Many of us could thank the welfare state personally for our move from working class to middle class. Those of the Americans who had made it out of poverty and even the ghetto had done it by themselves. For them, welfare was a net that trapped, not a safety net one could bounce out of, and 'welfare' was a derogatory term distinct from the more dignified notions of social security or public sector education.

Yet even in Europe, there is growing reluctant acceptance that the welfare state we have needs reshaping if it is to survive. Although many citizens on the Continent protest at welfare reforms, their politicians – privately if not publicly – agree that welfare isn't working.

One reason is that it is becoming more expensive than voters are willing to fund through their taxes. There is nothing wrong with a government whose expenditure is equivalent to 50 per cent of the economy as long as its citizens are prepared to pay taxes that are also equivalent to about 50 per cent of GDP.

But, as discussed in Chapter 8, borrowing to pay for the growth of the welfare state has left governments hostage to the financial markets. Steady increases in taxation are running into voter resistance as the ordinary person's trust in politicians to spend money wisely has crumbled. The traditional welfare system in Western democracies is proving unable to accommodate the profound economic restructuring resulting from weightlessness.

The embrace of welfare therefore no longer helps the people who are most disadvantaged, nor does it temper the growing social and economic inequality we face in modern economies. Just as in America, in the cities of Europe, especially those with poor immigrant communities forming natural candidates for the role of outsiders, the failures of the welfare state are all too obvious. There has been in effect a depletion of social capital.

A restructuring of the welfare state is inevitable. Some kind of consensus is beginning to emerge to this effect in the Anglo-Saxon economies but not yet in continental Europe. Governments there are torn between the demands of prudent finance and the continuing desire of voters for the same kind of social cushion that has been in place for the past 50 years. In the end European politicians will also have to face the need for forms of social protection and inclusion better suited to the new uncertainties of the weightless world.

Building New Jerusalem

It all began with the most honourable of intentions. The British welfare state was born of Sir William Beveridge's 1942 report on the means to defeat the 'Five Giants': want, disease, ignorance, squalor and idleness. The new Labour Government discussed the report at 28 cabinet meetings during the years 1945–6. Only one of the 28 discussed cost. And as Sir Kingsley Wood, Chancellor of the Exchequer in the previous (war coalition) government had pointed out in a secret memo, the Beveridge scheme was open-ended in terms of expenditure. It would not be financed by the proposed 'national insurance' contributions.[3] However, the welfare state was not the outcome of a cost–benefit analysis of how best to improve Britons' well-being. It was the result of a vision of a just society. So, across the Atlantic, was Franklin Delano Roosevelt's New Deal and its 1960s successor, Lyndon Johnson's Great Society.

Such was the extent of poverty and lack of opportunity in the immediate pre-war years that it is impossible to fault the vision that led to the creation of modern welfare states. Compare the lot of today's poor with the situation in the late 1930s. One of the classics of reportage, George Orwell's *The Road to Wigan Pier*, presents a graphic account of the filth, hunger and misery of being poor before World War II. Take this typical passage:

> '*As you walk through the industrial towns you lose yourself in labyrinths of little brick houses blackened by smoke, festering in planless chaos round miry alleys and little cindered yards where there are stinking dustbins and lines of grimy washing and half-ruinous WCs …*
>
> '*I found great variation in the houses I visited. Some were as decent as one could possibly expect in the circumstances, some were so appalling that I have no hope of describing them adequately. To begin with the smell, the dominant and essential thing, is indescribable. But the squalor and the confusion! A tub full of filthy water here, a basin full of unwashed crocks there, more crocks piled in any odd corner, torn newspaper littered everywhere, and in the middle always the same dreadful table covered with sticky oil cloth and crowded with cooking pots and irons and half-darned stockings and pieces of stale bread and bits of cheese wrapped round with greasy newspaper.*'

America's Depression was even better recorded thanks to the employment of writers and photographers in government schemes in order to monitor the state of the union, although John Steinbeck's classic novel *The Grapes of Wrath* is one of the best-known accounts of the tragedy of the thirties.

There are certainly inner-city pockets of deprivation, especially in the US, that can rival those conditions. And all modern industrial nations still have their homeless and down-and-outs. However, most people who are poor, most of today's *exclus*, have homes in far better physical conditions than pre-war slums. They have some heat and light, access to free schooling for their children and cheap healthcare, and in many cases telephones, TVs and cars. They are still poor, but there has been an improvement in their basic material conditions of life. Compare Orwell's urban squalor with a description from the 1980s. Paul Harrison writes of grim conditions in more than a fifth of the housing stock in inner-city Hackney, one of the UK's poorest boroughs: 'Sodden basements, leaking roofs, draughty windows, perpetually peeling paper and crumbling plaster. In human terms damp, cold, rheumatism, respiratory diseases and depression.'[4] Yet the scale of the problems and awfulness of the conditions he describes in his book clearly has nothing on the 1930s.

Even so, the elimination of poverty like this does not seem too much to demand of a welfare state in a rich economy. The trouble is that much of the improvement in basic conditions had taken place by the end of the 1960s. The additional welfare spending since then has delivered fewer clear benefits for the people it is supposed to help most. A recent study by the International Monetary Fund (considered unacceptably free market by some, but nevertheless reliable in its statistics) assembled the figures for government social expenditure and social indicators over long periods of time.[5] Almost all of the improvement in the most basic measures of progress – infant mortality, life expectancy, literacy rates – had taken place by 1960. Meanwhile, economic indicators such as inflation, growth and unemployment performance have deteriorated since 1960. Moreover, the newly industrialised countries of south-east Asia have almost caught up with the OECD countries in terms of the basic social indicators but with a much lower proportion of government spending to GDP.

Nor are the newly industrialising countries more unequal in terms of the distribution of income than the Western economies, according to UN figures. The US and France, the two states whose revolutionary origins have bequeathed them an ideology of equality, are two of the most inegalitarian countries outside the third world.[6] True, most of us would still prefer to be poor in a rich country rather than a less rich one, because the level of income available is higher. Our underclass is better off. Even so, in the old industrialised countries we seem to have an inefficient welfare state. What it provides by way of a safety net comes at a high price, with high government spending and high taxes but at the same time declining social cohesion and no sign of an end to the war on poverty.

The excess baggage that we are paying for now consists for the most part of additional entitlements not included in the original vision. Of course, high unemployment in Europe is costing governments large amounts in benefit. However, the greater long-term financial burden is concentrated in pensions, health and social security benefits of various types. According to International Monetary Fund and OECD figures for a range of countries, these are the bits of social spending that have grown the most.

The growing cost

It is only since about 1960 that government spending, mainly social security spending, has increased relative to GDP in the industrial economies, and only during the past two decades that the pace of increase has become unsustainable.

In two cases – the US and UK – the overall size of government has actually not changed much. In 1975 it accounted for 33.5 per cent of US GDP and 45.2 per cent of UK GDP. By 1995 these shares were 34.5 per cent and 44.1 per cent, respectively. However, the composition had switched dramatically. In the US the social security share was up from 8.4 to 10.1 per cent, and debt interest had nearly doubled to 4.4 per cent. But the share of defence and other spending had fallen. In the UK social security was taking 12.2 per cent of GDP by 1995, up from 8.8 per cent 20 years earlier. Unemployment benefits accounted for 2 per cent, up from 0.4 per cent. But the share of government investment had fallen sharply and defence, transport and industry spending were down.

Other industrial countries have seen their total government spending as a share of GDP rise in line with the extra social security. For instance, the gov-

Fig. 11 Does the size of government matter? The size of government and government performance indicators in different country groups.

Indicator	Industrialised countries						Newly industrialised countries¶
	'Big' gov'ts*		'Medium-sized' gov'ts†		'Small' gov'ts‡		
	1960	1990	1960	1990	1960	1990	1990
Real GDP growth (%)§	3.2	2.6	4.0	3.3	4.6	3.3	6.2
Inflation (%)	1.7	5.4	1.6	4.3	2.3	6.1	15.3
Unemployment (%)	2.9	6.1	4.6	9.2	2.7	4.2	2.9
Income share of lowest 40%	15.6	24.1	16.4	21.6	17.4	20.8	17.0
Illiterate population 15+ (% of population)	9.3	2.9	13.3	4.6	2.2	0.5**	9.2
Life expectancy	72.0	77.0	70.0	77.0	71.0	77.0	74.0

*Belgium, Italy, Netherlands, Norway, Sweden (public expenditure more than 50 per cent of GDP in 1990).

†Austria, Canada, France, Germany, Ireland, New Zealand, Spain (public expenditure between 40 and 50 per cent of GDP in 1990).

‡Australia, Japan, Switzerland, UK, US (public expenditure less than 40 per cent of GDP in 1990).

¶Chile, Hong Kong, Korea, Singapore.

§Average of preceding five years, 1956–60 or 1986–90.

**1991

(Source: IMF: Tanzi & Schuknecht.)

Fig. 12   Major industrial countries: general government expenditures by category, 1975–1993 (percentage of GDP).

Country	Year	Expenditures					
		Total	Social security	Unemployment benefits	Defence	Interest	Investment*
Canada	1975	39.9	3.1	1.8	1.6	3.8	3.7
	1985	46.8	4.2	2.1	2.0	8.4	2.7
	1993	50.8	4.8	2.5	1.7	9.2	2.2
France	1975	44.2	17.4	0.4	3.3	1.2	4.5
	1985	52.5	22.1	1.0	3.1	2.9	3.4
	1993	55.0	23.6	1.6	2.7	3.7	3.9
Germany†	1976	48.8	18.9	1.2	—	1.6	3.5
	1985	48.1	18.8	1.3	—	3.0	2.3
	1993	50.4	21.3	2.0	1.7	3.3	2.7
Italy	1977	38.6	—	—	—	—	3.6
	1985	51.4	—	0.7	2.1	8.0	3.0
	1993	57.2	—	0.5	1.5	12.0	3.2
Japan	1975	26.8	5.9	0.1	—	1.2	9.1
	1985	31.6	9.5	0.4	0.9	4.4	6.7
	1993	34.3	11.1	0.3	0.9	3.8	8.6
UK	1975	45.2	8.8	0.4	4.8	3.9	8.4
	1985	44.6	11.6	1.9	5.0	4.9	3.6
	1993	44.1	12.2	2.0	3.8	2.9	2.9
US	1975	33.5	8.4	1.1	5.7	2.4	2.9
	1985	33.2	8.9	0.4	6.4	4.9	2.2
	1993	34.5	10.1	0.5	4.8	4.4	2.2

*Public investment in the national accounts.
†Data refer to West Germany through to 1989, united Germany thereafter.
(Source: IMF: Masson & Mussa.)

ernment sector in France accounts for 55 per cent of GDP compared with 44 per cent in 1975. Most of that increase is accounted for by an increase in the social security share to 23.6 per cent from 17.4 per cent in 1975. In Japan, the government share is up to 34.3 per cent from 26.8 per cent, with the share of welfare spending nearly doubling to 11.1 per cent of GDP.

Three components account for this growth in social spending. The biggest, pensions, is a special problem covered in more detail below. The others are health and, to a lesser extent, benefits for poverty relief including unemployment benefit. Education spending has grown markedly too, although not always categorised as welfare.

There is nothing wrong with this growth in itself. As the figures show, voters in different countries choose very different scales of government anyway – small in the US and Japan, big on the Continent. But citizens around the industrialised world have expressed over the years a preference for a growing welfare state. There is no surprise here. Many of the public goods provided by governments during the post-war era are what economists describe as 'superior goods'. That is, demand for them rises more than in proportion to income. Another way of putting it is to say that they are luxuries. Clean water, roads, defence, basic literacy – these are the necessities provided by the state. Once there, there is no need for their share of spending to expand.

But as former prime minister Harold Macmillan expressed it, 'It is a happy feature of a progressive society that the luxuries of one age become the necessities of the next'. Better health and education become more desirable the more prosperous the nation, and these are traditionally provided by the state. Increases in national income will be spent on these areas, so their share will climb. Nor do they come cheap. Better health care means expensive equipment, more staff in hospitals, new and costly drugs. Quality increases in health and education carry a high price tag.

There is no inherent reason why this should point to a fiscal crisis. New drugs and equipment tend to be very costly at first but their price falls as the market for them grows. So the price of health care does increase faster than the general price level, but not at a rate which a prospering economy could not afford.

The difficulty, though, is that citizens' willingness to pay taxes has not increased by quite as much, and it has become pretty clear that it has for now hit an upper limit. The tax share of national income has increased during the past 20 years, outside the US and UK, but not by as much as spending. Yet although the governments in countries such as France, Germany and Sweden clearly need to cut the size of their 'structural' or underlying budget deficits, which have grown uncomfortably high, it would be an exaggeration to say there is an overwhelming crisis in funding the welfare state. But what is absent is a real desire to pay the necessary tax increases.

In most countries – certainly across Europe – voters will tell polling organisations that they want more government spending on health and education. This is a consistent result. Yet there is no similarly strong evidence that they would be willing to accept a continuously increasing tax share in order to meet the rising social security bill. There is a political dilemma: we want the health care to be there; we do not want to pay higher taxes year after year, or at least not on the same terms as in the past. It takes a brave politician to draw attention to this contradiction in electoral preferences, although some have started to do so.

The failures of welfare

Even more striking, though, than the rising cost of the welfare state – where it is a real exaggeration to talk of financial crisis or catastrophe – are its obvious failures. Absolute poverty has diminished. But do we feel we live in a better society now than in 1960? Have we eliminated inner city ghettos? Reduced inequality and improved opportunity? Are crime rates lower? Children safer or better educated? It is hard to answer any of these questions with an unqualified 'yes'.

Sometimes it seems as though things are no better than the Victorian era. Jack Straw, then law and order spokesman for the Labour Party, used a 1996 pre-election speech to launch an attack on the groups of children who stand at road junctions trying to make money from cleaning car windscreens. A Labour Government would clear the streets of the menace of these 'squeegee merchants', he indicated.

Compare Henry Mayhew, the journalist who painted the most comprehensive picture of the miseries of nineteenth-century London, on the children who swept mud from road crossings in bad weather. He talks to a boy whose parents have died and whose sister cannot afford to keep him. He lives and works with a little gang who survive on the streets.

> *'I found the lad who first gave me an insight into the proceedings of the associated crossing sweepers crouched on the stone steps of a door in Adelaide, Street, Strand; and when I spoke to him he was preparing to settle down in a corner and go to sleep ... "I was fifteen the 24th of last May, sir, and I've been sweeping crossings now near upon two years. In the daytime, if it's dry, we do anythink we can – open cabs or anythink; but if it's wet we separate, and I and another gets a crossing – those who gets it first keeps it – and we stand on each side and take our chance."'*

It is far more sympathetic than Jack Straw's version, but the phenomenon is without doubt the same.

Inner city poverty, social breakdown, crime – they are not confined to the Anglo-Saxon cultures. French and German cities have seen their own troubles grow this past decade. In *Roissy Express* author François Maspero and photographer Anaik Franz chart the bleakness of the poorest Parisian suburbs. The Aulnay 3000, an mammoth concrete estate for 16,000 inhabitants dating to 1971 and the opening of a new Citroen factory, had to be renovated in 1979. By then most of the jobs had already vanished.

> *'Never again will Citroen create unskilled jobs; nor will anyone else. Meanwhile, at least an entire generation has lost its way: the youngsters who have been in limbo and still are, who have never known what it is to have a real job. They are now twenty, twenty five years old. ... They have learned to live some way or other, and badly. But they've learned. French-born Arabs or not, they are all in the same boat. Some tell the social worker: "I'll never scrape a scabby living, Arab-style." What's involved is not race but the image of the father who has given all his strength to life and finds himself unemployed, crushed, defeated. The sons want to be stronger than the rest. Because there's easier money to be had, sums that take away the desire to earn an "honest" living through jobs which most*

of the time make no more sense and for which you have to beg. Yes, there's easier money. Even if they don't get it themselves, they see others getting it, through break-ins or drugs.'

In one sense, descriptions like these are a commonplace. In another, they are a puzzle. After all, on most aggregate measures social conditions in the industrial democracies have increased enormously since the 1930s. Average incomes have increased for the poor as well as the rich. The condition of the housing stock has improved. Most of the poor have just about enough to eat and some consumer durables as well. State schools are better equipped. Although TB has reappeared in some cities, the deadly epidemics of diseases like diphtheria are in the past.

Today's sense of social malaise reflects not absolute deprivation but increasing inequality, and the concentration of economic and social distress in a relatively small number of urban areas. It reflects exclusion, the lack of the cohesion which was one of the by-products of the post-war welfare state. The increase in inequality in some countries during the past couple of decades is well documented.[7] Recent research suggests that deprivation is becoming ever more concentrated within the inner cities – and that the losers 'may become dislocated from mainstream social norms and values'.[8] This explains why it is particularly in the Western world's three most unequal countries – the US, UK and France – that the moral panic about the welfare state and its underclass is most pronounced.

The Thatcher experiment

It is particularly interesting that the British still feel that the welfare state needs fundamental reform, for the country has already experimented with some controversial changes. Margaret Thatcher notoriously told a women's magazine in an interview shortly after her third election victory in June 1987, 'There is no such thing as society. There are individual men and women, and there are families. And no government can do anything except through people, and people must look after themselves first. It is our duty to look after ourselves and then to look after our neighbour.'

The Conservative Government under her leadership had begun with a wide-ranging review of social security in 1984, early in its second term of office.[9] Few fundamental changes resulted, until the Tories' third term. The significant exception was the 1985 decision to encourage people to opt out of the top-up state pension, the State Earnings Related Pension Scheme, into private pensions, and to link SERPS to prices rather than earnings, which tend to rise faster. As discussed below, this resolved doubts about whether future taxpayers would pick up the increasing bill for state pensions, replacing it with doubts about whether future pensioners would have an adequate income.

More sweeping change waited until 1988. This year saw the introduction of the 'internal market', whereby local doctors have to buy services from hospitals and stay on budget, into the National Health Service; education reform, which permitted schools to opt out of local government control and introduced a national curriculum and national testing for primary schools; a review of social services which placed much central responsibility – for the mentally ill, for example – into the hands of 'the community'; and a housing act which put social housing more firmly in the hands of independent housing associations rather than local councils and encouraged the revival of the private rented sector by attaching housing subsidies to people rather than buildings.

None of these radical steps actually reduced the role of government in the welfare state, although they opened the possibility of privatisation further down the road. However, they all marked a significant devolution of managerial responsibility – not to local government from central, but to schools, hospitals, GPs, and housing associations.

This partly reflected the national consensus that health, education and social security ought to be in the main publicly financed through the tax system. However, as Nicholas Timmins writes in his magisterial history of the British welfare state:

'At the end of the Thatcher era a remarkable paradox was apparent. A woman whose instincts were to unscramble the NHS and to increase charges, to roll back social security and social services, and to return schools to selection and fee paying, had instead headed a government which found itself promoting reforms that, however controversial, were plainly intended to improve existing health, education and social services.'

He adds that the middle classes, rather than being driven to abandon the welfare state, found their concerns being addressed and the services improved. The rhetoric had changed, and for the first time the American equation of 'welfare' with 'dependency' entered the debate in Britain. From the late 1980s onwards policy-makers became much more concerned about the effects of social security on incentives to work. However, there was no great rolling back of the state under that most ideological of governments.

The Thatcher experiment can be interpreted as an attempt to shape the welfare state into a more flexible form better suited to the modern information economy – not that there was any master plan to do so. There can be no doubt that the devolution of managerial power to unelected bodies such as the boards of hospital trusts and self-governing schools has damaged the fabric of democracy.[10] It has devolved the responsibility without the accountability. At the same time, it was an instinctive reaction to the fact that fundamental economic changes are shrinking the arena of conventional politics. Governments do not have the answers, and neither do technocrats or bureaucrats, so let the 'customers' have more choice about what the state provides. Let the welfare state become a system of support that enables rather than blankets its citizens.

However, the British experiment has been undermined by the reluctance or inability of politicians to follow this to its logical conclusion. For central government has also vacuumed up lots of formerly local powers over housing and social services, health and education, making Britain one of the most centralised of industrial states.

The welfare state we have does not equip individuals for a world in which they, and not their government or their company, must bear most of the economic risks. This is as true of Britain and the US, where the rhetoric of self-sufficiency has been loudest, as of the Continent and Japan. Nor has it tackled the problem of including those excluded by the new economy, something which is becoming increasingly urgent across the industrial world for the preservation of some kind of social order. And this is just as true of the more interventionist Continental economies as of the Anglo-Saxon ones.

Next steps

Some of the elements of the necessary reform of the welfare state in the Western world are by now well known, although they appear wearing two different sets of political robes. One is the stakeholding model. The other is in the classic libertarian or self-help pattern. Both emphasise individual responsibilities. Both respond to some clear failures in the existing welfare state. These can be summarised as fraud on the one hand and dependency or the poverty trap (depending on your ideological preference) on the other. Both also show some awareness of key social and economic trends: more part-time and temporary jobs, more frequent job changes, a higher risk of spells of unemployment, and greater inequality.

Fraud is a useful weapon with which Conservatives can attack the entire basis of the welfare state, so many people would rather deny that it is a problem at all. Unfortunately this is not true. False benefit claims cost many billions each year in all the Western democracies. Frank Field, the Labour Welfare Reform Minister and one of the most radical left-wing thinkers about the welfare state, diagnoses the disintegration of the social trust that has upheld the Western democracies since World War II. He writes: 'One of the most obvious areas where trust is ceasing to operate is welfare. Others cheat so why shouldn't I? The benefits I receive bear no relationship to what I pay.'

Existing systems certainly make cheating profitable. In addition there is no tradition of proper, hard-headed, commercial auditing in social security. Governments have started to react to the latter shortcoming. The former is related to the question of the incentives created by the social security system.

It is a fact that most schemes make it extremely hard for people who have started to claim benefits to stop. The classic poverty trap is that for a wide range of low earnings, the loss of benefits that the out of work can claim will exceed the increase in their income. Most of the jobs into which unemployed people can move are low paid, and the take-home pay will be reduced by taxes and social security contributions, not to mention travelling costs and the expense of eating a meal out each day. For the work to be worthwhile, this has to offset not only the loss of the basic unemployment benefit or social security, but all kinds of extras such as help with housing costs, school meals, children's clothes, medicine and health care, right down to cheaper rates at the local swimming pool or cheaper bus fares. Work often isn't worth it. And despite a growing awareness of the severity of the poverty trap, studies suggest that it has got worse rather than better since 1980.[11]

Tapering the withdrawal of additional benefits for people on low pay is one way to lower the poverty trap. Paying in-work benefits to those on low pay is another. They both cost money, but experiments in the US and UK since the early 1990s suggest that they are effective in increasing the willingness of the unemployed to work. The Chirac government in France has followed suit with a bigger scheme starting in 1996.

The broader question is whether welfare systems have moved too far away from the original model of insurance intended by Bismarck or Beveridge. Modern welfare relies heavily on means testing, so that those most in need get the most benefits. It appears to be the most efficient use of public money. Unfortunately, it breaks the link between the contributions an individual makes and the benefits he or she receives. This not only encourages cheating, as Frank Field suggests, because there is no sense that it is 'my' money. It also means the system does not reward effort. If you do odd jobs to make a bit extra until you can find permanent work, you will almost certainly find your benefits reduced because of the extra income. If you have more than a minimal level of savings, you will not be eligible for benefits. For those who suffer several spells of unemployment there will be no incentive to save when in work. What's the point?

To restore the notion that what you get out of the social security system is related to what you put into it would mean greater inequalities between recipients of welfare. However, it would help reduce fraud. It would help encourage people to take jobs. They might be low paid, but very few people move into a higher-paid job without starting out on low pay. And very few people are happier unemployed than in work of almost any kind. Making it hard for someone to get onto the first rung keeps them off the entire ladder, undermines their self-respect and makes it impossible for them to have a sense of purpose and optimism. Tilting the balance away from means testing and towards insurance could not do all of this either, but it is a necessary start.

There is a further step with which many Anglo-Saxon politicians are toying, and that is compulsion. The welfare reform bill signed by President Bill Clinton in 1996 limits the period for which people can claim unfunded social security benefits to five years out of their lifetime (there is no cap on claiming unemployment benefits as long as enough contributions have mounted up). In New Zealand and Britain there are pilot workfare schemes, experimenting with withdrawing benefit for people who refuse jobs, and Britain's 'Job Seekers Allowance' makes receiving benefit dependent on proving that you are looking for work. The Labour Government's Welfare-to-Work scheme also involves loss of benefits for refusniks.

This all sounds pretty callous, but there is another way to think about it. Richard Layard, a left-leaning academic at the London School of Economics, has proposed a job guarantee for anybody who has been unemployed for more than a year.[12] His argument is that, although the public sector might have to create some jobs, the availability of an extra supply of labour would create extra private sector jobs – at a lower wage but still paying more than the social security benefit. Nobody likes low pay, but this sounds a lot better than long-term unemployment.

However, there is little difference in practice between workfare schemes and a job guarantee. In a well-run workfare scheme that tried to match people to appropriate jobs the compulsion would bind only on a small minority, some of whom would be those who were doing better by fiddling the system or operating in the 'underground' economy anyway. The types of jobs would be similar in each case, job guarantee or enforced job. They are not the kind I would want, but then I have never been out of work for a year or more.

To put the issue in proportion, there are seven times as many people in Britain claiming means-tested benefits as there are working in manufacturing industry. Almost half the population lives in a household depending on benefits. The proportion is similar in the US, where in 1995 there were 21.3 million households with no earners.[13] It does them no favours, for the very system that is supposed to provide a safety net to bar them effectively from the mainstream economy. And it does nothing for our societies to polarise them into the included and excluded, those who pay the taxes that pay the benefits and those who receive the benefits.

For both the left and the right wing there is a growing sense of urgency about the need to rebuild a sense of social cohesion, a necessary part of which is the reversal of the deep split between those who do not need social security and those who depend on it. They are two separate classes of people.

There is no swift and easy way to do it. It will require a slow shift away from means testing and back towards the insurance principle in social security. This does not imply privatisation although it allows it. But the government would need to compel people to pay insurance contributions even if a private company were providing the assurance. Equally, private insurance companies would have to be compelled to provide cover to people they thought were bad risks, as they are with car insurance or workers' compensation in the US. There will, too, be limits to how far private insurance can go. It would work for some kinds of health care or disability cover. It would not work for unemployment because the people who are most likely to need it would be least likely to find an insurance company prepared to take on the risk. The state will have to act as the insurer – but it is restoring the link between what you pay in and what you get out that matters.

Left-wing politicians are beginning to accept this. (Right-wingers, of course, have no trouble with it.) The Clinton Democrats and Britain's New Labour have forged the way. As Labour's then social security spokesman, Chris Smith said before the 1997 election victory: 'We do need to ensure that – based on the Beveridge insurance principle and taking place within a framework safely established by government – we are making it possible for additional provision to be made by individual citizens'. A new welfare state must roll back the tide of means-testing, he continued.[14]

Welfare reform also requires cleverer design of the tax and benefit system. In addition to eliminating the harmful incentives created by the poverty trap, there needs to be much more flexibility in the system. Just as the tax system makes new patterns of work more difficult (see Chapter 4), the structure of benefits is still designed for a world where you either have a full-time, permanent job, or you don't work. More and more people fall in between, and are left marooned by the traditional pattern of social security. The rules generally cannot adjust payments to varying hours or freelance work. It is either all or nothing. Unemployment benefits are not available to the self employed, so anybody going it alone cannot claim. Those on short-term contracts have to make a fresh claim each time they stop working, with all the aggravation and wasted time that process involves.

The re-introduction of self-insurance into social security could also allow the system to be made more flexible. It could be made to parallel what many people have to do now, namely save privately, but at the same time provide them with insurance against real disaster and bring them within the safety net available to other citizens working in conventional jobs.

Health and Education

The welfare state we have at the moment is not in a truly serious financial crisis. Most countries can cover their current bill. One of the problems highlighted earlier, though, is that there is a potential financial shortfall. Taxpayers are not willing to pay more and more for social security improvements, or pensions (covered in Chapter 7), nor for health and education.

The fact that these last two are classic examples of a superior good makes their potential funding problems the most serious. It is no coincidence that government spending on them has grown steadily, after taking account of inflation, across the industrial world. Nor is it a surprise that they are the most contentious aspects of the welfare state. Whenever an expensive new treatment becomes available, all those who might benefit want access to it. It is sometimes literally a matter of life and death. If using a computer is an essential skill that will help guarantee work, all parents want their children's school to have the necessary equipment and phone lines; but many state schools struggle to buy books and pay the heating bill, never mind powerful computers with CD-ROM drives.

The systems of provision vary very widely between countries, but the dilemma is shared by all. Either taxes will have to rise in line with demand for health services and schooling or people will increasingly have to pay themselves.

There are added complications in each case. In health, there is pretty clear evidence that provision by the state is more efficient. The public sector is better at controlling costs and a national health service costs less to administer. Thus the US spends 14 per cent of its national income on health care, the UK only 7 per cent, and on average Britons are healthier and live longer than Americans. On the other hand, health rationing has become extremely visible in the UK, and almost nothing arouses more public passion than the fear of being denied access to treatment because of a limited health service budget.

It is less true in education that the public sector is more efficient, but there the issue is the benefits to the economy as a whole derived from having a better-educated work force. There is a social benefit on top of the private benefit people reap from education in the form of higher earnings. Skills and a sophisticated general education are essential to the information economy and no government can afford to see its citizens under-invest in their own education.

So if there is one branch of the welfare state that will have to continue growing, it is spending on education. With education essential to individual economic success, higher public expenditure might even be repaid in the form of reduced demands on other forms of social spending in future. And with investment in human capital crucial to the growth of productivity and output across the economy as a whole, education spending will augment the ability to fund the welfare state.

It is hard to generalise about specific policies on health and education because they will depend on each country's starting point. But the key question is how to reconcile the limit to governments' ability to increase taxes with the growing demand for high-quality health care and education. The only candidate for coming between the immovable object and the irresistible force will be top-up private insurance. Until political parties once again start to win elections on the back of proposals to tax and spend more for these two branches of the welfare state, people will, by default, start to pay more for private health insurance and private schools if they are not having their health and education demands met. Or rather, those who can afford it will do so. The better-off will meet their own needs rather than contributing to the needs of all through the tax system.

Welfare and inequality

It is an unpalatable choice: either a crunch in government finances or diminishing social cohesion. Either social security, health and education budgets will grow beyond the willingness of tax payers to finance them, or the budgets will stay under control but people will have to pay for their own welfare as far as their bank accounts can bear it. And if social security and social provision become increasingly inadequate, social exclusion will become more widespread. What's more, this will happen at a time when technology is anyway tending to increase inequality in the industrial economies.

So although politicians fret about the tax bill for the welfare state, it is inequality that presents the most serious challenge.

This is where the dystopian visions derive their power. In Neal Stephenson's *Snow Crash* all of Western society has been privatised. The affluent live in franchised quasi-national enclaves with their own private police forces – luckily the cops accept all major credit cards. Mr Lee's Greater Hong Kong is one of the better quality franchises. Companies educate their own indentured workers and the Mafia is one of the major powers in the economy. Welfare? Well, it's everyone for himself and heaven help you if you don't have enough money for either a personal computer or the narcotics that bring their own form of escape. This is not only set in California, it is also science fiction: so we recognise that it is not really going to happen like this. But it is the kernel of truth in it that gives it its fictional power.

I predict that what will happen will be the return of politics. This chapter has described the areas of emerging political consensus about the reform of social security – the need to restore work incentives so that people who fall onto the safety net bounce back off it, the return to a sense of ownership and insurance. It has also discussed the need for greater flexibility in social security systems. These are by no means uncontroversial but they are still fairly technocratic arguments about improving incentives. They do address the problem of exclusion but they do not tackle the essentially political issue of social equality.

The cultural critic John Berger paints this new quasi-consensus in extreme colours. Since the end of the Cold War, the triumphant global market system, he argues, has been imposing on the world the optimum conditions – such as free trade and globalisation – for the further development of the market economy.

> 'These conditions, wherever they are applied, change the country's life, destroying local agriculture and communities, increasing unemployment, widening the abyss between rich and poor, and destroying social welfare. As this global plan advances, it increasingly demands a global depoliticisation. ... Our decoy politicians are the agents of such depoliticisation. Not necessarily by choice, but by compliance. They accept the global market's projection concerning the future as if it were a natural law.'[15]

Now, this is essentially the same as the *Snow Crash* vision. (Berger even accuses our political leaders: 'They would sell their grandmothers to get more cyberspace'.) It foresees a brutal market-based technocracy marked by extreme dislocation and inequality. Without sharing the view that 'the market' is a demonaic conspiracy, one can agree that there has been too little politics in modern policy debates, and that too many economic decisions are made outside our democratic political structures. Commentators are very prone to presenting problems as technical rather than political, and this is certainly true of the welfare debate. The political issue is the same as it always has been: how much responsibility do we have for the well-being of our fellow citizens?

At least in the absence of an answer to this difficult question, some of the easier problems can be ironed out. Some of the steps that can be taken to update the welfare state in the weightless economy are clear enough. Adopting the agenda of reform, making the welfare state work better, and being aware of its limitations, will make the political dimension all the clearer.

The limits of the twenty-first century welfare state

Economic revolutions bring incredible dislocations. Industries vanish and new ones emerge. People are more likely to have to do different work, work in different ways or different places. The skills they need for their own prosperity will change. Communities are destroyed, and new ones created. This happened in the Industrial Revolution. Millions left the land for the towns. For the first time ever they began to work for fixed hours outside their homes. They were paid a money wage rather than scraping a subsistence living. Some made fortunes, others continued to live in squalor, albeit urban rather than rural. Many millions left not only their home village but their country for a new start in the New World.

This kind of change is all inherently unpredictable and uncomfortable. It will put great strains on the welfare state, and anybody who claims to have a simple remedy is a charlatan. But that is no reason for not setting in train the kinds of reform on which many politicians can agree now. It will not appeal to the romantics who look back to the 1960s and early 1970s – those who, like John Berger, talk about 'resisting the global market'. It is too late for that. Besides, resistance boils down to protecting the privileges of some groups at the expense of others – middle-aged men who had full-time jobs in traditional industries rather than the young and women with less rigid patterns of employment; residents rather than immigrants; the first world rather than the third.

In a recent book Nigel Harris, a development economist, attacks the notion of what he calls the 'socialised state', the conceit that the purpose of the industrial nation state is to promote the well-being of a homogeneous and fixed population.[16] Not only was it always a myth, he suggests, but one increasingly impossible to sustain in a world where goods and capital flow freely. But adherence to the myth is leading people on the left to support protectionism and the control of immigration. Harris writes:

> 'The world economy, it seems, has by now passed the point of no return, and we are set upon the road to a single, integrated global economy, regardless of the wishes of governments or citizens. Indeed, any efforts to reverse the process spell catastrophe – and particularly for the central project – the employment at tolerable incomes of all those in the world who wish to work.'

The modern welfare state was devised for a static era with a political consensus cemented in place by the Cold War. It cannot survive in its present form, any more than the dinosaurs could survive the transformation of the climate. Reforms to introduce more responsiveness and flexibility would at least give it the chance of surviving in some form.

The next chapter takes a short detour to consider a specific welfare problem – pensions – before returning later to the need for a new vision of what governments should be doing to protect individuals from economic insecurity.

Notes

1. In *Losing Ground: American Social policy 1950–80*, Basic Books 1984.
2. *The Revolt of the Elites and the Betrayal of Democracy*, Norton 1995; *The Culture of Contentment*, 1992.
3. See *The Lost Victory*, Correlli Barnett, pp. 129–138.
4. *Inside the Inner City*, 1983.
5. *The Growth of Government and Reform of the State,* Ludger Schuknecht and Vito Tanzi, December 1995.
6. See OECD *Employment Outlook*, July 1996.
7. See OECD *Employment Outlook*, July 1996, on earned income distributions, for example.
8. See *New Inequalities*, ed. John Hills, Chapter 11.
9. This section owes much to discussions with Nicholas Timmins, author of *The Five Giants*.
10. Anyone who does doubt this should read *Ruling Britannia* by Andrew Marr.
11. See, for example, *Tax Benefits and Family Life*, Hermione Parker, Institute for Economic Affairs, 1995.
12. Centre for Economic Performance discussion paper, LSE, 1996. See also his book, *What Labour Can Do*.
13. 'Money Income in the US 1995', Bureau of the Census report, pp. 60–193, September 1996.
14. Writing in *The Observer*, London, 12 May 1996.
15. In *The Observer*, London, 17 December 1995.
16. *The New Untouchables*.

Chapter Seven

The Ageing of Nations

Two-thirds of all the people who have reached the age of 65 throughout all of human history are alive today. There could be no more arresting illustration of the effects of one of the most profound of economic forces: demographic change. The world population explosion means that one in ten of all the people ever born are still living. Greater life expectancy, mainly in the West, is raising their average age.

In thirty years' time, a third of the population in the OECD countries will be over 60 – nearly double the proportion in 1990. Yet there is a strange lack of urgency about the trend that will dominate industrial society above all others for the next half century. Although population growth is rapid in the developing world, the populations of the world's richest countries are growing older and, in some cases, getting smaller.

This is not a happy thought in a youth culture, and it is one pretty much ignored in the popular media. Mid-life crises are common enough in modern fiction, but the elderly do not much figure as its heroes and heroines. The average age in the most popular genre novels – crime, science fiction, romance – is well below the average age of their readership. It is hard to picture a grey-haired and wrinkled protagonist on the frontiers of cyberspace. On television the elderly feature in comedies but rarely in drama or soaps (unless it is a costume drama, for the Victorians respected their old). Despite the occasional marketing hype about the power of the grey dollar or pound, members of Generation X, the twenty-somethings born to sixties parents, get much more press than the bigger group of fifty-somethings and up. (*Mea culpa*, I'm a thirty-something.)

One of the few recent novels to explore old age is Doris Lessing's powerful *The Diary of A Good Neighbour*. The heroine meets by chance at the local shops the elderly woman she will end up caring for through a decline into fatal illness.

> '*She took one step, then paused, examined the pavement, then another step. I thought how I rushed along the pavements every day and had never seen Mrs Fowler, but she lived near me, and suddenly I looked up and down the streets and saw — old women. Old men too, but mostly old women. They walked slowly along. They stood in pairs or groups, talking. Or sat on the bench under the corner at the plane tree. I had not seen them. That was because I was afraid of being like them. I was afraid, walking along there beside her. It was the smell of her, a sweet, sour, dusty sort of smell. I saw the grime on her thin old neck, and on her hands.*'

In fact, the moral of Oscar Wilde's *Dorian Grey* is as fresh as ever: if you want the world to acclaim or even notice you, stay young in public and keep the wrinkles private. Yet hiding the ageing of our economies from public view will bring an end just as dramatic as in Wilde's fable. If the process is ignored, there will be an uncomfortable reckoning in the end. The increase in the average age of the population in the industrial nations, something that can be predicted *with near certainty* to occur during the next four decades or so, will have important economic effects, only a few of which have made it to the policy agenda. It would take a baby boom across the developed world within the next decade to alter this outlook. It is just possible that all the great parties planned for the end of the millennium will have that unexpected result — after all, my son was born nine months after I toasted the arrival of a new decade with champagne. But this hope would be a bit of a shaky foundation for economic policy.

The problem that has just about made it out of the darkness of the attic and in to the light of day is the strain that an increasing retired population will place on the public purse. The World Bank kicked off with a mammoth study called *Averting the Old Age Crisis* in 1994, predicting that demography meant current public pensions policies were doomed. There is money at stake here, so in the financial markets and corridors of power at least, the growing pensions burden has become a big issue. It is permeating the general consciousness too. Attempts to cut back state pension provisions have brought protesters onto the streets in Italy, while the actual reduction of public pension entitlements in the UK has left Britons vulnerable to cowboy financial salesmen and played its part in the loss of 'feel-good factor'.

The amount of pension to be paid, and by a shrinking number of productive workers, is a bad enough problem. But the ageing of the population has potential implications for economic productivity and growth that are both unspoken and entirely unfashionable. In an age of trendy environmentalism, a growing population is seen as a Bad Thing. But there are few examples of spurts of economic growth occurring without parallel surges in population growth.

A lot of the increase in the size of economies that has taken place throughout the course of history has taken place because of growth in the key 'factor of production': human labour. Whether the pressures of population growth forced the pace of technical change or whether higher infant survival rates and longevity were permitted by it, it has been a high birth rate and youthful population that have gone hand in hand with increases in economic prosperity. This is even more true of the east Asian 'tiger' economies today as it was of the German post-war economic miracle, fertilised by immigration from eastern Europe, or of the original industrial revolution. Although economists talk about growth in terms of technical change – the unexplained and therefore interesting bit of economic expansion over the years – the growth explained by there being more people, saving more, has been impressive.

What does it mean, then, that birth rates in some industrial countries have fallen well below replacement levels? That the over-60s will become the biggest group in the population? The easy although unpalatable part of the answer concerns what governments will have to stop paying for.

A pension time bomb?

Eavesdrop on any gathering of pensioners, and you will find that they hate paying taxes. No matter what their income, they feel they have worked hard, paid their dues, and the time has come for them to get their reward.

This is an attitude ingrained in our culture. It can be found in the Bible. 'Honour thy father and thy mother, that thy days may be long on the land which the Lord thy God giveth thee', say the Ten Commandments. Morally unchallengeable. That which has been promised unto pensioners, let it be delivered unto them. Or, as an economist might put it, industrial societies should not break the implicit contracts they have made to pay pensions out of tax revenues. This was the basis upon which they raised the taxes in the first place: even though governments have long abandoned the notion that 'national insurance' means what pensioners receive is related to what they have paid in, most individuals still make the link.

Unfortunately, a few figures show the impossibility of taking the most honourable course and honouring past pension promises made by governments to their electorates. Studies by the United Nations, the World Bank and the Organisation for Economic Co-operation and Development, covering the gamut of ideological starting points, have demonstrated that the public sector in most industrialised economies can not afford to meet its existing pension liabilities. Some researchers have dubbed it a 'pensions time bomb'.[1]

The position differs widely between countries – partly because the demographic trends differ, partly because of differences in state pension schemes. Take the demographics first.

The ageing of the population between now and 2030 will be most dramatic in Japan and some continental European economies – Germany, France, Italy, Austria and Benelux. It will be less dramatic in the UK, less still in the US, Spain, Portugal and Ireland. Ageing is the product of lower birth rates and increased life expectancy over many decades. The post-war baby boom in the US and UK has produced its own baby boomlet, while at the other extreme in the Mediterranean countries birth rates have shrunk dramatically – to an average of only 1.3 births per mother in Italy, for example. Life expectancy has increased everywhere in the industrialised countries during the past few decades – up from 67 to 73 for men between 1960 and 1990, and from 73 to 79 for women. Neither trend seems likely to go into reverse.

The implications for the potential burden on government spending are correspondingly varied. For all of the seven biggest industrial economies except the UK pensions expenditure will exceed contributions by substantial but varied amounts unless their governments change their current policies. In the UK, thanks to the less dramatic demographic shift and to government

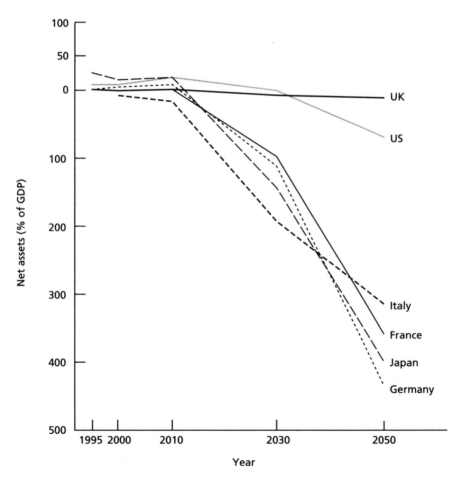

Fig. 13 Can our governments pay our pensions? Net asset positions of public pension funds. (Source: IMF.)

action that has made the state pension far less generous, the scheme should be in a small surplus towards the middle of the twenty-first century. The key step taken in the UK in the early 1980s was to link pensions to prices rather than earnings, so its welfare spending has not grown as a share of GDP. However, the US could have a pensions deficit equivalent to about four-fifths of its current national income by 2040, while France, Germany, Italy and Japan would face a shortfall equal to two to four times the current size of their economies.[2] The non-partisan Congressional Budget Office has estimated that the US Federal government deficit would have to rise to 26–37 per cent of GDP by 2030 if pension entitlements remain unchanged.

The UK does not entirely escape. It could have a different problem – too many pensioners on the poverty line. Although the country has about £500 billion invested in private and occupational pensions – more than the rest of Europe put together – so that on average the next generation of pensioners will be reasonably well off, that retirement income will be unevenly distributed. The minority that will have to rely on the minimum state pension will have a much lower income than the rest of their age cohort.

The OECD has calculated what sort of difference changes in policies such as less generous state pensions or later retirement dates would make to the potential burden on the public finances. What these calculations show is that the changes required will be quite dramatic, and most dramatic in the countries where opposition is likely to be stiffest.

For instance it would take a reduction in state pensions by more than a tenth relative to average earnings, or an increase of at least three percentage points of income in contributions by employees to the state scheme, or a rise of at least five years in the retirement age for the worst-affected countries to get close to financial balance. Although France, Italy and Germany have lower than average retirement ages and therefore have some scope to raise these, all three have generous pensions covering a large proportion of the workforce. Ageing voters could form a politically potent opposition to reform of the state pension system.

Yet doing nothing is not an option. According to one calculation, without any cuts in state pension funding, the government share of total output would rise to close to two-thirds in several countries, up from less than a half now. Only the UK and the countries with fast-growing and therefore more youthful populations – Ireland, Spain and Portugal – would avoid the trend.

That makes pensions one of the most urgent aspects of the broader re-thinking of the welfare state that is taking place in all developed countries. State payments to retired citizens have been the fastest-growing element of the biggest and fastest-growing component of government expenditure. For instance in the UK, which has cut back on government pension provision enough to defuse any crisis already, it still accounts for more than a third of the nearly £100 billion social security bill. The next biggest component, income support for the poor, accounts for only a tenth of social security. Paying for the basic retirement pension eats up a tenth of the British government's entire expenditure and about the same as all of its spending on education.

Caring for the old

Pensions are not the only issue for governments. For the first time long-term care for the elderly has emerged onto the policy agenda. The share of the very elderly, over-80s in the population is likely to double to about 6 per cent on average in the OECD. Their numbers in Japan will have risen 15-fold between 1960 and 2040, in the US tenfold. According to the OECD, someone aged 60 will have a two in five chance of needing a nursing home stay at some point during the rest of their life.

In the past there has been little need for long-term care. Existing old people's homes or long hospital stays met the demand with relatively few strains. Social policy was a matter of income support on the one hand and meals-on-wheels on the other. This will not be enough in the future. Hospital wards are both expensive and inappropriate for long stays. Residential homes are in short supply and inadequately regulated. Many are not equipped to care for ill or disabled residents. Local support services are creaking at the seams, caught between the pincers of budget cuts and growing demand. What to do about

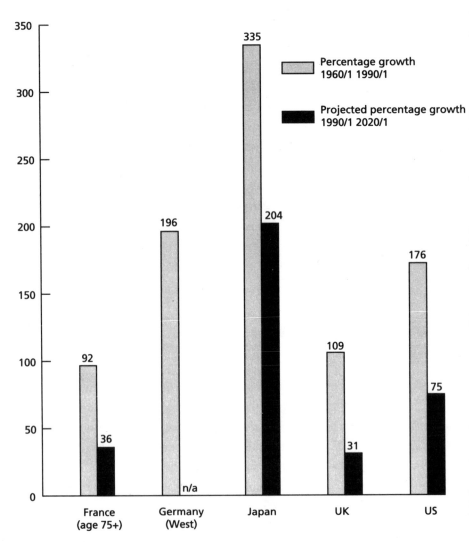

Fig. 14 Rate of growth of number aged over 80.

infirm parents has become one of the favourite moans of the middle-aged.

As with pensions, the consequences for the public finances of having the government foot the bill, as it still does in most countries through either general taxes or social insurance contributions, are ominous. Yet private insurance for long-term care, which has grown in Japan and the US, has proven of limited help. The policies are very expensive (around $2500 a year for a 65-year old rising to nearly $8000 for a 79-year old), they will pay out for only a limited number of years, and they suffer from a high rate of dropping out by policy-holders before they mature.

The political pressure for governments to improve long-term care will be enormous. The relevant group of voters is growing in size all the time. And as the far from soft-hearted economists at the OECD comment: 'For too many elderly people ... the pain and anxiety of becoming disabled are compounded by worries about paying for care'.[3] The high risk that many of us will need to pay needs to be factored into the policy debate. The construction of an affordable and flexible system of care that can cover its catastrophic costs is as urgent a challenge as paying for pensions.

The other costs of ageing

The arithmetic of the pensions and long-term care problem is unappetising but straightforward. Other questions raised by demographic change are harder to answer. Ageing populations could affect two fundamental economic forces: savings and productivity.

The total level of savings in an economy matters because it forms the pool from which investment is financed. In our world of international capital flows, investment can in theory turn to any pool of savings, so if one country has a shortfall it can import capital. However, the marked pan-industrial shift in population structure could have a big enough impact on the world's savings pool to create a savings shortage that would trigger higher interest rates and reduce investment.

Predicting savings habits is a tricky matter. Economists generally rely on the 'life cycle hypothesis' which supposes that people borrow as young adults, save in middle age, and run down their savings when retired. (Or perhaps, as Benjamin Disraeli put it in his novel *Coningsby*, 'Youth is a blunder, manhood a struggle, old age a regret'.) In other words, people use borrowing and saving to smooth their pattern of spending over their lifetime. This implies that ageing will tend to reduce national savings rates.

Research by Professor David Miles at Imperial College in London based on an empirical model consistent with life-cycle savings suggests that this will be true – but only after about 2035. Because the baby boom is middle aged and entering its prime years for saving, he finds that most OECD countries will enjoy a sharp rise in levels of savings and wealth until then. After that, however, savings will decline in all countries with a few exceptions such as Ireland and the US, and could fall catastrophically in some countries such as Italy and Denmark. Japan is likely to see its savings start falling from now on because of its older population.

The conventional implication drawn from these results is that the rich countries will start to import capital from the developing world from part way through next century. If this occurs, not only will it be a huge reversal of the current trend for the rich nations to invest in the rapidly growing developing countries, it also implies a slowdown in investment.

A related concern is the prediction by some economists that an ageing population will imply weaker growth in productivity (or output per head), and therefore slower potential increases in prosperity next century. At the individual level, productivity at work is generally assumed to rise with age up to a peak somewhere in early middle age and then tail off with the loss of youth and energy. This is based on a model where productivity is related to a person's investment in their 'human capital' – their stock of knowledge, skills, habits of mind and work, and usefulness in a working environment. Education and training raise human capital, so people become steadily more productive as long as they carry on learning. Experience also raises human capital, but diminishing returns set in. So once people pass an age where they have stopped learning and stopped adding significantly to their experience, their productivity will diminish. Their stock of human capital starts to depreciate.

There are accepted variations to this – mathematicians and computer hackers peak early, philosophers and novelists peak late. In general, though, an older population would be associated with a lower average level of productivity. This makes sense intuitively. If a majority of the workforce is past its prime, the economy will be less dynamic than one where the workforce is youthful. The middle aged do not take risks, start new businesses, dream up inventions, in the same way as the young. However, economist Richard Disney could not, in a comprehensive study, find firm evidence for this.[4] It might turn out to be true, but so far there are no signs that we need to worry enough to pack all our old timers back to college.

Conventional solutions

Time bombs have a habit of never going off. One clue to the future of our greying nations might lie in the well-known *Warning* by Jenny Joseph:

> 'When I am an old woman I shall wear purple
> With a red hat which doesn't go, and doesn't suit me.
> And I shall spend my pension on brandy and summer gloves
> And satin sandals, and say we've no money for butter.
> I shall sit down on the pavement when I'm tired
> And gobble up samples in shops and press alarm bells
> And run my stick along the public railings
> And make up for the sobriety of my youth.
> I shall go out in my slippers in the rain
> And pick the flowers in other people's gardens
> And learn to spit.'

To put it prosaically, it is perilous to make predictions based on the assumption that behaviour will never change. Old people might start behaving more like young people – and not just by staying out late and returning home to find their middle-aged children waiting up for them. For the gap in pensions funding is actually very likely to mean that the average retirement age will increase – it already varies widely between the industrial countries. Since the recession of the early 1980s men have been retiring ever earlier, with those of

50+ in declining industries unlikely to find work again and seen as too old to retrain. 'Early retirement' became the euphemism of choice for redundancy. However, that massive shakeout of the old industrial workforce in sectors such as textiles, shipbuilding, steel and coal was, to a large extent, a one-off. True, it has been spread over a couple of decades, and some industries in some countries still face it. Nevertheless, one of the forces driving retirement ages lower is past its peak.

A European Court ruling has already brought women's retirement age up to men's in some EU countries, including the UK, in order to make pensions more equitable. The US has mandated a rise in the retirement age from 65 to 67. These changes will be compulsory, but older people are likely to want to work longer when governments make it plain that a greater proportion of retirement income will have to be privately financed.

Later retirement or partial retirement will ease governments' difficulties in funding pensions and long-term care, but will not eliminate it. The state schemes in industrial countries were simply never designed to provide a decent retirement income for 15–20 years. They were drawn up by people in whom the memory of poverty and misery among the elderly in the 1930s was very fresh. Yet in the Depression a 65 year-old would not have expected to live very much longer – and at the start of the century almost nobody lived beyond 50.

Voter resistance to higher taxes in the Western democracies means that simply increasing the contributions paid by the work force to existing pay-as-you-go state pension schemes is politically out of the question. The size of government budget deficits – partly due to current pension spending – rules out borrowing more. So Western policy-makers have focused on the types of compulsory top-up introduced by Chile or Singapore. The emerging political consensus on financing the welfare state, discussed more fully in Chapter 5, points to a two-pronged shift: a return to the notion of contributions that insure an individual against his or her own future needs; and the replacement of state payments funded by borrowing with compulsory private saving, in fully funded rather than 'pay-as-you-go' pension schemes. That is, the past contributions of the elderly, rather than the current contributions made by people who are still working, will fund their pensions.

Chile's switch has attracted much attention. Its population ageing started around 1945, so that by 1980 government subsidies to the unfunded social security scheme already amounted to 3 per cent of GDP. They were forecast to increase tenfold by the end of the century. Therefore in 1981 the government introduced a system of individual retirement savings accounts with private pension funds to replace the pay-as-you-go state scheme.[5] Employees have to contribute at least 10 per cent of earnings, and the contributions are collected and deposited by their employers. There are also compulsory additional disability and life insurance premiums. The private funds compete on the size of these charges and their commission fees, and people are free to switch between funds.

The state's role is to regulate the system, and to provide a guarantee that everyone will have a minimum level of pension. But economists calculate that the scheme will typically deliver a retirement income equal to 55–60 per cent of earnings. Spells of unemployment would obviously reduce the pension. So would inadequate investment returns earned by the pension fund, although the funds should have no trouble delivering a high enough return over a working lifetime.

The big catch for the government with making the switch from pay-as-you-go state pensions to funded private pensions is that it still has to pick up the bill for today's pensions when today's workforce is paying into its own retirement savings account rather than paying social security contributions to the state scheme. The money has to come from other taxes or borrowing, of course. There is no way round the fact that the transition will make the public finances worse before it makes them better.

Despite the catch, most of the industrial countries will probably end up introducing something similar. Even in Britain, where there is no looming pensions crisis in terms of government finance because of the capping of the state pension and introduction of private pensions in the 1980s, there is still interest in reform because of fears that people are simply not saving enough towards their old age. It is an optional system, and millions will end up on unsatisfactory state pensions whose value will have been eroded because they are linked to prices rather than earnings.

Labour minister Frank Field has attracted cross-party interest with his proposal for a 'stakeholder' insurance scheme with both public and private elements. The state would make some minimum payments into it for those with low or no incomes. There would also be compulsory membership of a private pension fund, with contributions paid by both employees and employers, for top-up retirement income. Mr Field writes that the scheme would be much like the atrophied State Earnings Related Pension Scheme because of its universality. But it would be private and it would be fully funded rather than pay-as-you-go.[6] It would also, he argues, return to centre stage the universal motives of self-interest and self-improvement. His scheme 'should be viewed as the first, hopefully, of a number of schemes where social and individual efforts are collectivised in a manner acceptable to voters'. Collectivised or not, it also manifests self-help philosophy in a way that is equally acceptable to right-wing politicians.

All that remains is for political leaders to sell this idea to the voters. In individualist Britain and America it should not be difficult. In continental Europe the task looks likely to be much harder, despite the greater urgency of pension reform. Most Europeans see pensions as falling firmly within the domain of the state although they would probably not vote for the tax increases necessary to close their pensions deficit. Such is the passion about state provision of pensions that German, Italian and French citizens have demonstrated on the streets to defend it. Indeed, two million German civil servants marched in protest at the suggestion that they should merely start to contribute directly to their own pensions for the first time, foregoing 0.2 per cent of their annual wage increase from the year 2001. The civil service union claimed the demand was unconstitutional.[7]

A solution to the long-term care problem will be thornier still for two reasons. One is that the issue of family versus government responsibility is even more open a question than in the case of pensions. What role should relatives play in caring for the elderly, and what should happen if they refuse to meet their responsibilities?[8] Germany resolved the dilemma with the introduction of compulsory insurance for old age care in 1995, paid for through a payroll tax levied on both employers and employees, but so far it is alone. The other issue in long-term care is that advances in medical technology will make it increasingly expensive, and put it at the sharp end of the public debate about rationing access to health care.

The picture is complicated by the messy interaction between government assistance for the elderly and private insurance. Almost universally, the penalty for providing one's own care is the loss of whatever state support there is. In Britain, for instance, having assets (including a house) above a fairly low limit disqualifies the elderly from government funds for long-term care – a pretty binding trap for a nation where 60 per cent of adults are home-owners and the average house price is above the limit on allowable assets. It is a manifestation of the classic welfare clash between means testing, which concentrates resources where the need is greatest, and encouraging independence and self-help.

Despite these difficulties, top-up private insurance schemes look inevitable for all the rich countries unless their citizens rediscover an appetite for paying higher taxes. As more than half the entire European electorate will be over 50 by the year 2020, this might just happen. But it would be a recipe for conflict, as most of the workforce that would have to pay the taxes would be under 50. Of course, one possible way out of the impasse would be to rejuvenate the work force.

Lateral solutions

The emerging consensus on the solution to the pension problem – compulsory private saving – overlooks one thing. No matter how you rearrange the financing, whether lower pensions, higher contributions or saving, or a different private–public mix, the underlying demographic equation is unchanged. In economic terms the developed countries will require a shrinking active population to pay for a growing dependent population.

Sticking with the economics, the most direct solution would be to increase the working-age population: immigration. Some countries have long enjoyed the benefit of immigration. America was built on it. Germany has welcomed *gästarbeiter* when suffering labour shortages and more than done its duty by refugees. Even the UK, with a tradition of petty hostility to foreigners, has grudgingly permitted some waves of official immigration and is currently turning a blind eye to unofficial immigration from eastern Europe.

The economic evidence is that immigration is wholly beneficial to the host country. Immigrants on average contribute more to the public purse in taxes than they draw in benefits, at least until their families become assimilated in the host society. They are no more likely than other residents to commit crimes. They increase the host nation's average skill level and, rather than 'stealing' jobs, carry out the ones nobody else will take.[9]

Unfortunately, apart from the odd spot of political and racial tension an official open door policy might generate, it would take a huge number of immigrants to make much difference to the existing population structure. Only Australia, Canada and Germany have had high enough immigration rates − 5.7, 4.4 and 5.6 net new migrants, respectively, per 1000 people between 1990 and 1995 − to have had any impact at all on the average age of their population. It has not been a big impact, and yet the inflows have started to generate a vicious political backlash. It might be logical but it is clear why politicians would think it not worthwhile.

In so far as there is a rationale behind local hostility to immigrants, it tends to take the form of the fear that 'they' are stealing 'our' jobs. Thus getting a US Green Card requires proof that the would-be immigrant is not filling a job for which a US citizen is available. The fear is off-target, based on the 'lump of labour' fallacy discussed in Chapter 2. A new supply of cheap labour expands the number of jobs available, but cuts the wage paid. Immigrants do not steal jobs but they do compete down wages. A native San Franciscan might be able to afford an 'illegal' Mexican nanny, when once she would have gone without or opted for day nurseries because nannies' wages were too high before the latest influx of Hispanic immigration into California. It is obvious why the original pool of nannies would blame the Mexicans for taking 'their' jobs, but the jobs were not there before the Mexicans arrived.

Virtual immigration

Barriers to migrants are rising, not falling, these days. But technology will make borders futile. The combination of computer technology and cheap telecommunications means the industrial world has 'virtual' immigration. Any direct investment by a Western company in the third world is a partial substitute for importing cheap labour, but the benefits are offset to some extent by the cost of transporting the goods – whether Nike shoes or Motorola printed circuit boards – back to the country in which they will be sold. When British Airways bases its ticket sales operation in India, when American computer companies like IBM employ programmers there, the transportation problem is negligible. The economic effects will be just the same as if the companies brought thousands of Indian workers to the UK or US.

Virtual immigration is therefore cutting the wages of some groups of workers in the industrial countries – not just the nannies and domestics, but employees in manufacturing and traded services. On the other hand, it is helping the developed economies overcome their growing imbalance between active work force and retired population as long as the profits of those companies are eventually remitted to the elderly as pension payments. That will happen as long as pension funds are invested appropriately in companies which, paradoxically, tend to be criticised for exporting jobs to the third world as if it were a profoundly unpatriotic move.

The point about funding pensions is broader. If the ageing industrial countries invest their savings in the youthful and productive developing ones, the profits from the active work force in the latter will fund the retirement of the former. There is an example in the experience of France at the turn of the last century. Its labour force was static, and productivity growing no faster than in neighbouring Britain and Germany. About a half of French savings were therefore invested abroad, compared with a quarter of British and a tenth of German savings.

This is good news for countries like the UK and US, where private pension funds are heavily invested in shares rather than government bonds. Pension funds in continental Europe invest in bonds, which are less volatile but deliver lower returns over long periods of time.

All pensions involve transfers in an economic sense. The resources consumed by the retired are necessarily provided by those who are still working. But that transfer between generations can be more or less direct. One issue is who pays – the workers out of their current effort or the elderly themselves out of savings, their own past efforts? The other issue is which workers – the shrinking pool within national borders, or the growing pool in the developing world? If pensions are funded out of taxes, it has to be the former because foreign workers cannot be taxed. If they are funded out of private savings, the savings can be invested in dynamic, young economies and the profits repatriated in a mutually beneficial transaction between countries as well as generations.

A new framework

Current thinking about welfare, whether pensions or the broader framework, concentrates on the symptoms of change without addressing the fundamental changes in the world economy directly. New policy suggestions incorporate the need to restore the insurance motive to the welfare state, mainly because it is pretty obvious that the entitlement culture has eaten too big a hole in government finances and undermined the effort and self-respect of its recipients. But there is a deeper reason for making welfare more like insurance. It is because the financial and social risks people face have changed along with the technological foundations of our economies.

It is not new to observe that individuals bear more of life's risks themselves than was true 20 or 30 years ago. Both governments – through the pressures on their welfare budgets – and companies – through everything from the increasing use of temporary contracts or layoffs to the withdrawal of health and pension benefits – have transferred the burden of adjusting to bad luck to us.

Certainly this shift has gone hand in hand with free-market ideology, but the politics has been following rather than leading the way. This is why left-of-centre politicians like the Clinton Democrats in the US or New Labour in Britain do not propose turning the clock back. They grasp, at some level, that the world has changed too fundamentally. For information technology is reducing the domain over which governments and corporate bodies have any control. It is restricting the ability of governments to raise taxes, and of companies to protect their ideas. The industrial West will be forced to develop a new social contract that accepts technical realities, as explored in the next chapter – or perhaps those grim *Blade Runner* or *Black Rain* dystopias will come true.

Notes

1. See, for example, *The Pension Time Bomb in Europe*, Federal Trust, 1995.
2. *The Future of Savings and Wealth Accumulation*, by David Miles, Merrill Lynch, September 1996.
3. *Caring for Frail, Elderly People*, 1996.
4. In *Can We Afford To Grow Older*, 1996.
5. Details from Disney, Chapter 5.
6. In *Making Welfare Work*.
7. See report in the *Financial Times*, London, September 1996.
8. See *Social Protection for Dependent Elderly People*, OECD, 1995.
9. Figures in Chapter 8, *Managing the World Economy*, ed. P. Kenen.

Chapter Eight

Globalism and Globaloney

In the autumn of 1992 I was working from home, my son an infant under two. We had just moved to a house at the limit of affordability, for the property market had crashed and we reckoned that it was only at the bottom of a slump that we would ever be able to buy a big family house in London. It seemed a good idea but the mortgage did not bear thinking about. On Wednesday 16 September I finished work, printing out an invoice for an assignment I had just finished, and went downstairs to turn on the early evening BBC news.

Britain's Chancellor of the Exchequer, the unprepossessing Norman Lamont, was reading a statement to the television cameras that had gathered in Downing Street. In order to defend the pound's place in the European Exchange Rate Mechanism (ERM), he was saying, interest rates would rise from 12 per cent to 15 per cent with immediate effect. That meant an increase in the mortgage rate we were paying on our loan to more than 17 per cent and an impossible increase in our monthly repayment. We would lose our new home before all the boxes had been unpacked. I headed straight back to my desk to draft a letter to the building society that had made us the loan to say we could not pay them any extra interest and they should blame the Government for its mismanagement of the economy.

Luckily, I never had to post it. The same evening the UK left the ERM, along with Italy. Subsequently a number of other countries including France switched to much wider bands of permitted fluctuation against the core currency in the system, the Deutschemark. Many commentators in continental

Europe blamed the ERM crisis – soon named 'Black Wednesday' in Britain – on 'Anglo-Saxon speculators'. In their eyes it was the untrammelled power of international financial markets, unleashed by financial deregulation in the US and UK, which had torpedoed the centrepiece of European monetary arrangements after more than a decade of careful construction and management.

One of those speculators, who started the run that was estimated to have cost the British taxpayer more than £10 billion in the futile attempt to prevent a sterling devaluation, was George Soros. Anglo-Saxon only in the sense that he and the managers of his investment vehicle, the Quantum Fund, are based in the US, the Hungarian-born financier is a fervent supporter of the European project. Nevertheless, he argues that the ERM could not survive and defends the speculative attack on its weak currencies in September 1992 and again in August 1993.

European politicians indeed accepted this logic by pressing on with the plan to create a single EU currency. If it does happen – something that looks more uncertain as I write – it will be an experiment almost entirely without precedent in economic history. Previous currency unions have taken place between far more similar countries on a far less ambitious scale. The thought of binding the Deutschemark to the escudo, say, is one that some economists find truly mind-boggling. Escaping the scourge of the financial markets is not the purpose of this ambitious monetary union, but it is a spin-off that many will welcome.

For the markets have become one of the principal – and generally disagreeable – influences on economic policy in the 1990s, for industrialised and emerging economies alike. They have flexed their muscle again and again, vigilantes limiting the scope for democratically elected governments to pursue their chosen policies. As we all know from that new literary genre, the autobiographies of young men working in London and New York whose salaries are enormous multiples of their ages and sometimes even multiples of their telephone numbers, financial traders are irresponsible. They deal on rumour, on whim, according to whatever will maximise their own profit. The markets are manic, crazy, unpredictable. The spirit was captured by the hilarious account of a year at American investment bank Salomon Brothers by Michael Lewis, a one-time trainee bond dealer who has since retired to the quieter pastures of journalism. Lewis wrote at the end of the 1980s:

> 'Never before have so many unskilled twenty-four-year-olds made so much money in so little time as we did this decade.'

The trading floor was, and still is, an extraordinarily macho environment. That this is so is confirmed by the Salomons' slang for a successful trader:

> 'A new employee, once he reached the trading floor, was handed a pair of telephones. He went on line almost immediately. If he could make millions of dollars come out of those phones, he became that most revered of all species: a Big Swinging Dick.'

One of the bank's most successful traders was asked by trainees for the secret to dealing with the jungle law of the job. 'Lift weights or learn karate', he replied, according to the book.

The power of the financial markets

By all accounts, Lewis's memoir, *Liar's Poker*, with its tales of drinking and shouting, jokes and fights, was no exaggeration. What's worse, these testosterone and cocaine-fuelled bedlams in the heart of the world's great financial centres in New York, London, Tokyo and elsewhere trade *trillions* of dollars *every day*. The equivalent of Britain's GDP is traded daily in the foreign exchange markets alone, and the combined government bond markets are even bigger.

Many different types of financial deals form 'the markets'. Currency trading is the biggest and fastest-moving, dominated by London and, at a some distance, New York and Tokyo. Next come the markets for trade in bonds issued by governments, closely linked. Of these, the US Treasury bonds and German Bunds dominate, although London and Tokyo are also important centres. Stock exchanges, trading shares in companies in each country, are dominated by New York's market, Wall Street, followed by Tokyo and London, with Paris and Frankfurt eager to catch up. Some countries also have important markets in corporate bonds, or borrowing by companies rather than share issues. Then, on top of these basic financial instruments, is the trade in various derivatives. These range from well-established commodities futures dating back well over a century to the ever-more complicated options and futures traded on exchanges like the Chicago Board of Trade and Liffe in London.

Given their scale and compass, it is no wonder that the financial markets have come to seem a Frankenstein's monster, a creation of the richest economies that is fated to destroy them.

It is one thing for the power of the markets to deliver the finance ministers – and home-owners – of the wealthy European countries a nasty shock. But they presented an even more malign aspect at the turn of 1994 when an unexpected devaluation of Mexico's currency turned into a rout for the Mexican Government's entire economic strategy. For an impoverished population it meant misery. The crisis prompted the biggest international financial rescue in history, a $50 billion emergency loan package co-ordinated by the US Government, which feared that financial collapse in Mexico might spread north of the Rio Grande.

With hindsight, it was a crisis that had developed over several months, and some economists could claim with satisfaction that they had predicted early in 1994 that something like this would happen. The centrepiece of the Mexican Government's monetary policy was keeping a fixed exchange rate for the peso against the US dollar. It would guarantee that inflation was no higher than the US rate. The trouble was that the Mexican economy was still generating inflationary pressure, and the safety valve of a devaluation had been sealed off. The pressure of demand, due mainly to a growing Government budget deficit, was reflected in surging imports. Mexico financed the demand for foreign currency to buy imports by borrowing in dollars from overseas investors through issuing short-term bonds, called *tesobonos*. In a telling warning of impending crisis, its Government grew slower and slower through 1994 at publishing the figures for its stock of foreign currency reserves.

When something eventually had to give, and the Government announced a modest devaluation of the peso, the foreign 'hot money' fled. The peso halved in value, plummeting from three and a half to the dollar to more than seven to the dollar. Interest rates jumped. So did inflation. The Government had to slash its spending and rush through a privatisation programme in an effort to reduce its deficit. The International Monetary Fund imposed one of its classic austerity programmes.

In a country like Mexico where poverty is widespread, the consequences of this kind of crisis can be catastrophic. Inequality and hardship had already fomented a long-running revolt against government authority in the Chiapas region. Further unrest made it even harder to persuade US investors, or rather those obscenely overpaid bond traders on Wall Street, to refinance Mexican bonds. There is nothing like the presence of troops to put the wind up the capital markets.

Even two years after the initial crisis, the resulting job losses stood at a million while wages were below their 1982 level. Urban and political violence were still spreading, with soaring crime rates in cities and the emergence of reinvigorated guerrilla groups across a third of the country's territory. In the misery belt – Chiapas, Oaxaca and Guerrero – efforts to tackle basic social problems such as the 25 per cent illiteracy rate and absence of infrastructure ground to a halt.[1]

The US-led financial rescue achieved its aims, however. The peso eventually stabilised. So did inflation, and interest rates have been able to fall. The government deficit is shrinking and Mexico has paid back the emergency loans ahead of schedule. The IMF is happy.

Yet each crisis in the financial markets raises an insistent question. Can it be right for so much unchecked power to lie in the hands of speculators? Put it like that, and the answer is obviously not. But it is the wrong question, as a history of the development of the financial markets to their present state of influence demonstrates. It is a history inextricably linked to the post-war growth in the size of government. In the last analysis we have got the financial markets we deserve as a result of voting for governments that are spending more, much more, than we are willing to pay in taxes, and which have in many cases promised future spending on pensions that they will inevitably have to default on.

In this chapter I want to argue that the ur-weightless activity of trading in the financial markets has been able to expand so rapidly in the past 20 years because high levels of government borrowing have created the opportunity. Governments around the world have also fostered its growth by removing investment and credit regulations. Virtually every developing country now welcomes international capital with open arms. The arrival of the weightless world has been speeded, albeit accidentally, by government policy.

But those on the centre-left who imagine it is both desirable and possible to put the genie back into the lamp are profoundly mistaken. Not only have the markets become the only discipline on bad government fiscal policies and unsustainable increases in borrowing. They are also an agent of weight-lessness. They are helping hurry the transition.

This chapter looks at how the markets grew so powerful, why they are beneficial, and what governments should be trying to do to police them.

Markets go global

The huge global financial markets have developed since the early 1970s to finance large-scale borrowing by certain governments, mainly in the industrial countries – although increasingly they are financing private investment in 'emerging markets', with these flows setting a record $250 billion in 1995.[2] As a result, capital can be invested in almost any stock or bond market in the world at almost literally a moment's notice. Some developing countries have opted out of the global market by retaining restrictions on foreign exchange and foreigners' access to their domestic markets, but most countries around the globe are now competing for an international pool of savings.

There are two schools of thought about the development of a global capital market, which dates back almost two decades. There are those who claim the unprecedented degree of globalisation of international markets, both financial markets and markets for goods and services, has transformed the world. Companies face a new headwind of international competition, to a degree unimaginable two decades ago. The ability to transfer millions of dollars worth of funds at the touch of a key has transferred power from governments to financiers. Deregulation and technology have combined to change things utterly.

Then there are those to whom this is just so much globaloney. As discussed in Chapter 3, international trade and investment have grown steadily since World War II, but are nowhere near recovering the peak, in relation to the size of the world economy, that they attained at the turn of the last century. Information and communications technology make it possible now to transfer huge sums in seconds, but it only took perhaps three or four hours by telegraph in the Edwardian era.

The baloney school is right in some respects, but there were key differences to early twentieth century globalisation. First, people were then far more mobile than they are now; it was the era of mass emigration from the old world to the new. And second, Western money was invested only in colonies where it was controlled by other Westerners. International investment in autonomous and rapidly developing countries is new. International capital also used to finance mainly private investment, but at the end of this century it finances mainly investment by governments.

Some authors use the similarities to argue that (a) nothing fundamental has changed in the financial markets, and globalisation is old hat; and (b) governments can take steps to control the markets anyway. They are seemingly oblivious to the tension in holding to these two beliefs simultaneously.[3] Both are wrong. Something has changed – it is weightlessness, the irrelevance of boundaries, rather than globalisation, the whittling down of boundaries. The value in what the financial markets do lies not just in financing tangible trade and direct investment flows, but increasingly in dematerialised functions such as hedging risk. Moreover, governments cannot reverse technological change in the way they might be able to rebuild cross-border barriers. Much as he over-hypes it, Jean Baudrillard is intuitively right to think of the financial markets as having started to operate in a different sphere.

War, depression and then war again broke down the old nineteenth-century imperial order. International trade collapsed. International investment came to comprise the American bankrolling of western Europe and to a far smaller extent the British subsidy of its colonies and commonwealth. For global markets, 1945 was year zero. Under the Bretton Woods system established after World War II – named after the location of its founding conference – international capital flows grew slowly, limited by exchange controls. Intermittent balance of payments deficits in some countries were the main force driving the flows. It was not until after the Bretton Woods arrangements began to crumble that the growth in the financial markets began to head up the graph.

The birth of the Big Swinging Dick

A brief history of the recent growth of the international markets will demonstrate why their power this past decade or so has been fuelled by the growth of government. For what is really different about modern capital markets, what marks today's globalisation from the earlier version, is what those markets are being asked to finance. At the turn of the last century it was the great colonial infrastructure and extraction projects such as Argentina's railways and South Africa's mines. Speculative enough, but investment in real assets that provided some security. Today, the greatest demand on the pool of international funds is borrowing by rich governments to finance spending that their taxpayers are not prepared to stump up for. Nor is it generally capital spending that is expected to generate a future return, but rather current expenditure on everyday services. The payments on the borrowing will depend on tomorrow's taxpayers financing them instead of today's.

This pattern of borrowing in the international capital markets is a phenomenon dating from the 1970s. International capital flows grew at a steady pace for the first quarter century after the post-war Bretton Woods conference in the summer of 1945, and the 'offshore' Euro-market for short-term lending and borrowing on a large scale was well-established by the mid-1960s.

But the great leap forward stemmed from the OPEC oil crisis. The mainly Arab members of the Organisation of Petroleum Exporting Countries decided in 1973 as a result of the Middle East war to exercise their muscle by quadrupling the price of oil. It soared from $3 a barrel at the start of that year to $12 a barrel within 12 months. Additional increases followed, taking the oil price to a peak above $35 in 1980.

This left the OPEC countries with the happy problem of having more money than they knew what to do with. What they did therefore was lend it abroad to Western governments who vastly expanded their budget deficits in reaction to the severe recession induced by higher oil prices. By 1976 the IMF was imposing a remedial programme on the UK because of the size of its government borrowing and balance of payments deficit, and issuing severe warnings to other countries such as Italy. By then the 'recycling' of OPEC money had stimulated a high-octane spurt in the development of the financial markets.

The deregulation of international flows of money in the UK and US during the early 1980s certainly helped this continue. But more important was the fact that the demand for capital created by government deficits grew and grew. Ronald Reagan was a key culprit. After his election to the US presidency in 1980 Reagan slashed income taxes. He adhered to 'supply side' theories which predicted that lower taxes would stimulate effort and growth to such an extent that tax revenue as a whole would not fall, and there would be no budget deficit as a result of the tax cut. It was all absolute nonsense. The US government budget deficit ballooned from less than $6 billion in 1980 (or 0.3 per cent of GDP) to $115 billion in 1983 (3 per cent of GDP). It remained at just over $60 billion in 1995, although by then its share of the economy had shrunk to less than 1 per cent.

Where the Americans led, other industrialised countries followed. The cumulative effects of the OPEC crises, the two deep 1970s recessions and the even deeper one in 1981–2, and the cost of paying for high unemployment have never been unwound. Only Japan can claim a record of cautious government borrowing, and its economic and financial crisis this decade has

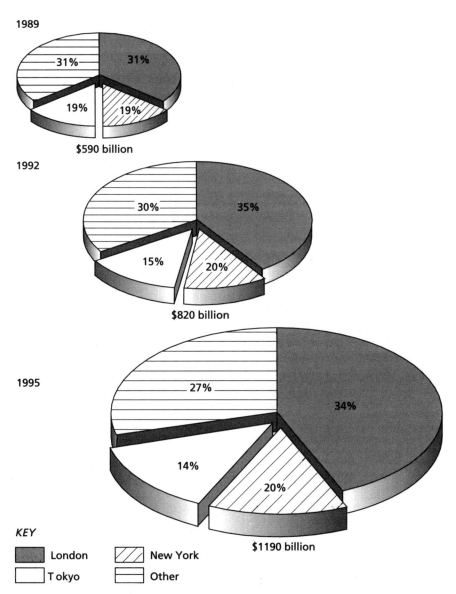

Fig. 15 Foreign exchange trading: average daily turnover. (Source: BIS Annual Report.)

undone much of that.

The result: total government borrowing in the form of issuing bonds by the industrial countries had reached $1.1 trillion in 1995, according to the

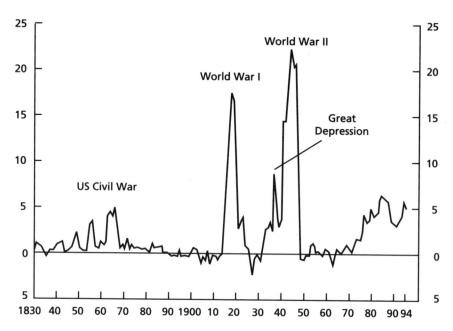

Fig. 16 G7 government budget deficit as percentage of national income. (Source: OECD.)

Bank for International Settlements, the central bankers' bank in Basle. Its increase since 1970 explains why these have been decades of unparalleled growth and profit in the financial markets. It explains the genesis of the Big Swinging Dicks with their telephone-number incomes.

This demand for funds is provided by the international pool of savings by the private sector around the world, a pool which has the alternative of lending to private sector borrowers. Investors via the financial markets have to bear in mind the current alternatives and also the likely future demands they will face for additional financing for governments. They are well aware of the unfunded pension liabilities many governments will have to start paying out after the turn of the century (see Chapter 6). It is no wonder that 'Anglo-Saxon' traders have started to get a bit edgy about governments that cannot seem to get their finances under control. So would a bank towards a customer whose loans grew ever bigger in relation to their income and who was starting to grumble about paying out so much interest to the bank.

Speculators as vigilantes

The view that globalisation due to technological developments and deregulation has brought about something new rests not so much on the existence or scale of international capital flows as on their apparent power. The modern financial markets judge governments – and private borrowers too – extremely severely. It has become commonplace to describe them as vigilantes. If a country strays at all outside the limits set down by the markets, punishment will be swift and harsh. The currency will drop like a stone in value. Governments are often compelled to react by jerking up interest rates, with all the pain that implies for their citizens. For all that, it is rarely enough to end the crisis. The only solution is for the beleaguered government to announce an austerity programme. It must accept the policy dictated by the markets.

For that is the rule set by the vigilantes. International money will be invested in countries whose governments do not spend too much more than their income. If their budget deficits grow too big, however, the punishment – massive and sudden withdrawal of funds – will be merciless. The episodes are numerous. Aside from dramatic examples such as the ERM crisis in 1992 or the Mexican crisis in 1994, there is a handful of runs on individual currencies each year. In 1996, during the approach to European Monetary Union, for example, Italy, Spain, Portugal and Sweden all experienced episodes of the withdrawal of financial market favour. They have suffered extraordinary devaluations, with currencies losing up to an eighth of their value within a few weeks or very short-term interest rates at extraordinary levels of 30 or 40 per cent. 'Emerging' markets fall into and out of fashion with global investors at the whim of fashion, or so it seems.

To critics of the untrammelled power of markets this is definitive proof that globalisation has undermined the powers of government. Although European governments have bound themselves to the fiscal disciplines set out in the Maastricht Treaty, the treaty creating the single European currency, opponents see this as surrender to the conservative orthodoxy of the international financial markets. As they see it, the effort to reduce government budget deficits below the 3 per cent of GDP limit set in the treaty, and outstanding government debt below 60 per cent of GDP, is exacting too high a price. It is deflating economies that had barely emerged from the 1991–2 recession and preventing unemployment from falling from destructive levels. Indeed, most of the jobs created in continental Europe since 1980 have been public sector jobs paid for by government spending – although, as the analysis in Chapter 2 showed, unemployment has causes and cures not linked only to macroeconomic policies.

This anti-market tendency is strong in France, where the once universally accepted *franc fort* or strong currency policy – running a cautious budget and interest rate policy in order to keep the French franc at a high level against the German mark – has come under increasing attack. The policy was the French establishment's reaction to the embarrassment of being forced by the markets to retreat from the 1981–2 Mitterrand experiment of reflating the economy. Yet the decade-old consensus has started to break down under the weight of the country's lacklustre economic performance.

For example, in the summer of 1996 the left-wing newspaper *Libération* ran a two-page spread on *la politique du franc fort*, using as an excuse the fact that the general price level had fallen slightly for the second month running as the economy continued to be lethargic and unemployment stayed high. Was France falling into an infernal spiral of deflation, the paper asked. 'Every time the French economy plunges, anguished discussions of falling prices come to the top of the agenda. Always with the same target in the line of fire: the *franc fort* policy.' It compared the strong exchange rate policy to the decision by Pierre Laval's government in 1934–6 to cling to the Gold Standard, the fixed parity for the franc against gold, which resulted in a far deeper Depression in France than elsewhere. The report concluded that Jean-Claude Trichet, the Governor of the Bank of France and symbol of the economy's subjugation to the financial markets, had lost the support of some members of the government and was in danger of finding the current of politics running against him.[4]

There is a strong current arguing in favour of taming the markets and continuing to run big budget deficits. Its proponents do not accept the restrictions on policies set by international investors. Members of this school of thought sometimes call for a tax on foreign exchange deals – the so-called 'Tobin tax' after Nobel Laureate James Tobin – to bring the markets to heel. Its supporters are mainly left wing, but it has orthodox financial support too. For instance, Wilhelm Nölling, a former Bundesbank Council member now teaching at Hamburg University, has argued that it would 'Make speculators think twice before attacking defensive walls erected by central banks and governments'.[5]

The idea is that such a tax would throw some grit into the machinery of foreign exchange speculation. It would be low enough not to inhibit currency exchanges that were needed to finance international trade or direct investment, but would eliminate a lot of speculative trades that depend on shifting large volumes of money to capture a tiny profit margin. It could also raise a lot of money – a tax rate of 0.5 per cent would raise $150 billion a year world-wide on one estimate.[6] Free-market critics of a Tobin tax rely on the argument that it would be hard to enforce because either traders would switch their business to the sort of haven like the Caymans or Bermuda that would be bound to opt out of the tax, or they would devise new financial mechanisms to get round that tax, such as new types of derivatives. The counter-response is that the bulk of foreign exchange trading by reputable banks would not leave London or New York because of the expense and bother, although even sympathisers admit the Tobin tax would have to be virtually universal and cover every form of foreign exchange transaction. The probable outcome would no doubt be somewhere in between. In fact, the most implausible thing about the tax is the political co-operation between dozens of countries that would be required to police and distribute its revenues. International regulators find it sufficiently hard to co-operate well enough to prevent downright fraud on a huge scale. It is difficult to believe it could ever work even if the arguments for introducing it were uncontested.[7]

Nevertheless, the notion of a tax on speculation has a superficial appeal on the grounds of democracy – can it be right to let the rabble of traders in London and New York dictate the policies of elected governments? But it is misguided for two reasons. One is that there can be no doubt that deficit financing by governments has been too high for too long. The other is that the untamed markets are the only voice exercised against excessive future taxes that will have to be paid one day to service current government borrowing. The markets are the voice of future citizens today.

Nor would it make sense. It presumes that the markets are over-mighty. In fact, financial traders are the pioneer cowboys on the frontier of the weightless economy.

More than sado-monetarism

These are perhaps controversial claims. The argument that the markets are right that government borrowing is too big, and countries which are not cutting the scale of their borrowing deserve to be penalised, is not one that has much popular currency yet. For some commentators – not all left-wing – describe the financiers' fiscal conservatism as 'sado-monetarism'. And it is clear that, no matter that higher taxes would be a real vote-loser, many people would see no problem with bigger budget deficits. In the UK, New Labour has been criticised by supporters for its over-riding concern not to make new expenditure commitments. In France and Germany the unions have taken to the streets to object to government spending cuts. In the US the quest for a balanced budget has been one of the political footballs of the 1990s, with Republicans and Democrats seeking to blame each other for welfare cuts each say are essential and the Federal Government closing down three times during one winter of brinksmanship in 1995.

Yet amongst the finance ministers and central bankers of the biggest industrial economies there is a new orthodoxy that recognises the need to cut budget deficits from the present levels. In 1995 they published, at the annual meeting of the International Monetary Fund, a study of the costs of high borrowing and the costs and benefits of reducing it. It concluded that the benefits in the form of lower interest rates exacted by the financial markets would probably outweigh the deflationary impact of cutting public sector expenditure.

It is not that these dignitaries are unworried about slow growth and high unemployment. The following summer, after another sluggish year for many of the big economies, the Bank for International Settlements warned about the danger of overdoing deflationary policies.

Yet the longer political leaders in the industrialised economies take to roll back the size of government borrowing, the longer they cheat their citizens and evade their responsibilities. This is not a right-wing stance against the traditional left-wing preference for big government, although the left is in danger of allowing radical right-wingers to capture the intellectual territory. It is hard for me, one of the thousands shouting 'Maggie! Maggie! Maggie! Out! Out! Out!' at demonstrations against Mrs Thatcher's early efforts to cut government spending, to admit it, but the public sector has grown to proportions that undermine growth and bequeath unsustainable problems to future generations, without succeeding in basic tasks of economic policy such as cutting unemployment, reducing inequality and boosting long-term growth.

In the UK case, it was successive Conservative administrations that were responsible for literally bankrupting the British Government. Prime Minister John Major doubled the national debt between 1990 and 1995. This made debt interest payments the fourth biggest category of government spending, a third the size of the total annual social security bill. The net worth of the central government – the surplus of its assets over its liabilities – fell from plus £20 billion when Mrs Thatcher first took office in 1979 to minus £152 billion in 1995.[8] This 'fiscal incontinence', as a former Conservative chancellor described it, ran counter to the party's philosophy and rhetoric. The Government was run over by the steamroller of the state. Governments elsewhere in Europe were even more badly flattened. In Italy, for instance, the government budget would be in surplus if not for debt interest payments. The country is trapped in a vicious circle of high debt and ruinously high interest, which in turn increases the debt.

The burden of welfare and interest is one which voters in many industrialised countries are ambivalent about. They want the public services but not if paying for them will require higher taxes. Some countries have been more successful than others at keeping growth in government spending and taxes in line. Others, such as France and the UK, have developed a public spending habit that is bigger than their tax base can sustain. Rather than face the politically unpalatable choice – cut spending or increase taxes – they have rolled up the debt for future politicians and voters to worry about.

Add in the prospect of future state pension liabilities, and next century's taxpayers are being asked to shoulder an impossible burden. The technique of 'generational accounting' shows how unfair this is. The technique assumes that benefits remain unchanged but future taxes are raised to make fiscal policy 'sustainable'. Calculations for the US – with a middling-serious ageing and pensions problem – show that a man who was 65 in 1989 would receive a net payment of $36,200 from the government on average. A man who was 25 the same year could expect to make a net lifetime payment of $220,100 to the government, and a new-born $102,000.⁹

The big government experiment has run for 50 years – long enough to accept that it has failed. Some of the reasons for the growth of the public sector were explored in Chapter 5. Defence spending during the Cold War era provided one of the original impulses. Far more significant in the long run, however, has been the expansion of the welfare state. Cost came a poor second as a consideration in its creation, and the original costs have increased enormously with the spread of entitlements beyond the original beneficiaries.

A sustainable future

A sustainable budget policy is as important as sustainable environmental management. A currency crisis can be thought of as the financial equivalent of a wrecked oil tanker or chemical plant explosion – a catastrophe that forces us to consider the weaknesses in existing policies and rules.

The time is now opportune to carry out an audit of the scale of government borrowing, the high-octane fuel firing the financial markets. For the end of the Cold War has brought the opportunity to reconsider more broadly what government is for. This is an opportunity so far grasped mainly by un-popular radical conservatives such as Newt Gingrich in the US and John Redwood in the UK, people who have little at stake in abandoning the no-tion of big government. It is a more painful process for those in the political mainstream who have seen the post-war development of the state as an essential social glue and fear its shrinkage would dissolve the cohesion of our societies.

The construction of a politics of replacing government spending with another form of social cohesion is well under way, however. As discussed in Chapter 4, Robert Puttnam, the Harvard academic, showed in his study of Italian regional governments that the effectiveness of government – how good the services they provide – had surprisingly little correlation with how much they spent. Clearly, a richer area has a bigger tax base and more available to spend on schools and roads. But the southern Italian regions had received trillions of lire more in grants than the northern regions and had less to show for it. Rather, Puttnam concludes, it is 'social capital', the historical accumulation of civic traditions and trust between citizens, that leads to good government. Money matters far less.[10]

One pessimistic conclusion from this research is that the economic performance of different societies depends on their history. If they want to get somewhere else, they shouldn't be starting from here. On the other hand, an extremely optimistic inference from this hypothesis is that it might be possible in some cases to cut government expenditure without doing as much social damage as seems likely on the face of things. It would depend on whether civic networks were available to fill the gap.

This is taking one suggestive piece of research too far, but there is another consideration. It is that, as discussed earlier, the technology-driven changes in industrial economies are making government policy increasingly irrelevant. The public sector domain is shrinking. There will perhaps be less for governments to spend on.

Taming the volcano

The one sure-fire way, then, of trimming the power of those financial speculators to undermine governments is for governments to leave themselves less at the mercy of the markets. If you want to borrow the equivalent of 5 per cent of everything your country produces every year, your lenders are going to be able to dictate terms.

Beyond that, however, there are measures that can limit the excessive movements in currencies and interest rates imposed by market crises. For the movements are sometimes excessive. Financial markets 'overshoot'. They take exchange rates to extreme levels unwarranted by the underlying economic conditions because they react so much faster than other markets, either markets for goods or labour markets, to changed conditions.

For example, in 1980 the pound appreciated by 25 per cent in value against a range of other currencies. It should have risen part of the way – investors were reacting rationally to the extraction of North Sea Oil and the Thatcher Government's tight macroeconomic policies. However, the extent of the appreciation was so great that it caused industrial devastation as British exports became too expensive abroad. Manufacturing industry collapsed to such a degree that the 1979 level of output was not regained until 1987 when the economy was booming. The level at the end of 1996 was only about 15 per cent above its 1979 peak.

It was the dollar's turn next. It rose fairly steadily in value to reach a peak early in 1985, 42 per cent above its 1982 level. In 1985 and again in 1987 the Group of Seven (G7) industrial countries agreed to take action to reverse these wild currency swings. Those agreements – the Plaza Accord and the Louvre Accord – hold one clue to effective management of the financial markets. Broadly speaking, taming the global markets will involve international co-operation. But the existing framework for international economic management is inadequate. The Bretton Woods system has broken down, and nothing has taken its place. *Ad hoc* interventions by a handful of the industrialised countries will not be powerful enough to govern the international financial markets. Even worse, they have neither clear aims nor political legitimacy.

The underlying problem was diagnosed by Lawrence Summers, then number two at the US Treasury, at a conference called in 1995 for the 50th anniversary of Bretton Woods. He said: 'With the passage of the communist threat an important adhesive binding industrial democracies to each other and their allies in the developing world has been lost'. The dissolution of the security glue means there is less need to co-operate and indeed there has been less co-operation. The policies and interests of the biggest countries have diverged while the US has become less willing to underwrite other countries' economies. At the same time, globalisation has started to have such a profound impact on individual economies that the need for international co-ordination has increased dramatically.

At the same conference Robert Keohane, Stanfield Professor of International Peace at Harvard University, argued that there are two possible paths for the world economy. Along one path, the constituencies for globalisation within each country created by the growing prosperity of the weightless world – the well-off elites and technocrats – would prevail. The self-reinforcing dynamic of internationalisation – more trade, free markets – would continue. Existing institutions would adapt to it.

On the other, the victims of globalisation, whether Mexican peasants or unemployed French textile workers, displaced north African refugees or America's hamburger flippers, would create enough political momentum to halt the process in its tracks. Professor Keohane argued:

> *'The global economic forces unleashed by liberalising political institutions are having profound and far-reaching effects on domestic politics, many of which may be as poorly anticipated as the collapse of state socialism was. We may only be living in the eye of the storm.'*[11]

The voice of apocalypse is making itself heard. It speaks in fiction. Take the racist lawyer in T. Coraghessan Boyle's *The Tortilla Kitchen*, a novel about the rumbling volcano of illegal Mexican immigration into California. 'What do you expect', he'd said, 'when all you bleeding hearts want to invite the whole world in here to feed at our trough without a thought as to who's going to pay for it, as if the American taxpayer was like Jesus Christ with his loaves and fishes.'

There is a backlash against the results of post-war financial liberalism, without question. Every industrial country has its economic equivalent of the seventh-day adventists. It makes it all the more urgent for those of us who think that post-war free global markets have a lot to be said for them to develop international institutions that will prevent them, along with free investment and trade, from inflicting too much collateral damage on vulnerable groups as they sweep all before them.

A Global Agenda

There will be several new elements in international economic management in the weightless world. Trade agreements will have to cover the kinds of things they have so far excluded as being too difficult, such as services, investment and the environment. The need is likely to expand, too, to cover moral and scientific dilemmas such as the rules for trade between countries that use slave labour and those that do not, or the framework for the use of biotechnology. Institutions will be needed to bridge the growing gap between the ever-smaller role of domestic governments and the ever-greater international space. Newly industrialising countries will have to be included as they catch up with the industrialised world in size and wealth.

It is probably also necessary for America to resolve its leadership dilemma. The Bretton Woods system worked for 50 years because the US took charge, not only providing the lion's share of the funding for international institutions but also acting as a powerful force for the liberalisation of trade and global markets. But America's political leadership has lost the singleness of purpose created by the Cold War. As in the 1930s, many politicians are willing to bend an ear to isolationists – there are votes in the redundant auto workers in Flint, Michigan. There is even the extreme right-wing militia fringe to keep a wary eye on. Some citizens think the International Monetary Fund and UN are fronts for an anti-American world conspiracy. Although sole US dominance of the international economic system is no longer either possible or desirable, America has to be internationalist in spirit.

Accomplishing this agenda of global management will not be easy. It was hard enough to reach agreement on the world's economic architecture in

1945 when only a handful of countries mattered. The architecture for the next half century will have to be less tidy, probably embracing regional agreements as well as global ones. The general problem of boundary disputes – the quest for self-determination, the quest for conquest – will affect economic and monetary arrangements. Eminent economist and internationalist Fred Bergsten, director of Washington's Institute for International Economics, has pointed out: 'In short, pluralism has replaced hegemony in undergirding the international economic order'.[12]

With good enough diplomacy, liberalising the increasingly important bits of international trade will be feasible. It is already under way under the auspices of the new World Trade Organisation (WTO). Decent progress on allowing international trade in services to grow – trade which often requires foreign direct investment – will be the best counter-argument to protectionists whose case is based on manufacturing interests. For expanding trade in services will help the industrial economies grow. However, the WTO will have to accomplish other things. For one thing, China must be persuaded to act in ways that will allow it to join.

More broadly, the organisation will also have to expand its role to cover areas that do not seem connected to international trade but are indeed so in the weightless world. For example, government's competition policies or public procurement policies can discriminate severely against foreign companies in areas which are currently growing extremely fast. Computer services, telecommunications and the media are the obvious examples, but it is also true of many other service industries that technology has made it feasible to export, including financial services. What's more, the difference between trade and direct investment has become pretty meaningless. The WTO will have to cover investment too. A start has been made on this by the OECD's multilateral agreement in investment, due to be agreed by ministers in May 1997, but that covers only the 27 member countries.

Thorny as it will be, the liberalising agenda for world trade could prove easier than co-operation in the foreign exchanges. For despite the protectionist urges discussed earlier in this book, most industrial country governments still agree about the direction they are heading: towards freer trade. In contrast, the occasional G7 agreements since 1987 to manage exchange rates have been *ad hoc*, and have taken place only in extreme circumstances when all members of the group were persuaded that the markets had got it so badly wrong that it would be in all their interests to take action. When turning a currency misalignment around requires three countries (the US, Germany and Japan, the G3) to spend hundreds of billions of dollars out of their currency reserves, this is easy enough to understand. The policy elites in the G3 also have a philosophical commitment to free markets, and are reluctant to intervene on principle.

It means that policy makers in the biggest industrial countries are reluctant to consider a more formal structure for managing exchange rates. Yet this would have two key advantages. One is that it would prevent currencies getting so far out of line that it would cost the central banks so many hundreds of billions to reverse. Having spasmodic intervention with no ground rules about when it should occur is to get the worst of all worlds.

The other improvement is that a system of 'managed floating' for exchange rates would bring some accountability to the international monetary system. The exclusiveness and secrecy of the G3 and G7 means that their actions have no political legitimacy. Ultimately, this undermines their stability. Better to have an explicit agreement about the ranges within which exchange rates can very – ranges which could move over time. Targets would need to be backed by both central banks' use of their currency reserves and by responsible domestic economic policy. Too big a government deficit, the engineering of a pre-election boom, high inflation – all would tend to make the national currency vulnerable to devaluation.

This would create a link between votes and the purchasing power of the currency – perhaps one of the most important economic indicators to expose to the ballot box. To see how target ranges for exchange rates would accomplish this, just think about France's *franc fort* policy. Successive French governments have made it a cornerstone of economic policy to keep the franc nearly level against the Deutschemark. Elections have brought an active discussion of the costs and benefits of the policy. Many French voters believe the costs, in high interest rates and high unemployment, are too great. Nevertheless, the policy is the result of an explicit political process. If the electorate shifts far enough away from it, it will probably be abandoned.

Conversely, the pound has floated freely against other currencies for more than 20 years with the exception of its two years in the European Exchange Rate Mechanism. Its purchasing power has declined dramatically, from DM12 to the pound in 1975 to a range between DM2 and DM3. With no target for most of that time, governments were not held accountable for the devaluation of the currency. By comparison, John Major's government paid a serious price in its loss of credibility after the 1992 crisis, when membership of the ERM had imposed a target.

Beyond currencies

It does not seem an excessive demand on our political leaders that they should try to agree on how to manage our currencies in a manner that leaves them less exposed to the whims of the markets. Yet the new communications technologies might well end up making formal exchange rates increasingly irrelevant.

The use of e-money will, if it becomes at all widespread, essentially privatise the national money supplies. Some Internet banking already takes place, through organisations such as the First Virtual Banking Corporation and DigiCash. Most banks on the Net carry out transactions in US dollars. Some use informal currencies similar to those that circulate in local exchange trading schemes (see Chapter 4). In both cases the world's central banks and authorised commercial banks have no role. The currency that matters in the world of e-money will be the one that thousands of individual users decide they trust. This could turn out to be US dollars – although they will be dollars that the Federal Reserve Board has nothing to do with and will probably not even be able to count. It could turn out to be virtual cowrie shells.

The central banks have begun to fret about this a little, but reassure themselves with the thought that there are so few monetary transactions on the Internet that even if use of e-money grows extremely fast it will take a long time before it becomes significant. They underestimate its likely growth. It was not long after the Bank for International Settlements published a reassuring assessment of the threat e-money posed to monetary control that the first financial company in London, Currency Management Corporation, launched a currency trading service on the Internet. It opened without authorisation from the local regulator, the Securities and Futures Association, but is nevertheless perfectly free to trade.

As Net expert Howard Rheingold points out,[13] money is already an electronic abstraction. Of course we still use a lot of the crinkling and jangling stuff in everyday life, but the bulk of the developed world's monetary transactions take place between computers. The technology for private currencies is already in place. Their emergence waits only for our monetary habits to change.

The biggest challenge

The dematerialisation of the economy means the structure of trade is changing so that trade rules will have to adapt. It also has the potential to transform what we understand as money. The one thing that will never dematerialise is people. People will be the biggest challenge to the existing international economic order.

The economic pressures on the world's poorest populations, which have led to large flows of refugees and legal and illegal migrants, have already shown signs of becoming one of the most divisive political issues of our times (see Chapter 7). The nasty politics of race is a winning card with some voters in the industrial countries, it has to be acknowledged. Even liberal politicians accept the need to put up high barriers against immigration, no matter that immigrants make a net contribution to their host country in both economic and social terms.

There are contrasting visions of the years ahead. There is a dark and unappealing prospect of conflict and terrorism, as the inexorable hordes pour out of their own starving and strife-fractured countries. No barriers can hold back the truly desperate, and rapid population growth means their numbers could grow to unthinkable proportions. But the barriers will be erected anyway.

The alternative vision would see immigrants enriching their new countries – as they always have in the past. The continuing growth of world trade, especially in the form of direct investment overseas due to the expansion of trade in services, will steadily bring greater prosperity to many developing countries and reduce both population growth rates and the desire to leave.

It takes a brave political leader to be unashamedly internationalist these days. The brighter path requires it, however. Those who think of themselves as political liberals have a duty to say so, loud enough to drown the voices of the fearful majority. Liberalism in one country is a contradiction in terms. We will only realise the full potential of the weightless world if we accept the logic of technology's removal of borders. And that goes for people as much as money and bits.

Notes

1. See *Financial Times* special survey, *Financial Times*, London, 28 October 1996.
2. *OECD Financial Market Trends,* June 1996.
3. Prime exponents of the wrong-headed approach are Paul Hirst and Graham Thomson, *Globalisation in Question.*
4. *Libération*, 14 August 1996.
5. *Financial Times*, London, 22 October 1996.
6. *An Evaluation of the Tobin Tax*, Paper presented by Philip Arestis and Malcolm Sawyer at the London Business School, September 1996.
7. For a rehearsal of all the arguments, see *The Tobin Tax*, ed. Mahbub ul Haq *et al.*, 1996.
8. See *The Independent*, London, 2 September 1996.
9. Auerbach *et al.* in *Tax Policy and the Economy*, ed. Summers and Bradford.
10. *Making Democracy Work*, Princeton University Press 1993.
11. Printed in *Managing the World Economy*, ed. Peter Kenen.
12. In Kenen, *op cit.*
13. In *The Virtual Community*.

Chapter Nine

Visible and Invisible Cities

The seer of weightlessness, novelist William Gibson, has made plain the parallel between the intangible world of cyberspace and our tangible urban world, between the virtual and the real. In one interview he said: 'The Internet could one day be seen as being something terrifically significant: something akin to the building of cities ... It's immune to legislation because it's post-national and post-geographical.'[1]

The post-geographical, invisible city of cyberspace, Gibson's matrix, 'lines of light ranged in the non-space of the mind, clusters and constellations of data. Like city lights, receding ...', will have the paradoxical effect of fuelling the growth of our existing cities, those agglomerations of traffic jams and pollution sited in actual geographical locations. Contrary to the popular view that communications technology will disperse people away from urban centres, turn us all into telecommuters, the weightless world will be one where cities resume the importance and economic dominance they have not enjoyed for a century.

Cities have always been the only places where significant economic activity occurs. Even in agricultural times, national wealth was concentrated in the towns and cities where merchants traded, in the palaces and guilds and, later, the coffee houses. Economics is urban. The countryside is a parasite on urban wealth. The economist Robert Hall put this in stark terms when he said that a city and a boom were essentially the same thing, one in space, the other in time.

This is something that is intuitively true when you consider the great cities. Sometimes early on Sunday morning I drive all the way across London from my house in the west to my office in the east. The journey starts in one of the affluent Edwardian suburbs of pleasant red brick houses, gardens and parks that expanded the city across such a vast area at the end of the last century. After a few miles the streets get narrower, the houses terraced and packed in tighter. A flyover takes me past the meanest parts of the inner city, the high-rise estates, prisons, railway sidings. Then through central London, its glitzy shops and impressive ceremonial prospects, and the City with its ostentatious wealth of monumental architecture, money made manifest.

East London is a constant bustle of rag trade enterprise, cafes, markets, patently much, much poorer than the neighbouring financial district but buzzing with energy and business, a lot of it down to immigrants. After that it's through the ring of inner city poverty, grey estates and litter blown across the streets, again before reaching the city's newest symbol of wealth and pride, the gargantuan Canary Wharf tower, the tallest building in the country.

There are many people who see Canary Wharf as an emblem of free-market capitalism gone wrong because its 1980s developers, feted by Margaret Thatcher, subsequently went bankrupt. Sadly for the critics, the place is not only thriving but also being steadily humanised by its history as the site of some of London's most important docks. The old buildings – a sugar warehouse built by prisoners from the Napoleonic war, the harbour master's house – and of course the timeless river, are woven in with the new. Symbolically, the 50-floor tower and its complex is almost entirely occupied by companies operating in the weightless economy – newspapers and TV stations, advertising agencies, law firms, investment banks, a financial services regulator, consultants and so on. One of the powerhouses of London's new economy has been built on the docks, the key site of the city's former economic pre-eminence.

Make a journey like this across any great city, and you cannot fail to be impressed by the variety, the amount of activity, the range of businesses, the numbers of people and the bustle. Jane Jacobs makes the same point in her classic book *Cities and the Wealth of Nations*. She notes that the key assumption in macroeconomics since the days of mercantilism has been that the nation state is the right basis for analysis; only Marxist theory was based on anything other than the nation. 'Nations are not discrete economic units,' she writes.

She goes on to argue that cities are the natural units, the milch-cows of the national economy, whose tax revenues fund subsidies to the rest, whose energy and creativity generate trade, innovation and economic growth.

The share of the world's population living in cities has climbed steadily from about one in seven people at the start of this century to more than two in five now. In the US the proportion living in city centres has not risen so quickly – from nearly 20 per cent in 1900 to nearly 30 per cent by 1990. But adding in the suburbs takes the share up from 25 per cent to nearly 80 per cent in nine decades. The number of cranes on the skyline of a country's capital is one of the best single indicators of the entire nation's economic growth rate.

Economic development means urbanisation. Efforts to find an alternative, rural path to prosperity have ended in either the mass starvation of the nation or the mass murder of its unwilling peasants by tyrants.

The giant stride in prosperity represented by weightlessness will revive the fortunes of the great cities of the industrialised world. In New York and London, which have some of the most intensively wired land on the planet, this is already evident. In both, the fresh burst of creativity in the music and film industries, in fashion, software, advertising, financial and business services – all of the most weightless industries – is without parallel in at least the last 30 years and probably longer. The magazine *Newsweek* spotted this at the start of 1997, splashing 'Cool Britannia' on its front cover, followed by a *Vanity Fair* special issue, 'London Swings Again!'. These editors did not get where they are today by misdiagnosing trends.

Weightlessness is generating both political and economic forces driving the renaissance of our visible cities. In turn, their impending burst of development is going to change the landscape of business and of government.

Why Hollywood?

What's so special about Hollywood that almost all of the most commercially viable films in the Western world are made there? The Anthony Minghella film *The English Patient* won nine Oscars in 1997. The story, as far as the news media were concerned, was that this was a British-made movie, filmed and partly financed in the UK, with English and French actors rather than a star US cast. As Billy Crystal, the ceremony's host, said on announcing another win by the movie, 'Aside from wheat and auto parts, America's biggest export is now the Oscar'. This sweep of the Oscars would certainly make the Hollywood career of *The English Patient's* director and actors. Crystal could make the joke only because the phenomenon of a foreign sweep of the awards is so rare.

The French film industry struggles defiantly to challenge the Hollywood hegemony, with some success because of its big domestic market for French language films, but without any hope of breaking out of the art house circuit in most other countries – and I say this sadly as someone who usually only goes to see a movie if it has subtitles. Eastern Europe's film industry has enjoyed a modest renaissance as Western directors exploit the cheap but highly skilled labour in Budapest, Warsaw or Prague.

Yet despite the huge cultural and language differences between the Western industrialised countries, each nation buys most of its movies from Hollywood. This is an extreme case, but it turns out that the production of almost everything is concentrated in just a few centres. Finance is one of the most important examples. It is the key paradox of weightlessness that its frontier industry, financial services, is the most concentrated in particular urban centres. London, Tokyo, New York are completely dominant. It is scarcely an exaggeration to say that the global markets have been midwife to the rebirth of these cities.

The pattern of geographical concentration in other industries is most pronounced in the US. For example, there are essentially only two centres for computing and software, Silicon Valley in California and Route 128 in Massachusetts. Similarly, two-thirds of car and auto parts production takes place in the mid-west, mainly in a few cities in Michigan, like Detroit and Flint. In Europe, it is concentrated in Germany, which accounts for two-fifths of total European production mainly in Wolfsburg, but France and Italy also have big car industries.

The phenomenon is not confined to the Western industrialised countries. Weightless production is triggering similar concentrations in Asia such as Bangalore's software industry. Indeed, there is greater scope for urban concentration in Asia, where there is a cleaner slate in terms of past production patterns.

The management guru Michael Porter has detailed many of the geographic clusters or concentrations in particular industries. He analyses, for example, the development of four industries since World War II – the printing press industry in Germany, patient monitoring equipment in the US, ceramic tiles in Italy and robotics in Japan.[2] Take tiles. Italian producers accounted for about 30 per cent of world production and 60 per cent of world exports of ceramic tiles in 1987, with a trade surplus on this one product worth $1.4 billion. The entire industry is concentrated around the town of Sassuolo in Emilia-Romagna. As well as tiles, the hundreds of supplier firms around the town make glazes, enamels, and equipment for tile-making.

According to Porter, the concentration was due partly to Italian design flair and to an important breakthrough in single firing technology right after the war. But Sassuolo had also been a centre for the production of crockery and earthenware since the thirteenth century. The tradition was kept up in a small way through to the end of the nineteenth century, leaving a handful of manufacturers by the mid-twentieth century. A construction boom after the war built on this small but deep foundation despite the absence of the primary material resource for ceramic tiles at the time – white clay – in the region.

From small beginnings, a world-beating industry grew. Porter's mammoth study gives many, many more examples of this pattern. Denmark: agricultural machinery, dairy products, food additives, industrial enzymes, telecommunications equipment. Germany: cars, chemicals, eyeglasses, optical instruments, pens and pencils, printing presses. Japan: home audio equipment, carbon fibres, forklift trucks, robotics, sewing machines, VCRs. Switzerland: banking, chocolate, pharmaceuticals, textile machinery, watches.

When you start to think about this pattern of geographical specialisation, its prevalence becomes mesmerising. Next time you are in the supermarket buying some everyday household item, look to see where it is made. Toothpaste? Ireland or Germany. Nappies? US or France. Bacon? If not home produced, Denmark. As for household items, so for almost every good or service produced in the world. For sure, every town has its accountants, shops, restaurants and hairdressers. But there is only one – or at most two or three – for anything that can be traded. And so we have Hollywood (movies), Seattle and Toulouse (aircraft), City of London (financial services), Paris and Milan (couture), Detroit and Wolfsburg (cars), Silicon Valley and Boston's Route 128 (advanced information technology).

Why cities exist

It was almost a century ago that the British economist Alfred Marshall noted that most industry was concentrated in specific districts: cutlery in Sheffield, cotton in the Manchester area, lace in Nottingham, not to mention coal in Newcastle. Marshall also set out the fundamental economic explanation, of which more will be said in a moment. The economics profession ignored this very fundamental fact about our economies for the next hundred years, only recently returning to it. Paul Krugman at MIT, Brian Arthur and Paul David at Stanford University, and in Britain Anthony Venables have pioneered the modern version of economic geography.

As some of these researchers spell out, the world is becoming more like the one Marshall described. The forces for geographical concentration are becoming stronger as the economy becomes increasingly weightless. There has always been only one Hollywood. Now there is also only one Microsoft, only one Novell, and before long there might be only one Citibank. But this is to run ahead.

Marshall saw three explanations for the existence of geographical clusters: these have a pool of skilled labour for companies to choose from and a range of companies for workers to apply to; they create a network of suppliers and specialised services; and they foster the exchange of ideas and information, encouraging technical progress. In his own words:

> '*Employers are apt to resort to any place where they are likely to find a good choice of workers with the special skill which they require; while men seeking employment naturally go to places where there are many employers who need such skill as theirs and where therefore it is likely to find a good market.*'

and:

> '*Subsidiary trades grow up in the neighbourhood, supplying it with implements and materials, organising its traffic, and in many ways conducive to the economy of its materials ... For subsidiary industries devoting themselves each to one small branch of the process of production, and working it for a great many of their neighbours, are able to keep in constant use machinery of the most highly specialised character.*'

and:

> '*The mysteries of the trade become no mystery; but are as it were in the air ... if one man starts a new idea, it is taken up by others and combined with suggestions of their own; and thus it becomes the source of further new ideas.*'[3]

These certainly apply to my dominant local industry, financial services in the City of London. Foreign banks opening offices in London often cite the availability of a skilled labour pool, and their employees have a choice of hundreds of potential employers. The subsidiary industries are there, from telecommunications companies and information providers such as Reuters to the huge range of fancy wine bars. Eavesdrop on a conversation in one of those wine bars, and you will hear plenty of shop talk.

Paul Krugman has translated Marshall's arguments into the language of modern economics, although it still boils down to the essence of any market, people going to trade where there are other people.[4] Geographical concentration is the result of what economists call increasing returns to scale, or what an engineer would describe as positive feedback. This means that the more a company does of something, the better it does. Expensive set-up costs, for example, generate economies of scale. A new aircraft engine costs $2–$3 billion to design, develop, test and put into production, but the second one costs only $50–100 million. Or there can be increasing returns in the marketing and distribution of a product: the bigger it gets, the better McDonalds does because customers know the brand and know what they are getting.

The most important kind of positive feedback in marketing exploits 'network externalities'. This term just means that a product becomes more beneficial to its users the more other people are using it, because it sets a common standard. There are countless examples of one product squeezing another out of the market entirely because of network effects – for example, the VHS rather than the Beta standard for video cassette recorders, the spread of the DOS operating system for PCs, the use of petrol or gasoline to power car engines, the QWERTY arrangement on keyboards well beyond the technological advance that meant typewriter keys would not get stuck with any other layout. These technological lock-ins are sometimes called founder effects and can last until the next big wave of technological advance overturns them.

Increasing returns or positive feedback create the basic virtuous circle that leads to the concentration of production in a relatively few places – towns and cities. Companies want to be in the place where there are the workers to make their product and customers to buy it. The market develops where the producers are.

Transport costs make a difference to the basic tendency towards geographical agglomeration. If they are too high, it will discourage an industry from clustering in one place because the cost of shipping the raw materials or the finished product elsewhere would be prohibitive. This is why the processing of raw materials like ores or sugar usually occurs very close to where they are dug up or harvested. Equally, a reduction in transport costs can often permit greater concentration in one place – a fact very relevant to weightlessness, where transportation costs are nearly zero.

A second wrinkle is created by barriers to the movement of people. If immigration restrictions were to stop enough people moving to an urban cluster, wages there would rise and there would be an incentive for companies to switch production to the cheaper and more distant location.[5] This might help account for the famous Bangalore software industry or the transfer of some backroom operations to developing countries by companies like British Airways. New geographical clusters then develop elsewhere.

Accidents of history

These elements of economic geography make it clear that most industries are where they are because of happenstance. Paul Krugman says: 'Important aspects of an economy are contingent, determined by history and accident'.[6] One of his favourite examples is the development of the US carpet industry around Dalton in Georgia after World War II, with 19 out of the top 20 firms in the town or its immediate area. Up to the war carpets were woven, but a new machine allowed the much cheaper production of tufted carpets. Dalton was the country's tufting capital because of a cottage industry that had developed from a tufted bedspread made as a wedding gift in 1895 by a young woman called Catherine Evans. In the late 1940s and early 1950s the small Dalton companies saw the potential of the new machine, suppliers such as dye companies sprang up, and the development of Dalton as carpet city USA snowballed.

Brian Arthur argues that this very typical process quickly becomes self-reinforcing after the first few firms move in. He cites the example of Silicon Valley, where a few individuals such as William Hewlett and David Packard started small computer businesses in the 1950s because it was close to Stanford University. Once they had started, others followed, and before long there were hundreds of businesses supplying each other and drawing on a pool of specialised labour. But Silicon Valley could have been near any one of another dozen university towns – as, indeed, Route 128 developed near Boston, drawing on MIT, Harvard and several other universities.

There are new examples of this classic pattern all the time. Take Toy Town in Los Angeles, for example. LA County already has one of the toy industry's giants, Mattel, in El Segundo. But Asian immigrants into city centre LA during the past decade or so have created well over 500 new toy companies, employing at least 6000 people – many of them Hispanic immigrants – and generating annual turnover in excess of $4.4 billion. LA's Otis College of Art and Design started running a bachelor's degree course in toy design in September 1996. The Asian entrepreneurs sell the toys through their links to the big and growing markets across the Pacific.

Brian Arthur writes: 'If small events in history had been different would the pattern of cities themselves have been different? I believe the answer is yes … To the degree that industry and people are attracted to places where people and industry have already gathered, small chance concentrations early on may have become magnified into today's configuration of urban centres.'[7]

Weightless geography

Geographers and historians have, perhaps not surprisingly, always found it easier than economists to link production to the specifics of time and place. David Harvey sees the conquering of time and space as an integral feature of capitalism. He writes: 'Capitalism as a mode of production has necessarily targeted the breaking down of spatial barriers and the acceleration of turnover time as fundamental to its agenda of relentless capital accumulation'.

Technological change, he argues, has played a fundamental role in shaping the arrangement of economic activity on the landscape. 'Each bundle of innovations has allowed a radical shift in the way that space is organised and therefore opened up radical new opportunities for the urban process.'[8]

I believe that the weightless economy, the product of the latest technological wave, will renew concentration in the great cities. This is an argument that many people find counter-intuitive. At an abstract level, the philosopher Jean Baudrillard suggests that the modern economy is becoming steadily more and more divorced from the real world. In fact, there is a separate virtual economy, he suggests. 'Our only reality is an unchecked orbital whirl of capital which, when it does crash, causes no substantial disequilibrium in real economies ... Money hyper-realized circulate[s] in a space which is inaccessible – but which consequently leaves the world just as it is.'9

Or, as one of the characters in *Microserfs* puts it in an e-mail message to a friend: 'What's with these mutual funds and pension funds? I REFUSE to believe that money put into a bank in 1956 is *still* money in 1994. 1956 money may still technically be there (wherever 'there' is) – but it's undead money.'

At a more mundane level, the European Commission's 1994 Bangemann Report predicted that ten million teleworking jobs would be created in Europe between 1992 and the year 2000. The subsequent Delors report on unemployment saw telecommunications as a source of jobs in rural or peripheral areas. Amongst policy makers the view that modern computer and communications technologies permit work to be moved out of cities is certainly widespread. For example, the French Government has deliberately tried to make a small and otherwise unimportant town in northern Brittany, Lannion, the country's telecoms centre. The work could be anywhere, technically speaking, and Lannion needed work.

John Goddard, a geographer at the University of Newcastle, has put it like this: 'In public and private services, the use of telematics [i.e. information and communications technology] is breaking the traditional geographical linkage between local demand and local supply of services'.10 And there are certainly examples of big companies dispersing their workforce in this way. Telephone operators, for example, are unlikely to sit together in one big building in the centre of town any more. Some sit in offices far removed from the big cities they mostly serve. Some work at home. Technology has made homeworking possible in many new areas, especially the kinds of secretarial and routine white collar jobs that big companies have cut.

William Mitchell from MIT claims: 'The very idea of a city is challenged'.11

Even Danny Quah writes: 'Cities might still exist, but they will be places where people go to spend time with other people, not places where people go to work and produce economic value'.[12] He argues that the dematerialisation of economic output, with the irrelevance of transportation costs that implies, means: 'The natural marketplace for dematerialised objects is essentially unbounded'.[13] He reckons that loosens the ties of geography.

Yet the fact that it can and does happen in some cases that work has been dispersed from an old city centre location to a suburban one does not spell the end of the city or the city centre as we know it. If weightless production can occur anywhere, it might as well all take place in the centres where it has already started. We are more likely to see the kind of massive urban agglomeration that features in William Gibson's fiction, his Boston–Atlanta Metropolitan Axis, the Sprawl.

The reason I argue this is that weightlessness is dramatically increasing the scope of increasing returns to scale and decreasing transport costs. Both tend to favour more rather than less clustering. In the introduction I gave one example, in the increasing dominance of London in financial services despite the fact that its activity takes place in cyberspace. The role of very low transport costs – the cheapness of the phone calls needed to move money around the globe – is clear in financial services. Banks are increasingly able to concentrate all their trading in one place to exploit the undoubted economies of scale, the pool of skilled staff, because it costs almost nothing to ship the finished 'product' – the electronically registered financial transaction – to the right computer in the right place.

What is true of financial services is true of any service where the product can be delivered over the wires – or rather, the fibre-optic cables. There is therefore huge scope for more geographical concentration in many parts of the entertainment business or the media, and in professions where advice is increasingly being delivered via technology rather than in person – law, accountancy, medicine and teaching for example.

Suppose Harvard University were to decide to admit online students, delivering lectures and tutorials via computer and video links. Its superb brand name would enable it to capture a big share of the market for online studentships, and the university would be able to grow. Already a big employer of academics in Cambridge, Massachusetts, it would hire more and more of them. The town would become even more of a centre for the education business than it already is. Perhaps this example is a little far-fetched, but it illustrates well the point that the ability to ship weightless 'products' at almost no cost could boost existing urban centres.

Edward Glaeser at Harvard offers another argument in favour of an urban renaissance. He argues that telecommunications may be complementary to face-to-face contact rather than a substitute for it. This means cities will become more important as communications improve in quality and become cheaper. His research indicates two conditions that produce this result. Communications will favour the cities if urban residents use them more than rural residents; and if the value of interaction between people increases, say because the ideas that need to be exchanged become more complex and creative. He and a co-author write:

> 'The rise in the New York multimedia industry may be a sign of big cities' comparative advantage in facilitating the difficult information flows involved in cutting-edge industries ... As telecommunications improve, the demand for interactions of all varieties should rise, and the role of cities as centres of interactions should also increase. After all, the most famous modern agglomeration of industry, Silicon Valley, has occurred in the industry with the most direct access to the latest and best information technology. This agglomeration probably occurs because that industry relies so heavily on interactions and has so much knowledge to be transferred across firms and individuals.'

Increasing increasing returns

An increasing proportion of business in the weightless world is becoming subject to increasing returns: information is a limitless resource. There are two worlds of business, as Brian Arthur sees it – the traditional processing of materials or information to add value to them and the businesses that are knowledge-intensive with relatively little emphasis on resources. The division is not the same as manufacturing versus services. Data processing is a service, for example. The advanced industrial economies are becoming steadily and heavily dependent on the increasingly weightless, knowledge-intensive segment.

Many of the products or services of the weightless economy are interdependent. They are used in groupings – computer operating systems, software, modems, telephone cables and mobile phones, for instance. An equally important force is the prevalence in weightless economics of network externalities, the benefit that users of a product derive the more users there are, and infinite expansibility, the property that allows one person to use a dematerialised commodity without it detracting from anybody else's use of the same thing. It is feasible for one company to supply an entire global market – you only have to think of Microsoft, supplying a huge proportion of the world market for operating system software for personal computers from its Seattle campus.

Products such as software are virtually costless for their originator to reproduce but costly for people to use because they require the purchase of compatible hardware – network externalities become very important. Customers only want to have to buy one set of kit to use software or listen to music or watch videos. Getting in first, being biggest, will give one company an almost unassailable market position. The geographical configuration of the software business is probably sealed from now until the next technological revolution.

However, the cost of hardware and cabling, and the perceived importance of access to it, is leading to the wiring of our cities at an astonishing pace. Public buildings such as libraries and schools, cyber-cafes, business centres have joined the 'information superhighway'. In the industrialised countries, a lot of the infrastructure has already been put in place. It is in our towns and cities. The cost of cabling other areas to the same degree is prohibitive. To quote *Neuromancer*.

> '*Program a map to display frequency of data exchange, every thousand megabytes a single pixel on a very large screen. Manhattan and Atlanta burn solid white. Then they start to pulse, the pace of traffic threatening to overload your simulation. Your map is about to go nova. Cool it down. Up your scale. Each pixel a million megabytes. At a hundred million megabytes a second, you begin to make out certain blocks in midtown Manhattan, outlines of hundred-year-old industrial parks ringing the old core of Atlanta.*'

People need people

It will not do to get too carried away with the high-tech aspect of weightlessness. There are non-technological reasons why cities are going to become more important in the weightless world. Essentially, it will be down to the growth of the social economy, the creation of jobs in community and personal services. These are the kinds of service jobs that cannot be exported to some distant place, but do have to be undertaken where there are people demanding those services. In other words, people need people.

As Paul Krugman wrote in his mock retrospective of the late twentieth century: 'The jobs that could not be shipped abroad or handled by machines were those that required a human touch – face to face interaction between people working directly with physical materials. In short, they were jobs best done in dense urban areas'.[14]

The entire, huge social economy and personal service sector, one of the twin-engines of weightlessness, are tied to the places where there are already lots of people. The new economy is going to be more urban than ever.

City government

One of the best computer games in existence, if game is the right word, is *Sim City*. The game provides a basic landscape and gives you an initial budget. You start building your city in the year 1900, providing the basic infrastructure. If you do the right things, people move in, the tax base expands and the city grows. Keeping it healthy requires the addition of more schools, libraries, parks, police, power stations at just the right pace and in the right mix. Too little of any one kind of public service, and people will start to move out. Too many departures, and you have to resort to issuing bonds for finance, which tips you onto a downward spiral of raising tax to service the debt, and driving more and more citizens away. *Sim City* has always seemed to me a wonderful model of the problems involved in actually running a city. In our household we have managed to get one city thriving until 2035, although most tend to implode well before that thanks to my son's worrying preference for deficit financing. 'Just issue a bond, mummy!' he'll say.

The industrial nations offer varied models of how much power they devolve from central government to regional and city governments. France and the UK are highly centralised, Germany and the US federal. In most countries an empirical rule of thumb about the number of cities of a certain size holds true: the number of cities with population above a certain level falls in proportion to that size. Thus the US has 40 cities of above a million inhabitants, 20 above two million and nine above 4 million (Houston having been a bit laggardly). But both France and the UK have too few big cities: Paris and London dominate because of the high degree of government centralisation.

Discussions about the correct distribution of governmental power tend to focus on the balance between regions and central government. In the US the issue is the Federal Government's tendency to absorb or trespass on states' rights. In the UK the important constitutional debate is about the devolution of power to regional assemblies. Most of the writers who have discussed the end of the nation state have assumed that what power remains to politicians rests in the regions. As Mathew Horsman and Andrew Marshall point out in their book,[15] the nation state is 'historically robust'; but they see regional governance as the way forward, writing of the re-emergence of older regional loyalties in Europe – the Basque country, the Tyrol, the 'Atlantic Arc' of Ireland, Wales, Cornwall, Brittany, Galicia – not to mention separatist movements in northern Italy or northern Belgium.

For many people, however, regional identity is a non-event. To the extent that they do not identify with their nation, they will identify with some unit far smaller than a region – with their city, its football team, its speciality dishes, its finest buildings. Liverpudlians do not feel like north-westerners or Londoners like south-easterners; the Venetians are Venetian before they are Padanian; Parisians are completely unique, as anybody who has spent more than a few hours there will know. Regional pride is the consolation prize for people who don't belong to a city.

Economists have come up with some principles for the level to which policies should be devolved, most recently applied in the context of the European Union's debate about subsidiarity – should economic decisions be taken at EU, national or regional level?[16] It is a question of balancing the advantages and disadvantages. Decisions made at the centre can be more efficient – for example, if there are economic spill-overs like pollution created in one region but affecting another, or if there are economies of scale such as provision of a defence umbrella. It can be fairer, too. We might think it important to redistribute tax revenues from rich regions to poor ones. But decentralisation can improve efficiency when it is informed by better knowledge of local conditions and preferences, and it can be more democratic because citizens have more leverage over local politicians – they know more about them and their votes will matter more in local elections.

In general, various decisions will be best taken at different levels of government. But it is clear from the discussions of the advantages of the local that if a region has these advantages, a city will have them in spades. If there is an economic case for devolution, it will be for devolution of power to the most local level at which the superiority of better information is combined with minimum economies of scale in taxation and public infrastructure. That means the big urban agglomerations.

City government will become more important than national government in the weightless world. Industries will choose cities, not countries, and will deal with urban and not national governments. The devolution of power only makes sense if it is applied locally enough both to gain all the benefits of superior local knowledge and to meet local preferences adequately. There is generally no sense in devolving political decisions to a region – it is still too big and too distant to deliver these advantages.

Besides, a regional structure fosters the subsidy of poor regions by rich ones under the national umbrella. It is the regions in longest receipt of subsidies that trail furthest behind the national average. Italy's *mezzogiorno*, despite decades of funding from both the EU and the national government, still has GDP per capita less than three-fifths of the north's. Extremadura in Spain does little better despite subsidies almost as extensive. The US federal structure involves some cross-subsidy of poor states by rich ones, but not as much. With 3 per cent of the US population willing to move state each year, economic disparities between states persist but are smaller than between European regions.

Switch to a pattern of city government rather than regional, and the fruitless subsidies would become a thing of the past. Cities do not need subsidy from the centre, and given responsibility for their own success, they have the potential to regenerate their surrounding regions.

I was surprised to find support for my view that cities rather than regions will be the economic and political powerhouses of the weightless world in the work of the management theorist Professor Charles Handy. In his bestseller *The Empty Raincoat*, he writes: 'The city is replacing the nation state as the focus of our identity and our way of connecting with society'. He adds that our cities are in a mess. They are often crumbling physically, polluted and congested, with run-down areas of unacceptable poverty. There is little reason for civic pride in most of today's big cities. 'They should be given back the responsibility for their futures,' he says. The case for transferring economic powers – the power to tax, to issue bonds, to invest and plan infrastructure – to cities is overwhelming.

I got another surprise at a lecture given by John Gummer, the minister responsible for London in the UK's Conservative Government – which had, after all, abolished the Greater London Council, the elected body that had formerly run the city. He said: 'We cannot allow London to divide itself, and increasingly divide itself, into two worlds'. It was not acceptable, he said, that there should be high unemployment within three miles of vacant jobs in the city. 'A lot of Londoners do not share in the very successful economy. The better the thing that they are being left out of, the more the resentment builds up.'[17]

The problems common to inner cities in the industrialised West are not going to be solved by central or federal government, whose sole idea for applying technology to urban problems seems to be to install more and more surveillance cameras. Politicians and bureaucrats who scarcely ever leave central Paris have no idea what to do about problem estates and racial tension in Marseilles and Toulon – they have little enough imagination about their own poverty-stricken suburbs in Aubervilliers or Aulnay.

Our cities are poised for a huge surge in economic growth. The last time this happened, at the end of the nineteenth century, was another era of terrible inequality and poverty. It was also an era of civic pride and responsibility, when many of the municipal buildings, transport networks, sewage systems, electrical cabling and parks still in use were first created, built or installed. Give cities their head now, and the fibre-optic cables, educational institutions, Internet connections and urban structures needed in the weightless economy will be put in place.

We will be able to return to patterns of life common before the tyranny of the suburbs. People will live closer to their work. Affluent professionals and less affluent creative artists are already reviving the inner city in all the great capitals. Fewer people will commute. The delights of coffee house or cafe society will return. Children's voices will be heard again in city centres as families move back in. Inhabitants will start to demand parks, clean streets and decent traffic management. The inflow of people will in turn ginger up city government.

What it requires is for central government to accept the inevitable and devolve power – something I explore further in Chapter 10.

Notes

1. In *The Independent*, London, 24 October 1996.
2. *The Competitive Advantage of Nations*, Macmillan, 1990.
3. *Principles of Economics*, 1890.
4. See Krugman's *Geography and Trade* for the full explanation.
5. See *The Rise and Fall of Regional Inequalities*, Diego Puga, CEPR paper no. 1575.
6. In *Geography and Trade*, MIT Press 1991.
7. In *Scientific American*, February 1990.
8. In *Justice, Nature and the Geography of Distance*.
9. 'Transeconomics' in *The Transparency of Evil*.
10. Conference speech in London, May 1995.
11. In *City of Bits*.
12. In 'The Weightless Economy' column in *Centrepiece*, February 1997.
13. In *The Invisible Hand and the Weightless Economy*, CEP discussion paper, March 1996.
14. In the *New York Times* magazine, October 1996.
15. *After the Nation State*.
16. See, for example, *Making Sense of Subsidiarity*, Begg *et al*.
17. Speech at Future London conference, 11 December 1996.

Chapter Ten

Redesigning Government

The opinions of the philosopher Jean-Jacques Rousseau, one of the early architects of democratic thought, are as fresh now as they were two and a half centuries ago. In an early work, *Political Economy*, he wrote: 'If politicians were less blinded by ambition ... they would realise that political authority has its main source of power in the citizens' hearts'. We are all democrats now; it would be hard to find a politician to disagree with that statement. Yet the pressing problems governments face today, the inequality, poverty, urban squalor and unemployment, are a function of the collapse of political legitimacy in the Western democracies as well as of the fundamental economic trend towards weightlessness.

The two transformations, political and economic, go hand in hand of course. As the last chapter argued, the dematerialisation of value means the economically efficient scale of government has changed, and it has become increasingly clear that national governments cannot manage the national economy as effectively as they have in the past. Even so, the failure of mainstream politicians to acknowledge that the world is a different place has handed those in favour of free markets and a minimal, night watchman state easy victories.

For there is no question that in an increasingly weightless world, with a dramatic increase in the scale and scope of uncertainty, markets play an essential role. There is no possibility of corporatism, of management from the centre of the national economy. Free markets send crucial price and demand signals, and in effect devolve decision-making to the most dispersed level possible. When we cannot even measure or monitor what is happening in the economy, or where it is happening, there is no alternative.

In this chapter, however, I want to make the case for a different role for governments. We need to replace the nanny state of the post-war years with a teacher state, rather than the night watchman. Or, to use a different description, following Anthony Giddens, we need to create a public domain that 'does not situate itself in the old opposition between state and market'.[1] Later, I give examples of what shape of government this might be, but let me start with an everyday illustration of what has gone wrong with the state, involving one of my closest friends.

Jennie is typical of somebody working in the weightless economy. Once a full-time accountant, she now spends a lot of her time bringing up her three children. On top of this unmeasured contribution to the economy, she also makes and paints furniture and gifts to sell at craft fairs. It is as classic a weightless activity as computer programming; she is selling creativity.

The British government, without meaning to, makes it as difficult as possible for this busy and hard-working person to provide for her own economic security. As a married woman not working in a formal job she is not entitled to make any form of pension contributions, and instead has to save without the tax relief available on pensions policies. She is discouraged from growing her tiny business because it would quickly run into the red tape and tax net. It is not worth looking for a job – or at least a job in the formal economy – because she could not afford to pay another woman to look after her children out of her after-tax income. If she did get a part-time job and then became unemployed she would almost certainly not be entitled to claim benefits despite paying taxes. She must operate mainly in the social economy, where she 'trades' services like child care and helping people who have similar businesses to hers.

The nanny state we still have makes life extraordinarily difficult for people like Jennie because it was designed for a fixed world of male, full-time work, which has been consigned to the dustbin of history. The rules cannot accommodate the new, flexible pattern. The night watchman state would respond by shrinking the tax and benefit net to the point where it did little to influence people's choices. The teacher state might, on the other hand, encourage every individual, regardless of their marital status, sex or source of income, to save for their pension by offering tax relief on incomes paid out of their personal retirement plan in old age. In addition to the one person, one pension framework, private but regulated, the government would provide a minimal state safety-net pension for those who had not provided for themselves.

There is nothing original about this suggestion. It is the way debate about pensions has evolved in the UK during the past few years, and is likely to be introduced. It is not dissimilar to what happens in the US, although there large numbers of old people live in poverty because of holes in the safety net. Continental Europe and Japan, with its gigantic pension headache, might follow suit. But it is a good example of teacher state design. What structure of tax and regulation will allow people the most flexibility and opportunity?

This thinking must be extended across the entire range of what governments do, across the welfare state, across regulation, public investment, the tax system and planning laws. We do not need a withdrawal of government so much as a redesign. Nannies make judgements for their protégés and tell them what to do. Teachers let their pupils think for themselves. They provide the stable framework in which people can take on the responsibility for their own judgements and decisions.

Why nanny doesn't know best

Most of this book has dealt with the economic aspects of weightlessness, but it is necessary to stray into political territory. How is fundamental economic change reacting with the political structures of the advanced industrialised countries? The usual, even clichéd, response is that it is all a matter of globalisation, the breaking down of national boundaries to trade and investment combined with the technology that allows companies to take advantage of this. Governments and individual citizens have therefore lost power *vis à vis* global corporations. So it is not that traditional government actions and decisions have become less desirable; they have, rather, become less possible. The old left might hanker after the traditional big government solutions but they are no longer feasible – and some writers spend much energy debating precisely how feasible or infeasible.[2]

This mistaken analysis is what has handed the apparent intellectual victory, certainly since the dramatic implosion of traditional communism and socialism in 1989, to the radical right, the free marketeers. But the growing social tensions and economic inequalities in modern economies, which have provoked a backlash against Reagan or Thatcher style free marketry, indicate that even if eastern European maximum state intervention in the economy did turn out to be a disaster, minimal government is not the right answer either.

In *Beyond Left and Right* Anthony Giddens also uses the concept of globalisation to explain why we need to think about government in a fresh way. But he does acknowledge that globalisation is not just more of the same, even more of the international links than existed before. 'The current period of globalisation is not simply a continuation of the expansion of capitalism.' He uses two concepts that mesh beautifully with weightless economics. The first is 'manufactured uncertainty', the idea that the advance of human knowledge has made the world chronically unpredictable. He gives the example of global warming. The course of human activity and the resulting greenhouse emissions and thinning ozone layer have created the warming phenomenon which is causing climate change. Humans have altered nature with the result that we can no longer take nature as being something 'out there', a fixed environment. We have no idea how minimal or catastrophic the results will be.

In the economic sphere, the course of development has taken us down a path of increasingly weightless and dematerialised production. This means that for the first time there is no economy 'out there' either, no fixed framework of activity within which people have a finite set of choices to make. For economic growth is no longer about growing more food or making more things, about processing physical resources. It is about people performing a growing variety of services, having more ideas, being more creative or entertaining, designing goods to be more beautiful and more useful. 'What is increasingly being produced are not material objects but *signs*.'³ Growth is in a sense more or less what we imagine it to be.

That this makes the world more unpredictable can be seen from the fact that we are not yet able to measure or perhaps even *define* the weightless economy. The clear distinction between work and home, work and play, is vanishing – of which more will be said later. The growth of the social economy (in that space between the market and the public sector) is another facet of the same phenomenon.

The uncertainty that results from the fact that the economy is increasingly the product of our skill and imagination, and cannot be defined in the familiar ways, is linked to another concept used by Giddens and other sociologists. This is *reflexivity*, the idea that the way we react to reality in turn alters the reality we are all reacting to. Economists would call this general equilibrium, the economic outcome where all the feedbacks and reactions between one person and another, one company and another, have been worked through. It is difficult even to prove that an economic general equilibrium exists, never mind establish what it is like. There might not be a stable outcome, a steady state in which an economy can rest. Having defined the idea of general equilibrium, most economists have subsequently ignored it.

Weightless economies are above all reflexive economies. Consumers' choices between the services and goods on offer changes the range of choices. Small, everyday decisions – what to watch on TV, what kind of savings account to open, what toy to buy your child – are swiftly analysed by the broadcaster or bank and alter programming decisions or the design of new products. Because the economic value of production lies increasingly in the parts that are most about matching consumers' dreams and desires – the design or creative content. We are a whole world away from being able to choose any colour car we want as long as it's black.

It is obvious that in this sort of economy, conventional economic management by national governments is just irrelevant. Formal politics barely touches most people's lives, and conventional policies cannot engage with the kinds of economic uncertainty they face. The inherited welfare state, designed for a national economy dominated by conventional jobs in industry, which has come to be identified with the very idea of 'government', is equally irrelevant. Our governments can't control their national economies, can't remove the extensive new economic uncertainties we face, and do not know any better than the rest of us what is happening in the economy. No wonder a disaffection with politics as usual has emerged across the Western world since the late 1980s. The less politicians and the institutions of the state have kept up, the more they have fallen into disrepute.

The clear conclusion is that in a weightless world, political and economic decisions are bound to be widely dispersed. The centre, the government, does not have the answers. It probably does not know the questions either. We have gone beyond nanny's reach into the age of anxiety.

The geography of politics

If every action has an equal and opposite reaction, then globalism means a revival of localism – or so the usual reasoning goes. While it is certainly true that one reaction to the crumbling of national economic boundaries has been a surge of interest in economic devolution – whether on the part of the Scots or Lombardians, or in a more radical way by environmentalists or autarkic militias – thinking of it in these terms is a bit one-dimensional.

The last chapter explored the ways in which weightlessness is altering the location of economic activity. It argued that in several ways it will boost the importance and growth of some big cities. It will lead to the increasing concentration of certain activities in certain places, often building on historical accident. This reinforces the case for transferring some aspects of economic management from national to city governments. In many ways, although it applies everywhere, this is an argument directed more towards the most centralised Western nations, the UK and France. These two countries have fewer big cities than could be expected given their population size because of their excessive centralisation on the capital.[4]

Both capitals, London and Paris, are and will continue to be hugely important cities in the weightless world, alongside New York, Bombay, Tokyo,

Berlin. All these cities are wired-up ferments of creative interaction. They will consolidate their existing leads in their particular areas of strength, whether that is innovative financial services and the music business in London, or industrial design in Tokyo, or movies and software in Bombay. These massive international cities will be where much of the economic growth we are poised to enjoy in the next half century will take place. They will be joined by other urban centres of weightless activities, perhaps Seattle with its software industry, Montpellier with its high-technology parks, Edinburgh with its financial services.

All of them ought to enjoy a much greater degree of self-government than they do now. What business does a centralised national bureaucracy have running any of them? They have varying degrees of freedom to run their own affairs now. London has no elected mayor as I write, although it is due to get one soon, whereas the mayor of New York is a political force to be reckoned with. But at a minimum, all middling to large cities ought to have many of the economic powers that national governments reserve for themselves.

For example, the share of taxes raised and spent within any city should be higher than it is now. (Cities have always subsidised the surrounding economy, as Jane Jacobs points out, so they cannot expect to keep all of the tax revenues raised from their inhabitants.) Planning of the transport infrastructure should be almost entirely a local matter – it sounds obvious enough, but no British city could build a relief road or lay some new tram lines without permission from a central government minister. Cities ought to be able to issue bonds to finance investment projects.

Much of this is already possible in federally structured countries like the US and Germany, but economic devolution will need to go much further in the weightless world. There are two reasons for this. One is that there is a growing advantage to making decisions with better local information. The other is that localism will be the foundation stone for rebuilding trust in government.

Take the need for closer access to information first. The calculation about where it is most efficient to locate responsibility for economic policy involves weighing the economies of scale and equitability of centralisation against the efficiencies arising from exploiting local knowledge and meeting local preferences.[5] Weightlessness is tipping the scales decisively in favour of the latter. Take taxation, for instance. For most of the past century, it has made sense for the national government to levy most taxes. There are definite economies of scale in the administration of the tax system. Patterns of economic growth were very predictable, so running the system from the centre generated stable growth in revenues too. In addition, national taxation has the great merit that revenues can be redistributed from richer to poorer regions.

The first and last points still apply and mean that there will be a place for national taxes for a long time yet. But industrial restructuring is shifting the patterns of activity, making tax revenues unpredictable and shifting spending needs. For example, it is harder to collect value added or sales taxes on weightless activities. It is not impossible, but requires closer, on-the-ground monitoring of business.[6] At the same time, the growth of the social economy and failure of the welfare state are transforming needs for public expenditure. It would make sense to retain a national income tax system to finance central government spending – defence, police, the legal system and so on – and combine it with a local value added tax to finance local, social spending. It will be easier to monitor those needs and collect those taxes at a more local level.

And it would still allow redistribution of resources, given that almost all urban regions are a patchwork of widely varying districts. Central governments have failed utterly in tackling urban ghettos. These concentrations of poverty, unemployment, lack of infrastructure, social and cultural deprivation and absence of economic activity present horribly intractable problems. There is not going to be a one-size-fits-all solution that can be worked out in the capital. Each inner-city problem area will need a different patchwork of approaches. In one it might be altering road layouts to prevent youths racing stolen cars. Another might need to demolish tower blocks or projects and build a different style of housing with fewer long walkways and more green patches. Another might need improved public transport links to another area of the city where work is available. All will need to develop links with companies based in the same city to negotiate jobs for local people. There is no way the central government can know. It will be a matter of experiment, pilot schemes and listening to local demands. And politicians in those towns and cities, as a matter of both pride and the well-being of all their citizens, will have a much stronger incentive than central government to make these experiments work if they have the authority to do so.

The other merit in a serious devolution of economic policy making is that it would start to repair people's diminished trust in their government. It is not that we have become any less patriotic. But we don't feel the same about our politicians or political institutions. In all the industrial democracies this loss of respect has been various and widespread, from Italy with its *tangentopoli* scandal and the uncovering of the embrace between the state and the Mafia, to the Perot phenomenon or upsurge in militia activity in the US, to the astonishing landslide victory for the New Labour party in the UK – and for Martin Bell, an independent 'anti-sleaze' candidate – when the electorate gave its emphatic verdict on the 18-year record of the previous government.

Take these reports from one newspaper on one day, chosen at random. In one, Thierry Flandin, a regional councillor for Donzy in the Nievre, was reported to be worried about the national mood. 'There is a disaffection from politics, from the state itself, which goes deeper than anything he can remember. It is partly the result of the many political–financial scandals. It is partly a sense that decisions are being taken out of the hands of elected politicians and being taken over by Europe or the markets.' M. Flandin said: 'We know in our hearts that France needs to take a crucial step forward'.[7]

A few pages further on, Silvio Berlusconi, head of Italy's Fininvest business empire and former prime minister, gave his reaction to the 18-month suspended prison sentence passed on another top businessman, Cesare Romiti, chairman of Fiat, for payments to politicians from an illegal slush fund. Berlusconi said: 'I'm sorry about the verdict because I know that for many companies these financial donations are necessary to be able to keep working. We all know this.' The reporter concluded that the *tangentopoli* scandal had changed nothing, and the popular revulsion over the corruption of the Italian state had probably come to nothing.[8]

The philosopher Gillian Rose argued that one of the failings of conventional politics has been its failure to acknowledge the centralised state's monopoly of power which was formerly dispersed across a range of quasi-independent institutions, including local government and community groups. The growing irrelevance of conventional politics has also been mirrored in the spread of interest group and lifestyle politics, especially among young people. A sort of alternative opposition movement has developed, embracing environmentalists, animal rights groups, local activists and human development organisations.

The loss of trust in political institutions is one reason why funding the welfare state has become so difficult. People do not want to hand over a quarter or a third of their income to politicians they do not trust to spend it wisely. This resistance has been understood by more thoughtful politicians. One suggestion has been to earmark tax increases for particular areas of spending, such as schools or health care. However, 'hypothecated' taxes like this have the drawback that it might not make sense to spend, say, all revenues raised from taxing cars and petrol on building roads. They also invariably merge into the general public finances within a few years.

Trust can be rebuilt much more effectively by taxing and spending closer to home. Taxpayers would literally be able to go and see some of the things their money was being spent on. There is an appetite for tighter accountability and closer scrutiny which can be met by a radical devolution of government. The time is ripe for a rediscovery of civic pride. It happened at the end of the nineteenth century, when the civic monuments of the Industrial Revolution were built as an expression of economic vibrancy. It could happen at the end of this century too.

The new school rules

I have argued that governments must cede power in two directions. One is acknowledging the role of markets because of the inevitable uncertainty that is the product of the weightless economy. In many respects, such as creating jobs or fostering national champions or controlling trade and investment flows, government intervention is no longer possible. No government can know enough for this classic type of intervention to work. Similarly, the traditional welfare state does not work any more. It makes no sense to compensate people for the loss of full-time, permanent jobs in given industries when that is not how most people work. As Giddens puts it: 'Welfare institutions have their beginnings in the effort to create a society in which work, meaning paid labour in industry, has a central and defining role'.

Most Western governments have accepted this case for markets – perhaps to excess. But with the dominance of the idea of globalisation, and the loss of power to the market this has come to stand for, few have turned their attention to the other direction in which they will gradually lose power – namely, to more devolved levels of government, at least in big cities. The theme of localism will come to be as prominent as globalism, however.

So what is there left for national governments to do? One answer is that they must create the framework for the teacher state. This will have a lot to do with setting out rules of behaviour. It will involve mediating between the global and the local, and maintaining economic institutions – at a minimum, making markets work properly. Let me give four examples here.

International financial regulation

The financial markets represent the ultimate weightless economic activity, located as they are in cyberspace. The popular view that the markets are the playground of lawless fiscal vigilantes is an exaggeration but there is a grain of truth in it. There have indeed been extraordinary scandals. Rogue derivatives trader Nick Leeson lost nearly £1 billion and brought down Barings Bank, one of the oldest and most blue-blooded in the City of London. Copper trader Yasuo Hamanaka did not topple Sumitomo in Japan, but caused it severe embarrassment as well as losses of billions of dollars. Proctor & Gamble lost $102 million after tax on two derivatives transactions arranged by Bankers Trust in 1994. It alleged that the bank had not explained the risks, although the matter was settled out of court two years later. Derivatives also bankrupted Germany's giant engineering group Metallgesellschaft.

Nor is it just a matter of cheating and scandal. It was perfectly legitimate flows of international capital that caused the Mexican crisis at the end of 1994. Co-ordinating the regulation of the financial markets is, rightly, one of the top items on the agenda at all the international meetings of ministers and central bankers. National regulators will need to exchange information and act for each other far more often than they have in the past.

National pride still gets in the way, unfortunately. The American government has dragged its feet over a proposal from other countries in the Group of Seven industrial countries to choose a 'lead regulator' for each bank – a regulatory institution in one country would be responsible for co-ordinating information and calling meetings about the banks for which it had the lead role. Cynics also reckon the $50 billion rescue package for Mexico only worked because the Americans were unequivocally in charge. The US Treasury certainly offended other governments at various points during the rescue because of its high-handedness. These kinds of obstacles must be overcome. Governments will have to co-operate to police multinational banks, enforce contracts, co-ordinate rescues when a bank or country is in danger of going under, and even lend each other vast amounts of money in emergencies.

In *The Transparency of Evil*, Jean Baudrillard portrays the global capital markets as an extreme phenomenon divorced from real economies. 'Our only reality is an unchecked orbital whirl of capital, which, when it does crash, causes no substantial disequilibrium in real economies ... The realm of mobile and speculative capital has achieved so great an autonomy that even its cataclysms leave no traces.' It is a neat idea to see the financial markets as so hyper-real that they do not impinge on ordinary folks, working and shopping and eating and sleeping. But wrong. Any Mexican could correct Baudrillard, any of the people who relied on the charitable trust funded by Barings, or anybody whose pension fund lost value as a result of the drop in Proctor & Gamble's share price. Regulating financial markets on a global scale through co-operation is one of the key tasks of governments.

Building the information superhighway

This is a slightly tongue-in-cheek way of saying that governments need to guarantee the infrastructure in a modern economy. The infrastructure ranges from conventional things like bridges, roads, airports, hospitals and schools to requirements like a fibre-optic cable network, through to new, weightless infrastructure like the school and university system and networks of people.

This does not necessarily mean that they have to pay for it all or own it all. But they will often need to subsidise investment in all these varieties of infrastructure. If people are to cope with uncertainty, they need some certainties about the framework. It is a minimum requirement for governments to guarantee that it is adequate. Just as bridges must not be allowed to collapse, phone systems must have had enough investment and work reliably. This type of infrastructure needs to be regulated so that everyone has access, charging is fair and disputes can be resolved. The planning and regulation of infrastructure will turn out to be the single most important task of governments. This kind of social investment overcomes one of the textbook examples of why markets fail – when the return to society as a whole far exceeds the return an individual investor could hope for.

What is new is that infrastructure investment is increasingly international. Just as in the case of financial markets, national governments will need to negotiate international agreements. A good example is the attempt to reach a world-wide agreement on the assignment of Internet domain names, the on-line equivalent of street addresses. Previously, it was always a question of first come, first served for names in the relatively few 'domains' available to private users, either *.com* or country specific variants of *.co.uk*. A few entrepreneurs had wisely bought up a lot of obvious names and then offered them for sale to the obvious user at a much higher price. An agreement would allow an escape from this type of blackmail by creating a much wider range of suffixes. The first attempt failed, but this is exactly the kind of negotiation governments are needed for.

Other examples would be air travel, where the investment required covers air traffic control, air space agreements and safety measures; and telecommunications, where there will be a growing need for common standards and pricing. Anything that concerns how we connect with each other around the world is a candidate for government involvement, monitoring and regulation.

Educational and professional standards should be included here. Although people do have an incentive to invest in their own education and training because more highly educated people generally earn more, there is a good case for seeing investment in people's skills and attainments as an investment in weightless infrastructure. Weightless industries need large numbers of people with creativity and skill and a high standard of education; and it will benefit the economy as a whole if schools, colleges and universities can deliver these high standards.

At least this is not a difficult case to argue. One thing politicians in the Western countries have learnt from rapidly industrialising countries like Korea is that an emphasis on education is an important ingredient in economic miracles. Education has been, on paper at least, an important policy priority for several governments, including Tony Blair's. It has also been a theme of the Clinton administration, following the advice of Robert Reich, its former Labor Secretary, who pointed out that the brains of its people were the least mobile and most fertile natural resource any modern economy could hope for.[9] Investing in brains would pay big dividends, he suggested. Harvard University professor Edward Glaeser has put this very succinctly: 'Computers are not a substitute for human brains. Rather, they work together.' Brain power leverages computer power.[10]

The difficult part is knowing how to put it into practice. It is going to require a mix of setting appropriate standards and channelling adequate resources into schools and universities. People are certainly willing to pay large amounts of money for their children's education, but as in other areas do not necessarily trust the political process enough to pay for it in the public sector through taxes. This is something that varies so widely by country that it is impossible to generalise. The one sure bet is that education will everywhere be one of the hot-button issues in politics for years to come.

One crucial aspect will be providing equal access to new technologies.

Now is absolutely the time to prevent a gap opening between the digital haves and have-nots.

Rules for international trade and investment

The international community has kept in mind for the past 50 years the lessons of protectionism in the 1930s and the subsequent world war. Enormous diplomatic effort has been focused on delivering progressively freer trade and capital movements, in order to avoid the danger of a return to that damaging isolationism and conflict that characterised the disastrous first half of this century. The reward has been an enormous increase in prosperity for those industrial nations that have engaged in the international system on the terms laid down by its policemen, notably the International Monetary Fund. The recession of the early 1990s brought challenges to the free trade, free investment, free market system, however. Protectionist voices were raised, by politicians like Pat Buchanan and troublemakers like James Goldsmith (a man whose shoddy and ranting books suggest he got far more respectful a hearing than he deserved from the French technocrats who would prefer to carry on directing the economy from the centre).

Many experts subscribe to the 'bicycle theory' on trade negotiations: without keeping up the constant motion they fall over. There were successive rounds of removing trade barriers under the auspices of the General Agreement on Tariffs and Trade, progressing from simple manufactures to complex services. It has been replaced by the World Trade Organisation (WTO). Its task is more difficult than overseeing the removal of tariffs and quotas on tangible goods. In an increasingly weightless world, guaranteeing free trade becomes less to do with trade in the sense of shipments of items across boundaries, and more to do with co-ordinating national policies that have international spillovers. For example, trade in engineering consultancy, say, or telecommunications services will be hindered by governments that set technical standards that differ too much from everybody else's. Before weightlessness, it would have astonished industry ministry officials to be told that specifications for the type of concrete to be used in bridges could amount to an illegal hindrance to free trade.

The WTO, and its member governments, will find themselves negotiating over competition and technology policies, over rules for government purchases of goods and services (public procurement), and increasingly over protection of the environment and human rights.

Keeping up the momentum is necessary to improve prosperity, not only for the already rich countries but also for the still poor ones. For weightlessness gives poor countries a chance to leapfrog their way into a higher economic league. This is partly because multinationals are investing more in operations in the third world. Nike subcontracts to Indonesian shoe manufacturers, Indian programmers write software code for US computer corporations or run the back office for British Airways' ticketing operation. These are familiar examples of how the multinationals can save money by paying much lower than Western wages and the locals get better jobs at higher than local wages.

It is also because there will be unexpected sources of value in the weightless world. And just as the oil reserves of the OPEC countries turned into a bonanza for them in the mid-1970s, some poor countries might have what turns out to be a valuable resource. This could be just large numbers of young people, for the OECD countries are already importing large numbers of them on the quiet, and as discussed in Chapter 7 there will be more demand for 'imports' of unskilled workers to fill some categories of jobs. Equally, it could be a type of music that will sweep the world and enrich its performers; or tourism for that matter.

Environmental regulation

Concern for the environment is a luxury. People who live in poverty care much more about getting enough to eat this season than about protecting the soil in the long term. Those living in developing countries will want to get their fridges, cars and hairsprays before they start to worry about greenhouse emissions. It is the richest countries in the world that care the most about the environment – they have done the most to despoil it in the past, but can also afford to think about it from the midst of their plenty.

Weightlessness offers hope that future growth in the rich part of the world will not put the same pressures on the environment. The great thing about dematerialised production is that it does not use physical resources. The natural resource cost of financial services is extremely low compared to steel mills; they use less power, fewer raw materials and emit fewer pollutants. Of course, we have not stopped being consumers; but rather than wanting to own more and more cars, we want to own the same number, just better designed and engineered. We do not want an ever-increasing number of pairs of shoes, but want the ones we have to be exquisitely beautiful or comfortable and have the right brand name attached.

This is the sense in which optimists like *Wired* magazine can talk about the end of scarcity. According to its manifesto: 'Today's leaders scorn the possibility of a golden age in which economies are based on limitless ideas, not limited materials. They refuse to see that abundance, not scarcity, drives the future.'

The tricky thing for governments will be international agreement over environmental standards because Western governments are in a weak position to demand from developing countries higher environmental standards during the course of industrialisation – are we to tell the Indians and Brazilians that we can have a car for every two households but they cannot? The signing of the Rio Agreement on reducing greenhouse gases was a great achievement. Policing and enforcing it has been difficult and disappointing. And there are other areas of environmental spillover where there are no agreements. Can and should countries export toxic waste? Build more nuclear power stations – or be trusted to run their existing plants? The promise of the weightless world is vulnerable to ecological catastrophe. Although we do not know what the price of an explosion worse than Chernobyl would be, the ultimate costs in well-being and wealth could be enormous.

Out of the welfare net

These tasks – setting regulations, reaching international agreements, setting standards – are the backroom work of government. Most of the hard work is done by civil servants and experts, and there seems to be little role for politics beyond the obvious choice between engaging with the world and closing it off. There is only one option. It is all very worthy but pretty boring. Surely there is more to government than that?

On the domestic stage, the task for governments is to transform themselves from an administrator of the welfare state on behalf of passive recipients into an investor in active citizens able to create their own welfare. The outlines of how they should go about this are beginning to emerge.

Earlier I gave the example of pensions. Most Western economies face a funding crisis in the state provision of pensions. Those, like the UK, that do not face the corresponding problem of the likelihood of having large numbers of pensioners living in poverty. During the next 50 years those of us who are some distance from retirement will change our behaviour as a result – retire later, save more.

But there is, nearly, a consensus about how the government should restructure pension provision in the most helpful way, with a bottom state tier, a low flat rate for everyone, and a top-up individual tier, properly administered and regulated. This second tier could be run privately or publicly – there might be advantages in government-run schemes. It would, however, be a pension linked to individual contributions invested in a fund, rather than paid for out of current taxes. This would mark a return to the original welfare state principle of insurance against a fairly predictable risk, namely old age.[11]

Similar principles could apply to other types of risk – the lifestyle risks where there is enough predictability for the principle of self-insurance to apply. This would probably work for old-age care. It could work for some kinds of health care too, such as childbirth, varicose veins or prostate troubles. Most voters still think of welfare as 'national insurance' and it need not prove difficult to reintroduce the notion.

There is significantly less agreement about what governments should be doing about the other aspects of the welfare state, about its post-war aims of redistribution and social assistance. It is not straightforward to insure against unpredictable risks in an age of general uncertainty – that is how many governments got into such a fiscal pickle. This lesson must be learnt. The government is not the answer. The social security safety net, designed 50 years ago and patched up meanwhile, has become a net that traps rather than a net that saves. The welfare state, across the rich countries of the world, has patently not reduced inequality, not redistributed incomes and not eliminated concentrations of poverty. We could scarcely do worse by the poorest sections of society if we eliminated most of it.

As discussed in Chapter 5, the operation of the social security system positively hinders the expansion of the social economy, which is where more and more people will find some of their income, employment and social support. It is an urgent priority in welfare reform to eliminate the restrictive rules and poverty traps that current systems suffer in proliferation. Some of this will be a matter of scrapping the kinds of regulations with which officials like to keep their supplicants in order. For example, there is no excuse for rules that forbid benefit claimants to undertake voluntary work or go on training courses. They should be abolished immediately. It might mean a few people draw state handouts when they might have taken paid work instead – a small price to pay for eliminating the incentive to cheat and lie, and for engaging other claimants in a more productive use of their time.

Another malign effect of most social security systems is the poverty trap. This means that it is usually not worth benefit recipients taking a job because the pay is too low to compensate for the sudden loss of a whole range of benefits as well as income support – rent or mortgage payments, health treatments, free school meals and cheap uniforms for the children, right the way through to cheaper entry fees to the swimming pool and no fines on library books.

One solution is to phase out benefits slowly for people who move from unemployment into a job – fearsomely expensive, complicated, and involving intrusive means tests. Another is not to pay so many benefits in the same form in the first place. It is a perhaps unpalatable truth that long-term unemployment exists where long-term unemployment benefits are paid. Where they are not paid, like the US, people take whatever work they can when their benefits run out. Is it better to have them in bad jobs or on the dole for months or years?

This is a real political choice. My view is that bad jobs are better; they might just lead on to not quite such bad jobs, and psychological surveys show that nobody is unhappier than the unemployed. Both the US and the UK have got to the point where political opinion across much of the spectrum agrees, and schemes that withdraw the option of remaining unemployed and on benefit have been introduced. The results have been dramatic. In both countries official unemployment has fallen to the lowest levels for nearly 20 years. A lot of cheating of the system has been forcibly eliminated, and benefit recipients have either moved into jobs or into the social economy. Opinion in continental Europe is far from reaching this stage, however. It clings to the myth that if only the social engineering could be fine-tuned it would be possible to turn the clock back.

The underlying problem is the fact that the welfare state is built around the notion of The Job. The full-time job reliably paying enough to support the whole family. Anthony Giddens writes: 'Unemployment can't even exist without a basic element of subjective experience: to be unemployed one has to want to have a paid job. And not just a job; virtually no-one who is unemployed would take *any* job that was available.' The era of The Job, an artefact of factory capitalism, is drawing to an end.

Giddens seems to envisage some form of job-sharing as a solution. This has been a popular proposal in France, where the government introduced a subsidy for companies that increase their workforce by 10 per cent by reducing working hours for existing employees. But this falls into the trap of assuming there is a fixed pot of work available to be shared more or less fairly – the 'lump of labour' fallacy, as economists call it. It does not escape from the tyranny of thinking about people's options in terms of jobs and not-jobs.

For an alternative vision, let's turn to science fiction. Neal Stephenson's view about how people will make their way in the world in *Snow Crash* is at least as plausible as the jobbist outlook. It starts with a very a distinctive and American view of the role of government. The Federal Government in a future USA has put all Federal buildings in Washington DC out to a tourism concession.

> *'Government should govern. It's not in the entertainment industry, is it? Leave entertaining to Industry weirdoes – people who majored in tap dancing. Feds aren't like that. Feds are serious people. Poli sci majors. Student council presidents. Debate club chairpersons ... The kinds of people who would feel most at home on the dark side of a one-way mirror.'*

It's a little extreme, but those who are on the receiving end of government – receiving social security – will identify with the spirit of it. The most junior clerk in a benefit office will make sure the 'customers' are in no doubt where the power in the relationship lies.

The Feds are the only people in the novel who have what we would recognise as a job. Others work on tasks which they are then paid for. The protagonist, Hiro, finds pieces of information which he sells. And delivers pizzas. Heroine Y.T. is a courier, although as she lives with her mother this need not provide her with a full and rounded income. Other characters include a rock musician and a computer programmer. It is a world closer to the mediaeval order where people invested in a craft skill which created the basis for them to earn a living than to the passing modern world of selling your time to an employer for a fixed amount of money.

Futurology is a risky business, best done in fiction. But I will hazard a prediction that in another half century's time relatively few people will spend all their working time for long periods with a single employer. There will be a wide variety of patterns, from the Charles Handy type of portfolio career for the affluent and highly qualified executive to the modern equivalent of mediaeval craftsmen – freelance writers, TV producers, piano teachers, plumbers; from the unskilled who are shunted from job to bad short-term job as a cleaner or hamburger flipper, to people who stay entirely in the social economy, working in their own family and neighbourhood.

Do we need welfare, social security, in this kind of world? Probably not.

Government resources could be better focused than on trying to glue back together a disintegrating world of full-time, permanent employment. If it is to spend, better to spend on giving people anything they want by way of training or child care – preventive spending – rather than paying benefits – palliative spending – except when it is absolutely necessary. A switch to preventive spending would do better at reducing inequality and equalising opportunities than the welfare trap the Western economies have accidentally created.

The end of clock time

One of the badges of the weightless world is that economic activity can take place anywhere. At a minimum, modern technology and communications mean the link binding work to workplace is crumbling. Businessmen carry their laptop computers and mobile phones everywhere, engineers and drivers are attached to pagers. A writer, record producer or advertising executive can be thinking about her work anywhere. It is increasingly people, not places, who define an organisation. And the work attaches itself to the person not the place.

The clear divorce between home and workplace, between leisure and working hours, that has characterised the industrial economies, is drawing to a close. In a classic article the historian E.P. Thompson described the evolution of how people understood time as the Industrial Revolution progressed.[12] Before the factory era, people described a length of time as how long it would take to do something. Eight hours would be 'a sleeping-time', a minute or so 'a pissing-time'. Then came factories and clocks. What workers were selling was not their knowledge, skill or craft, and what they could accomplish with it, but their time. Time was therefore money, and punctuality everything. This reached its apogee under Taylorism, the religion of time-and-motion studies.

There are still plenty of factories in the Western economies where employees are cannon fodder, required to process as many of whatever it might be as possible for every minute of the shift. There are security guards and care workers who are kept to the clock or, like junior doctors everywhere, beyond it. But there are fewer and fewer of them in increasingly weightless economies. More people are selling not their time but their skill or creativity. Employers are increasingly judging and paying them for their ideas rather than their presence. The people who are still selling their presence can often decide for themselves when they will work. Newspaper proprietors do not care whether or not they see a columnist every day as long as the column appears on time and is a good read. A trader in the financial markets has to be on-line at his terminal at particular hours when the markets he deals in are open, and often at home too; but most will plan to work like this for a few years and retire from it when they choose, as their pay makes this pattern possible.

In fact, the range of work patterns is expanding dramatically. Although many professionals complain now about putting in ultra-long hours at work, this is probably transitional, as they and their employers adjust to the fact that more work does not have to correspond to more hours.

Governments are learning the lesson that many big companies have taken to heart during the past five years. Businesses have learnt that it is no longer possible to run a huge, centralised organisation because the central brain cannot monitor or respond to the huge volumes of information in the weightless world. Survival requires decentralisation and dispersion. Similarly, it makes no sense to employ factory fodder. Employees must have the responsibility for taking decisions and for organising their own use of time.

Indeed, increasing numbers of workers are using technology whose unit of time is the nano-second — about half the workforce already in the US. According to sociologists Scott Lash and John Urry: 'It follows that when many important activities take place below the threshold of human consciousness, then social time as structured by the clock becomes progressively less relevant to the contemporary organisation of human society'.[13]

It will become plain impossible, as the range of possible working patterns expands, to sustain existing social security systems. It will become too unclear what being out of work means or exactly what the government is supposed to be compensating people for. The framework is too rigid. If our political leaders want to regain our trust – our hearts – they must become as flexible as we will be in the weightless world.

The weightless future

'To study unemployment and its effects you have got to go to the industrial areas ... It is only when you lodge in streets where nobody has a job, where getting a job seems about as probable as owning an aeroplane and much less probable than winning fifty pounds on the football pools, that you begin to grasp the changes that are being worked in our civilisation.'[14]

He was describing Britain in 1937. But George Orwell's classic description of economic misery and social trauma 60 years ago could, with due allowance for poetic licence, apply today in many of the industrial world's cities.

Most citizens of the industrialised world face threats and upheavals arising from this century's new industrial revolution. Unemployment is stubbornly high. Inequality is growing. People are insecure in their jobs and incomes. The future of pensions and the welfare safety net is under threat. Crime is on the increase. All around, especially in our cities, we see social and physical decay.

It is not hard to identify the forces generating this state of uncertainty. There is the breathtaking spread of information technology. There is the ageing and shrinking of Western populations in contrast to the youth and growth of third world countries. And there is the upheaval in political thought triggered by the fact that capitalism won the Cold War but cannot solve the economic crisis.

It is not surprising, then, that apocalyptic prophesy is back in vogue. Most commentators on our economies are pessimistic.

Their pessimism is full of paradoxes, however. The end of work is nigh; yet human knowledge and people are the key to success in business. We are heading for a crisis in paying for pensions because there are too few people of working age; yet mass unemployment is here to stay. High technology is making workers obsolete; but we are undermining our own industries with our demand for labour-intensive imports.

This book has argued that it is perverse to be pessimistic about huge advances in technology that enhance human creativity and effort, or about political developments that hold out the promise of minimally decent living standards for millions of the world's poor for the first time ever. We are not necessarily heading for twenty-first century economic apocalypse.

What we do face, as in Orwell's time, and as in the last industrial revolution, is a mammoth problem of transition and distribution. The world is a riskier place. People in the industrialised world are ill-equipped to deal with their loss of security and are governed by profoundly undemocratic economic institutions. Individuals must have a greater stake in shaping their own future if they are to be equipped to cope with new economic uncertainties.

This requires a redrafting of the economic policy map. Just as the political importance of the nation state has declined, so has its economic influence. Policies need to be shaped internationally and locally as well as nationally. This is a debate whose resonances are obvious in Europe, where the structure of power in the EU and its defences against the outside world are amongst the most bitterly contested political issues. But it is just as important in North America, where anti-government, anti-federal and anti-international forces are gaining strength.

Elsewhere George Orwell wrote: 'The energy that actually shapes the world springs from emotions – racial pride, leader-worship, religious belief, love of war – which liberal intellectuals mechanically write off as anachronisms, and which they have usually destroyed so completely in themselves as to have lost all power of action.'[15]

The world today is rocked by emotions fierce enough to threaten the real achievements of the post-war era. Emotion won in the 1930s. It has already had its victories in the 1990s. Anybody who values peace and economic progress has a duty to address the nuts and bolts of policies that might chip away at economic problems – and to turn a deaf ear to the siren voices of apocalypse.

Notes

1. *Beyond Left and Right*, Introduction.
2. See, for example, Hirst and Thomson.
3. Lash and Urry.
4. I am grateful to Paul Krugman for pointing this out.
5. See, for example, *Making Sense of Subsidiarity*, Begg *et al*.
6. See Neil Barrett, *State of the Cybernation*.
7. Report by John Lichfield, *Independent on Sunday*, London, 18 May 1997.
8. Report by Andrew Gumbel, *Independent on Sunday*, London, 18 May 1997.
9. In *The Work of Nations*.
10. In *1997 Global Competitiveness Report*, World Economic Forum.
11. See Report published by the Joseph Rowntree Foundation, edited by John Hills, Autumn 1997.
12. *Time, Work Discipline and Industrial Capitalism*, Past and Present 1967.
13. *Economies of Signs and Space*, 1994.
14. *The Road to Wigan Pier*.
15. *Collected Essays*, Vol. 2.

Bibliography

George Alogoskoufis, Charles Bean, Giuseppe Bertola, Daniel Cohen, Juan Dolado & Gilles St Paul (April 1995) *Unemployment: Choices for Europe*, Centre for Economic Policy Research, London.

Anonymous (1996) *Primary Colors*, Chatto & Windus, London.

Brian Arthur (February 1990) 'Positive feedback in the economy', *Scientific American*.

Brian Arthur (July/August 1996) 'Increasing returns and the two worlds of business', *Harvard Business Review*.

Correlli Barnett (1995) *The Lost Victory*, Macmillan, London.

Neil Barrett (1996) *The State of the Cybernation*, Kogan Page, London.

Roland Barthes (1957) *Mythologies*, first published Editions du Seuil, Paris.

Jean Baudrillard (1993) *The Transparency of Evil*, Verso, London.

David Begg, Jaques Cremer, Jean-Pierre Danthine *et al.* (November 1993) *Making Sense of Subsidiarity*, Centre for Economic Policy Research, London.

T. Coraghessan Boyle (1996) *The Tortilla Curtain*, Bloomsbury, London.

Moshe Buchinsky & Jennifer Hunt (February 1996) *Wage Mobility in the US*, National Bureau of Economic Research Working Paper 5455, National Bureau of Economic Research, Cambridge, MA.

Daniel Cohen (1995) *The Misfortunes of Prosperity*, MIT Press, Cambridge, MA.

Michael Connors (1996) *The Race to the Intelligent State*, Capstone, Oxford.

Steven Davis, John Haltiwanger & Scott Schuh (1996) *Job Creation and Destruction*, MIT Press, Cambridge, MA.

Ralf Dahrendorf, ed. (1995) *Report on Wealth Creation and Social Cohesion*.

Paul David (May 1990) The Dynamo and the Computer, *American Economic Review*.

Richard Disney (1996) *Can We Afford to Grow Older?* MIT Press, Cambridge, MA.

Friedrich Engels (first published 1845) *The Condition of the Working Class in England in 1844*.

Amitai Etzioni (1993) *The Spirit of Community*, Simon & Schuster., London

Frank Field (1994) *Making Welfare Work*, Institute of Community Studies, London.

Robert Frank & Philip Cook (1995) *The Winner-Takes-All Society*, The Free Press, New York.

Jostein Gaarder (1995) *Sophie's World*, Phoenix House, London.

John Kenneth Galbraith (1991; first published 1958) *The Affluent Society*, Penguin, London

John Kenneth Galbraith (1992) *The Culture of Contentment*, Sinclair Stevenson, London.

Jess Gaspar and Edward Glaeser (1996) *Information Technology and the Future of Cities*, Boston University working paper.

Jeffrey Gates (1996) *Revolutionising Share Ownership*, Demos Arguments no. 8, Demos, London.

William Gibson (1984) *Neuromancer*, Voyager Books, London

William Gibson (1986) *Burning Chrome*, Voyager Books, London.

Anthony Giddens (1994) *Beyond Left and Right*, Polity Press, Cambridge.

George Gissing (first published 1891) *New Grub Street*.

James Goldsmith (1994) *The Trap*, Macmillan, London.

John Gray (1993) *Post-Liberalism*, Routledge, London.

Paul Gregg, ed. (1997) *Jobs, Wages and Poverty*, Centre for Economic Performance, London School of Economics, London.

Lawrence Grossman (1995) *The Electronic Republic*, Penguin, London.

Ben Hamper (1992) *Rivethead*, Fourth Estate, London.

Charles Handy (1989) *The Age of Unreason*, Arrow Business Books, London.

Charles Handy (1994) *The Empty Raincoat*, Hutchinson, London.

Mahbub ul Haq, ed. (1996) *The Tobin Tax*, Oxford University Press, Oxford.

Nigel Harris (1996) *The New Untouchables*, I.B. Tauris, London.

Paul Harrison, (1983) *Inside the Inner City*, Pelican, London.

David Harvey (1996) *Justice, Nature and the Geography of Difference*, Blackwell, Oxford.

John Heilemann (March 1996) 'The new economy, stupid', *Wired* magazine, San Francisco, CA.

John Hills, ed. (1996) *New Inequalities*, Cambridge University Press, Cambridge.

John Hills (July 1997) *Rowntree Title*, Joseph Rowntree Foundation, York.

Paul Hirst & Grahame Thompson (1996) *Globalisation in Question*, Polity Press, Cambridge.

Mathew Horsman & Andrew Marshall (1994) *After the Nation State*, HarperCollins, London.

Peter Huber (2 December 1996) 'Cyber Power', *Forbes*, New York.

Mike Hudson (1995) *Managing Without Profit*, Penguin, London.

Jane Jacobs (1984) *Cities and the Wealth of Nations*, Random House/Viking, London.

Jane Jacobs (1961) *The Life and Death of Great American Cities*, Jonathan Cape, London.

Thierry Jeantet (1986) *La modernisation de la France par l'Economie Sociale*.

Peter Kenen, ed. (1994) *Managing the World Economy*, Institute for International Economics, Washington, DC.

Paul Kennedy (30 May 1996) *Analysis lecture*, BBC Radio 4.

Paul Krugman (1993) *Geography and Trade*, MIT Press, Cambridge, MA.

Paul Krugman (1994) *Peddling Prosperity*, Norton, London.

Paul Krugman (1996) *Pop Internationalism*, MIT Press, Cambridge, MA.

Milan Kundera (1996) *Slowness*, Faber & Faber, London (first published in French 1995).

Scott Lash and John Urry (1994) *Economies of Signs and Space*, Sage, London.

Richard Layard (1997) *What Labour Can Do*, Warner Books, London.

Charles Leadbeater (1997) *The Rise of the Social Entrepreneur*, Demos, London.

Doris Lessing writing as Jane Somers (1983) *The Diary of a Good Neighbour*, Vintage, London.

Michael Lewis (1989) *Liar's Poker: Two Cities, True Greed*, Hodder & Stoughton, London.

Alain Lipietz (first published in English 1992) *Towards a New Economic Order*, Polity Press, Cambridge.

Edwin Luttwak (9 May 1996) 'Buchanan has it right', *London Review of Books*.

Jay McInerney (1992) *Brightness Falls*, Bloomsbury, London.

David Marquand (July 1996) *The Great Reckoning*, Prospect, London.

Francois Maspero (1994) *Roissy Express*, Verso, London (first published by Editions du Seuil, 1990).

Henry Mayhew (first published 1851–2) *London Labour and the London Poor*.

Edmond Malinvaud (1994) *Mass Unemployment*, Blackwell Publishers, Oxford.

Andrew Marr (1995) *Ruling Britannia*, Michael Joseph, London.

Paul Masson and Michael Mussa (December 1995) 'Long-term tendencies in budget deficits and debt', IMF Working Paper.

Pamela Meadows, ed. (1996) *Work out – or work in?*, Joseph Rowntree Foundation, York.

David Miles (June 1996) *Savings and Wealth*, Merrill Lynch.

David Miles (January 1997) 'A household level study of the determinants of income and consumption', *Economic Journal*.

Hamish McRae (1994) *The World in 2020*, HarperCollins, London.

Geoff Mulgan, ed. (1997) *Life After Politics*, Fontana, London.

Nicholas Negroponte (1995) *Being Digital*, Hodder & Stoughton, London.

Richard O'Brien (1992) *The End of Geography*, Royal Institute of International Affairs, London.

OECD (1991) *Technology and Productivity: the Challenge for Economic Policy*, Organisation for Economic Co-operation and Development, Paris.

OECD (1992) *Technology and the Economy: The Key Relationships*, Organisation for Economic Co-operation and Development, Paris.

OECD (1994) *OECD Jobs Study: Evidence and Explanations*, Vols I and II, Organisation for Economic Co-operation and Development, Paris.

OECD (1996) *The Knowledge-Based Economy*, Organisation for Economic Co-operation and Development, Paris.

OECD (1995, 1996, 1997) *Employment Outlook*, Organisation for Economic Co-operation and Development, Paris.

George Orwell (first published 1936) *The Road to Wigan Pier*.

John Philpott, ed. (1997) *Working for Full Employment*, Routledge, London.

John Plender (1997) *A Stake in the Future*, Nicholas Brealey, London.

Michale Porter (1990) *The Competitive Advantage of Nations*, Macmillan, London.

Diego Puga (February 1997) 'The rise and fall of regional inequalities', Discussion Paper 1575, Centre for Economic Policy Research, London.

Robert Putnam (1993) *Making Democracy Work: Civic Traditions in Modern Italy*, Princeton University Press, Princeton, NJ.

Robert Putnam (January 1995) 'Bowling alone: America's declining social capital', *Journal of Democracy*, **6** (1).

Danny Quah (March 1996) 'The invisible hand and the weightless economy', Centre for Economic Performance working paper, London School of Economics, London.

Danny Quah (July 1996) 'Twin Peaks: growth and convergence in models of distribution dynamics', *Economic Journal*.

Danny Quah (October 1996) *Discarding Non-stick Frying Pans for Economic Growth*, Centrepiece, Centre for Economic Performance, London School of Economics, London.

Gregory Rawlins (1996) *Moths to the Flame*, MIT Press, Cambridge, MA.

Robert Reich (1991) *The Work of Nations*, Simon & Schuster, London.

Howard Rheingold (1994) *The Virtual Community*, Secker & Warburg, London.

David Ricardo (first published 1817) *Principles of Political Economy and Taxation*.

Jeremy Rifkin (1995) *The End of Work*, Tarcher/Putnam.

Gillian Rose (1996) *Mourning Becomes the Law: Philosophy and Representation*, Cambridge University Press, Cambridge.

Nathan Rosenberg (1982) *Inside the Black Box: Technology and Economics*, Cambridge University Press, Cambridge.

Jean-Jacques Rousseau (1994; first published 1755) *Political Economy* (transl. Christopher Betts), Oxford University Press, Oxford.

Edward Said (1994) *Representations of the Intellectual*, Vintage, London.

Lester Salamon, Helmut Anheier, Wojciech Sokolowski & associates (1996) *The Emerging Sector: a statistical supplement*, Johns Hopkins Institute for Policy Studies, Johns Hopkins University, Baltimore, MD.

Lester Salamon & Helmut Anheier (1996) *The Emerging Non-profit Sector*, Manchester University Press, Manchester.

Juliet Schor (1992) *The Overworked American*, Basic Books, New York.

Joseph Schumpeter (first published 1942) *Capitalism, Socialism and Democracy*.

Gill Seyfang and Colin Williams (February 1997) 'LETS make money work for people rather than profits', *Kindred Spirit*.

Neal Stephenson (first published 1992) *Snow Crash*, Bantam, London.

Bruce Sterling (1988) *Islands in the Net*, Arbor House.

Susan Strange (1996) *The Retreat of the State*, Cambridge University Press, Cambridge.

Vito Tanzi & Ludger Schuknecht (December 1995) 'The growth of government and reform of the state', IMF Working Paper.

Vito Tanzi (1996) 'Globalization, Tax competition and the future of tax systems', IMF Working Paper no. 141.

E.P. Thompson (1967) *Time, Work Discipline and Industrial Capitalism*, Past and Present.

Nicholas Timmins (1995) *The Five Giants*, HarperCollins, London.

Gillian Tindall (1995) *Celestine*, Sinclair-Stevenson, London.

Robert Tressell (1986; first published 1955) *The Ragged Trousered Philanthropists*, Grafton Books, London.

William Turner (1992) *Riot! The Story of the East Lancashire Loom Breakers in 1826*, Lancashire

County Books, Preston.

Thorstein Veblen (first published 1899) *The Theory of the Leisure Class*.

Sallie Westwood & John Williams (1997) *Imagining Cities*, Routledge, London.

Jeffrey Williamson (March 1996) 'Globalization and inequality then and now', National Bureau of Economic and Social Research Working Paper no. 5491, National Bureau of Economic and Social Research, Cambridge, MA.

Wired (1996) 'The WIRED Manifesto', *Wired* magazine, San Francisco, CA.

Adrian Wood (1994) *North–south Trade, Employment and Inequality*, Oxford University Press, Oxford.

Index